TO THE HOOP

IRA BERKOW

TO THE
HOOP

THE SEASONS
OF A
BASKETBALL LIFE

Ivan R. Dee
CHICAGO

Library of Congress Cataloging-in-Publication Data:
Berkow, Ira.
    To the hoop : the seasons of a basketball life / Ira Berkow.
        p. cm.
Originally published: New York : BasicBooks, c1997.
Includes index.
    ISBN 1-56663-548-9 (alk. paper)
    1. Berkow, Ira. 2. Sportswriters—United States—Biography. 3. Basketball players—United States—Biography. I. Title.
GV742.42.B47A3 2004
070.4'49796'092—dc22   2003062702

For my brother

For my mother

Contents

To the Hoop

Prologue

*I*t felt as though I had stumbled into heaven.

In January of 1992, I had checked into the Hyatt Regency Hotel in Minneapolis, the press headquarters for Super Bowl XXVI, and had been given a room on the sixteenth floor. I was on assignment as a sports columnist for *The New York Times* to cover the Super Bowl, but my thoughts were not focused on football. I had discovered that on the fifth floor of the hotel was the Greenway Health Club, which boasts a regulation-size basketball court. It is well-lighted and well-constructed, and several good leather basketballs are available. As someone who has played basketball regularly since the age of seven or eight, heaven was having my own gleaming basketball court just an elevator ride down from my room.

The first night I was in town, I went down to the club in T-shirt, shorts, and sneakers, paid a fee, and played. There were satisfying full-court games with a good group of players. The next night only two other players showed up. One was a television producer from Detroit whose name I didn't catch. The other was Rick Telander, a sports columnist for the *Chicago Sun-Times*, a former Northwestern University defensive back, and an enthusiastic pickup basketball player. The three of us began a game in which whoever has the ball is guarded by the two other guys. At one point I had the ball and Rick closed in on me. I took one step to begin my dribble and heard a popping sound, like the shell of a Brazil nut being cracked.

"What was that?" Rick said, stopping.

"I don't know," I said, holding the ball. "But I think it was me."

I felt something curious in my right knee, though it didn't hurt. "Let me try a jump shot," I said. I couldn't jump.

"I think I'd better quit," I said and I left the court limping slightly.

The next day my knee throbbed. In fact, I could hardly walk. I visited the orthopedist for the Minnesota Timberwolves, Dr. David Fischer. My X rays showed nothing. Dr. Fischer said that there had probably been a strain on my ligament and suggested physical therapy. When I got home to New York, I consulted another orthopedist, who agreed. I did therapy for several months, and yet nothing improved. So I took a magnetic resonance imaging test at the New York University Medical Center, lying for nearly in an hour in a cylinder as claustrophobic as a cocoon.

A few days later the doctor, Jeff Weinrib, with whom I had often played basketball on the nearby courts at NYU, called to inform me of the results.

"You've severed your ACL," Jeff said.

"What does that mean?" I asked.

"Means your basketball playing days are over."

"It does?" I couldn't believe it.

"I'm sorry," he said.

Without an ACL—an anterior cruciate ligament—there is no spring in the leg. The ACL is the rubber band, so to speak, that connects the thigh to the calf. Jeff said that I was too old to undergo reconstruction since results could hardly be guaranteed and the recuperation period of more than a year wouldn't be worth it at my age, fifty-two. Unbowed, I spoke with several surgeons, and every one agreed with Dr. Weinrib. But they all said that I should have arthroscopic surgery to "clean out" the cartilage, which was also torn up and which caused me a lot of pain when I walked.

Of course, there were many injuries and illnesses I could have been afflicted with that were much more serious than this, but the idea of never playing basketball again rocked me. It was like having something integral ripped from me, and for the first time I found myself peering into the canyon of death. After all, the paradox of maturing is that you must also come to grips with the reality of the final buzzer. Mortality beckons.

But I couldn't accept that this was the end of the road of my basketball life. I mean, I knew I still had a lot of missed shots left in me. And there still were places I wished to play, like that gorgeous outdoor court in Laguna Beach, California, which I drove past one day, admiring skillful players against a backdrop of brightly colored umbrellas on the sunny beach and sailboats on a sparkling ocean.

I had played basketball since I was a small boy, first tossing a rubber ball into a paper bag that I had hung atop a door in my apartment on Springfield Avenue on the west side of Chicago. I can still hear the downstairs neighbors, the Heifetzes, banging their ceiling with a broom as my ball bounced and thundered on the linoleum floor above them. To their relief, I soon moved on to school-yard and playground basketball.

Growing up, I spent hours by myself shooting, working on

my moves—sometimes dribbling haphazardly on a rock-strewn dirt surface—and working particularly on my jump shot. I can still feel the sweaty ridges of the ball on a hot, sunny summer's day as I shot with shirt off. And I recall lofting shots on a playground court on a winter's evening, snowflakes falling on my face, under yellow streetlamps, in gloves, knit cap, and coat. I can still feel the texture of the ball retrieved from a snow bank after it had bounced awry from the netless hoop. And, with the ball now a little wetter and a little heavier, and shooting with snow flicking away, I could still dream that one day I might drive through whole teams or flip a pass behind my back to a cutting teammate in the inimitable fashion of Bob Cousy of the Celtics. Or just pull up and drain the "J" from 20 feet away. Swish! Yeah! And the ball plopped back into the snow.

And while I never became a pro—never close—I did become a starting player on my high school and college teams and later played for my regiment in the army and in various amateur leagues and tournaments. Even now, in my so-called middle age, I was still playing in pickup games in parks and school yards and gymnasiums long after many of my friends had stopped playing altogether.

My work as a sportswriter takes me far from my home in New York City, and I have played ball around the country, as well as in other parts of the world. I once played several half-court pickup games in a gym in Athens. One of the players asked me to compare basketball games in the States with those I had just played.

"The only difference," I told him, "is that you guys argue in Greek."

Once, in pursuit of a story, I phoned Wayne Embry, the general manager of the Cleveland Cavaliers. Embry, who is just a couple years older than I, had been an outstanding

NBA player. In the course of our conversation, I mentioned that I still play basketball—sometimes full court.

"Give it up, man," he counseled. "Give it up."

My eighty-two-year-old father also sounded a discouraging word. "You're not a spring chicken anymore," he told me on more than one occasion. "And you know we have a history in our family." He didn't have to add that my grandfather, an aunt, and an uncle have all died of heart attacks and that he himself had to undergo quadruple bypass heart surgery.

Others I've met have looked at me with upraised eyebrow. "When are you going to grow up?" they ask.

"When are you supposed to?" I reply.

I like Picasso's attitude. "Youth has no age," he said.

This is certainly true in the arts, among other avenues, where the "childlike" quality as opposed to the "childish" quality—the sense of curiosity, of wonderment, of striving toward dreams—is cherished.

At bottom it remained pleasurable for me to play basketball, an activity that gave me joy when, in retrospect, life was relatively free of the physical and mental aches and pains of midlife.

I asked my long-time friend and former high school teammate, Barry Holt, a Chicago attorney, why he still plays basketball.

"I guess because I still can," he said.

Within limits, to be sure. But in our fashion.

Sometimes I wondered whether I was trying not to recapture my youth but in a way to reinvent it and to improve upon it. I would look back with some dissatisfaction on my life as a young basketball player, always thinking I could have been better. Or even should have been better. No matter how good one becomes, I have found, there is always some frustration. There were kids who wished to be high school players who never made the team, high school stars who did not become college stars, college stars who never made the pros, and pros who felt they could have done more in the NBA. Some of these people may be quite successful in life after basketball, but they never forget those earlier heartbreaking experiences.

At one point, I thought I had retired from basketball. I was in my midtwenties and I had resolved to accept the biblical injunction. "Well, yes," I figured, "it's time to put away childish things." So I quit basketball to play grown-up sports. But golf held little interest for me because the only time you break a sweat is when you crawl in and out of the canopied cart. Swimming was lonely. And I was disqualified from bowling because I didn't have a beer gut. But I played squash and tennis and enjoyed both. Perhaps because of the lack of team play in those sports and the avoidance of even incidental contact, neither was as satisfying as basketball. And I jogged. Not marathon jogging—just three or four miles. Enough so that when I had my blueberry cheesecake after dinner, I felt I deserved it.

I once tried skiing. I bought a ski jacket, I rented skis, I clop-clopped to the ski lift, and up and up and up I went, to the top of a mountain in Aspen. My instructor, a Swedish blonde, showed me how to hold the poles, how to hold my body, and then told me that the first thing I "moost" learn was to fall down while on skis. It was very difficult, but finally I plunged successfully into a nearby bank of snow. After absorbing a few more fundamentals, I decided I had had enough skiing for a lifetime.

I asked my instructor how to get down from this mountain. She said I had to ski down: "Ees only vay." I looked down, and it felt as if I were at the top of the Empire State Building and this was straight down. I glanced to my right. "Look," I said, "no one's going down on those lift chairs!" She told me no one goes *down* on lift chairs. I ripped off my skis and flew to the lift. I imagine that she was right behind me to try to tackle me. I jumped on a lift chair, and all the way down I passed people coming up on the lifts, clutching their poles: little girls, matrons, college boys, old men looking merry behind sparkling sunglasses, all gleeful anticipation beneath their stocking caps. Some shot me disbelieving looks or just snickered. But about halfway down a man looked sympathetic.

"What happened?" he asked, as we passed in the sky, "broken bindings?"

"Yes, yes," I blurted out, "broken bindings!"

All the rest of the way down I shrugged at the passing skiers. "Broken bindings," I said.

"Oh, what a shame."

"Yeah," I said, "brutal."

But I missed playing basketball. I missed not only the competition and the camaraderie, the occasional team play and the delight in making a good move, but also the very feel of the ball: the comfortable 10 ounces, the knobby leather, the ridges where the fingertips habitually search, like a blind man touching braille, to enhance the spin on the shot.

It took me about a year to admit this to myself, but finally I did. For a time I wondered if it was some kind of addiction. The photographer Walter Iooss Jr. used to tell me that he had a basketball Jones—though he has since discarded hoops for tennis and, alas, water skiing. Yes, water skiing! Once, though, Walter and I played one-on-one in Chicago on a windy day. He was born and raised in New Jersey and so had been deprived of the experience of playing basketball outdoors in the Windy City. I threw in some shots that, under the circumstances, he thought were unseemly, if not in fact unsportsmanlike. He fixed me with a glare. "You damn meteorologist," he said. Music to my wind-blown ears.

But playing basketball all these years has certainly taken a toll, especially physically. I was once hit so hard in the nose that I had trouble breathing for a month; another time I was hit so hard in the solar plexus that I had trouble eating for a month. I have strained my back, developed painful heel spurs, torn a rotator cuff in my shoulder. I have banged up my fingers, my hands, my elbows. I have torn ligaments in both ankles, and sometimes even stepping in the slightest crack in a sidewalk would cause my vulnerable ankles to buckle, sending me tumbling to the ground and spilling the contents of whatever I might be carrying all over the street. I would have to grab for support at anyone who happened to be nearby, risking a punch in the mouth in the bargain.

Even before severing my ACL in 1992, I had suffered torn ligaments in both knees. My first arthroscopic surgery, in the late 1970s, was on my left knee, but only to repair strained ligaments. And after that first operation, I was soon back playing, though somewhat more carefully than before.

"At this stage," said Barry Holt, who still plays in fifty-five-and-over national tournaments, "it's not so much knowing what you *can* do, it's knowing what you *can't* do."

So it is. I tailored my game to my limitations. I boxed out for rebounds instead of attempting to jump and perhaps landing, disastrously for me, on another player's foot. When defending, I tried to analyze my man's moves, for as the former New York Knick star Walt (Clyde) Frazier once explained to me, "Everyone has a certain rhythm that he dribbles to." I took that also as an insight into life itself. Basketball can have that effect on me.

When I was thirteen years old, I came across the instructional book *Basketball for the Player, the Fan and the Coach* by Red Auerbach, the cigar-smoking coach and savant of the Boston Celtics. I studied it and began to understand in rudimentary fashion that the philosophy of basketball has its roots in the philosophy of life. "Remember," Auerbach wrote in his section for coaches, "regardless of the system of play you use, proper balance is important." I know that after examining the universe, Copernicus came to roughly the same conclusion.

I have found that in the wide variety of people I have played with—from Wall Street whizzes to drug dealers, from seventy-year-olds to teenagers—I have developed a deeper understanding of the world through hoops. While some may see the world in a pebble or a grain of sand, I believe I can get a sharp glimpse of humanity from a pickup game of basketball. Through the game I have had an unusual opportunity to look into the soul of others, as well as, the spirit and wisdom willing, my own.

When I was in my thirties, I collaborated on a book with Walt Frazier called *Rockin' Steady: A Guide to Basketball and Cool.* And on the few occasions that we got to play one-on-one, I was impressed by the vast differences between the amateur and the pro. Whenever he felt challenged, Frazier, on defense, suddenly expanded before my eyes, as if he were being pumped with air. He not only got closer, but he also got taller and wider—even the hand that he raised to rebuff my shot seemed to grow as big around as an archery target. On offense he astonishingly shifted into higher and higher gears.

Playing basketball, it was clear, was one of life's great pleasures for me, like the dawn breaking over a lake or blueberry cheesecake, a lilting clarinet, a clear-as-a-stream sentence, a woman's touch. To be sure, though, the game can sometimes be a torment. Numerous times I've dragged myself home after having shot at an unfriendly rim or having played with younger, swifter players who tried to slam-dunk and ignore the open man—who, occasionally, was me, with hands extended, waiting for the pass that never came to shoot the shot that was never lofted. A particular low point was when a younger player *on my own team* took the ball from me while I was dribbling and turned and shot. Something like that could drive a man to introspection, or worse. And many times I have come home and announced to my wife: "That's it. Never again."

But there has always been one more time.

I still savor the memory of coming home on a summer's evening from a good outdoor game, my body agreeably tired and sore and my T-shirt drenched with sweat. On one such occasion I stopped, politely, to say hello to Mrs. Douglas, a neighbor, who was walking her two small white fluffy poddles. I was leaking happily from every pore. "Do you mind?" she said. "You're dripping on my dogs."

Regardless, I retained a longing for basketball.

That was why the arthroscopic surgery to repair cartilage in my knee troubled me so. How much damage would be found? Would I never play again? Had I laced up my last pair of sneakers?

I put off the operation for nearly a year, but finally I relented. The next thing I knew (so it seemed), I lay flattened on a gurney in the recovery room at Columbia-Presbyterian Hospital on the Upper West Side of Manhattan. Part of my brain was still befogged from the anesthesia that had been administered, but the other part was clear as a bell. My surgeon, Dr. Stuart Hershon, came by to see how I was doing.

"Your knee looked worse than I thought it would," he said, solemnly.

"Oh?"

"You'll be able to walk fine, but you're going to have to be careful about the activities you engage in." He knew about my primary sports interest because we had discussed it earlier, and he addressed it.

"I think you should not play basketball again," he said.

I raised up on my elbow and looked at him. "I think I need a new doctor," I said.

I did not need a new doctor. After three days on crutches following the operation, and a week of walking around with my newly scoped cartilage, I began to jog. I was feeling good. Should I try basketball?

The other doctors I had consulted were skeptical about my playing ball, and so was my wife, Dolly. After the operation Dr. Hershon told her that I should never play again, and she urged me to heed his words. "Life is making adjustments," she said wisely. "You'll find something else that you can love and throw yourself into." Somewhere in the recesses of my mind, I recalled a boyhood friend, Ted Schwartz, carried home by another friend and me after he had sprained his ankle in a playground game, and his mother, in apron and in tears at the front door, wailing, "Teddy, the ball will kill you!"

Dolly and the doctors feared that the ball might cripple me.

Was I vaguely hearing what the French call the *chant du cygne*, or swan song? I was at a crossroads. Should I risk playing basketball again, despite the serious consequences if I reinjured my knee? Should I take life by the scruff of the neck or hold it at arm's length? And if I did play, how would I play? Through the years I had made adjustments and concessions to age and mobility. What about now? I mean, even a street player has his pride!

When I visited Dr. Hershon in his office, I asked him about it. "You're determined," he noted. I said yes. He didn't look happy. "You can do serious damage to your knee, you know that," he said. "You can have an early case of arthritis. It might impair your walking."

But even as he spoke, I knew that Stuart Hershon had

overcome injury, too, as a defensive end on the Harvard football team. In a game against Brown during his senior year, 1958, he chased down a ball carrier and tackled him before he reached the goal line. But the runner's cleats scraped across Hershon's face, and as he lay on the ground, his face was bleeding all over the 20-yard line. Hershon was removed from the game and had "fifty-one sutures," as he later told me, sewn from forehead to chin and looking like an understudy for the Phantom of the Opera. But he and the team trainer devised a special mask for his helmet for the next game. "I was a senior and we were playing Yale," he said. "I'd been looking forward to that game all season. I wasn't going to miss it for anything."

"Doc," I asked in his office, "isn't there some kind of brace I might be able to wear for my knee?"

Hershon shrugged. He said that there was a Lenox Hill brace that has proven effective, "if you want to take the chance."

I had a plaster cast made of my knee so I could get a personally fitted brace, which cost $795. About a month later, when I first strapped on the serious-looking blue plastic and Velcro-strapped apparatus, I wondered whether I had made the right decision. The brace was bulky and looked heavy, though it was in fact lighter than it looked—about two pounds. But like a racehorse with only a little lead weight added in his saddlebags, I hoped I'd get used to it.

The operation, plus the brace, in effect might allow me a second life at basketball. Once something you love is taken from you forever, or so I thought, and then is miraculously returned as a kind of gift, even short-term, it is to be embraced, not taken for granted. If I could play again, I would savor playing the game more than I ever had before.

I knew that every time I stepped onto a basketball court it

would be an adventure: Would the knee hold up? Would the brace inhibit me? I decided I would try not to think about it. For two years I worked on bringing my game back to its presurgery level, but as a new basketball season approached in the fall of 1995, I hit upon an intriguing distraction for myself. Not only was I going to play, but I was also going to try to play a better game than I ever had. I hoped to reach another level.

I determined to do something I've only occasionally done in basketball, and that is to be a consistent and effective driver. I've always had a good jump shot, but for reasons ranging from motivation to skill (or lack of both), I have invariably reined in my drives in the lane or along the baseline. It was just more in my rhythm to stop suddenly and pop. But the more I thought about it, the more convinced I became that it was time to try to get deeper into the game, literally and figuratively, and, as they say around the courts, go to the hoop.

I wanted to do this for several reasons. One was to see whether you can in fact teach an old dog—or a middle-aged dog—new tricks. Another was that if I could do it, I'd be just that much more effective and perhaps extend my basketball life even further. And third, there was a kind of embarrassment factor. A young black player whom I played with in the school yard near my home in Manhattan once complimented me on my shot. "But how come you don't go to the hoop more?" he asked. I extended my right leg and allowed him to feel the brace under my sweatpants. Severed ACL, I explained. But I knew that wasn't the whole reason. The fact was, I didn't *think* drive. I thought jumper.

I resolved to watch the good drivers and ask about technique—I know that many players take a long first step and throw the ball a little farther out to dribble than in other circumstances, and go hard! I would practice, try it in games, see what happened.

But there was also an aspect beyond versatility, and that was virtuosity. It was a word that Itzhak Perlman, the renowned violinist, used when I interviewed him for a profile in the *Times*. Perlman, so enthusiastic a basketball fan that he once cut short a European tour to see Michael Jordan's return to Madison Square Garden in 1994, compared Jordan to Yascha Heifetz, saying that in the throes of creation, whether it's a drive shot or a concerto, the virtuoso goes to a higher level. "It's like playing a phrase," Perlman said, "and you don't know what you're going to do until you do it."

I wasn't fooling myself; I understood I was neither Michael nor Yascha. But beyond that I knew I would be confronting my own self-image and reality. I would have to make adjustments even as I strove to broaden my game.

I didn't want to be dumb about the extent of my partial handicap. That is, I wouldn't exactly emulate any of the devil-may-care professional athletes I had interviewed over the years: Vinnie Pazienza returning to fight for the middleweight championship after he had suffered a broken neck; Jackie Fields, the onetime lightweight champion, who fought despite being blind in one eye and risking what sight he had left in the other; Troy Aikman, the Dallas Cowboy quarterback, who returned to his job after suffering three concussions in one recent season.

But neither did I want to be Steve Blass, the Pirates pitcher, who became so frightened of hitting a batter that he lost all effectiveness, or Paul Blair, who, after being hit in the head with a pitch, began to shy away at the plate and was soon out of baseball.

Perhaps I'd take my guidance from the Bard or Bobby Knight or whoever it was who said, "I dare do all that may become a man; / Who dares do more is none."

. . .

Not long ago I was talking to a woman in her thirties, who said she didn't remember the 1960s. I said, "I can remember the 1940s."

She stared at me. "How old are you?" she asked.

I told her. "Gee," she said, "you're very well preserved."

Time speeds. As I write these lines, I am fifty-six years old, and when I look in the mirror, I see a brown-haired man graying at the sideburns, considerably more weathered than the teenager I used to observe, with more wrinkles at the eyes and mouth. Sometimes I wonder where that kid went, but it's not something I'm forlorn about—not for very long, anyway. It's actually a double-edged sword: that fresh-faced youth had so much to learn. On the other hand, I think, my God, this middle-aged guy is *still* learning.

Basketball, like writing, has helped keep me from feeling I am growing too old too fast. When he turned eighty, Carl Sandburg said, "I should like to think that as I go on writing there will be sentences truly alive, with verbs quivering, with nouns giving color and echoes."

There is something to that. All of us think, tomorrow we will be better.

Some other physical facts: I'm six feet tall, give or take a millimeter. Probably "take," since I'm sure I've begun to shrink somewhat, as the spinal cord begins its normal compressing in aging and the shoulders sag, but I haven't noticed it yet. The hair on my head remains curly and unruly, a matter of genes rather than grooming. I weigh about 195 pounds, some seven or eight pounds more than I'd like to weigh, but I've found it gets harder to lose weight as one gets older. Also, the desserts look better and better. My doctor told me it isn't so much what you eat, but the portions. "Cut back about half," he said.

I'm always interested in other people's diets, to see what might help me. One year as Thanksgiving approached, I became curious about what William (The Refrigerator) Perry, the nearly 400-pound lineman for the Chicago Bears, was planning for his holiday dinner, and what he had eaten the previous Thanksgiving. He told me he had gone to his in-laws for dinner and described the turkey and chicken and roast beef and various types of potatoes and, of course, the numerous cakes and pies on the table. "What did you eat?" I asked.

"A little bit of everything," he said.

"A little bit of everything or a lot of everything?" I asked.

"Both," he said.

Another time I was in a baseball press box when Stan (The Man) Musial, the former St. Louis Cardinal batting star, came through. An old friend of his noted how trim he looked. "How do you do it, Stan?" the man asked.

"I push away from the table when I'm still just a little hungry," he said. "I never overeat."

I find that I am somewhere between The Refrigerator and The Man in my gastronomic habits. But sometimes too much Fridge and not enough Man hurts my game. I know from experience, and not just physics, that the lighter you are the more spring you have in the jump shot and the longer you can go. So much of the shot, after all, is in the legs.

My job as a sports columnist, meanwhile, has also fed my personal basketball world—in a noncaloric way. When I watch games, I'm looking not just for the story, but also for the masters' secrets—to steal a move, if I can. Not just Kareem Abdul-Jabbar's extension on his sky hook, or how a relatively slow Larry Bird compensated by making amazingly economical moves, but even trying to copy Michael Jordan's flight to the basket. And not when he was aloft. Jordan is famous for his aeronautics, but I have marveled at how *low* to the ground he gets when he dribbles to the hoop, slicing between and around and, in some ways, through defenders and then coiling and springing. The best athletes often maintain that kind of low center of gravity, that flexibility, that body control—the way the pitchers Tom Seaver and David Cone thrust off the mound, the way Barry Sanders explodes through the line, the way Mike Tyson steamrollers into opponents.

It turned out that not only couldn't I get as high off the ground as Jordan, but I also couldn't get as low to the ground as he did. But that didn't mean I couldn't improve my game, for example, by bending a little lower and going hard, as one does in a rainstorm.

The idea of attempting to fit parts of someone else's game into yours was first made clear to me in college, in a literary way. By then I had begun to dream of being a writer, having long given up the notion of replacing Bob Cousy in the backcourt of the Celtics.

Full of youthful nerve, I sent a couple of the stories I had done for my college newspaper to the great sports columnist Red Smith and asked for suggestions on how to write better. Out of the blue. And he wrote back! He was gentle but candid in his assessment, saying, well, that I needed work. But he offered this piece of general advice: "If you can take one move, as we say in boxing, from ten like Mark, Matthew, Luke, John, Shakespeare, Hemingway, Thurber, E. B. White, Ibsen, and Edgar A. Guest, you'd be a helluva writer."

Now, thirty years later, I was about to try to follow Red's advice again—this time on the basketball court.

Home Courts

*I*t's a tight full-court game as the October dusk descends and the nearby trees with their lemon-yellow and russet leaves darken. From the basketball court behind the New York University Medical Center on the east side of Manhattan, the players in their motley array of shirts and shorts might see the cars and hear their rumble and honk on the close-by F.D.R. Drive. An occasional toot from a tugboat on the East River, the whir of a helicopter landing at the 34th Street heliport, an ambulance siren heading for the emergency ward at Bellevue, a block south, all add to the ambience. Some cars have their headlights on, and the lights in the hospital windows are also beginning to glow. The warmth of the late day meshes with the fumes from the automobiles and copters as the players run and sweat and hustle for the ball and for position, oblivious to nearly everything else around them.

A handful of guys are waiting for the next game, standing or sitting along the chain-link fence, and the losers will have to sit while the winners take on the newcomers. So there is pressure to win. There is no referee, of course, and players call their own fouls and infractions. Players are free to dispute calls, and they do so frequently.

"The ball hit the top of the backboard, it's out!" cries one player.

"Top of the backboard is in play!" shouts another.

"It isn't!"

"It is!"

Another player gets bumped while taking a shot from the top of the key.

"Foul," he grunts.

"Chump call," says his defender.

"Careful," says the first guy, "or your mustache is goin' in your mouth."

There's also the desultory pat on the ass for a good move. "Nice take," says an opponent.

The players, like their wardrobes, are also a mixed bag. On this day there are some medical students, a radiologist, a cardiologist, a cook from the medical center's kitchen, a lab assistant, a security guard, and a few teenagers from the projects about a half mile away. Some in the game have played college or high school ball, some haven't. They range in size from S to XXL. There are blacks, whites, Asians, even an Indian from Bombay. Most of the players are in their twenties, a few in their early thirties. One is over fifty.

I'm the only player in long sweatpants, since I'm somewhat self-conscious about wearing my brace. The gray at my sideburns is enough to reveal age, or infirmity, and I don't need a bulky brace to add to it. Sometimes under the boards I'll bump knees with someone.

"What the hell was that?" he asks.

"My brace," I tell him.

Another time I was running up the court, and a teammate, ambling alongside me, asked, "Do you have a mouse in your shoe?"

I said, "No, why?"

"Because something is squeaking," he said.

"Oh?" I said, and kept on as if I had no idea that the unseen brace under my sweat pants needed oiling.

In my white New Balance sneakers (I wear this brand since it is one of the few that has widths and not just lengths) I have placed orthotics because I once had heel spurs. Nobody sees them, either.

This is the court where I frequently play my outdoor pickup games. It is a long, full court with nets on both baskets, always a plus for a pickup player. One basket is regulation height, but the other is slightly shorter—the winning team has its pick of baskets and usually chooses the lower one, a somewhat easier target. A standard game can be from eight to twelve baskets wins. In this game, it is twelve. There are no free throws in pickup hoops. There is a small hump in the cement near midcourt, and the regulars there know to avoid it. A new player has a surprise bounce in store. Most of the players are regulars, though, and the personalities and talents are quickly discerned.

I've been coming to this court for twenty years, and I've made friends. Some know I write for a newspaper, some don't. But once you're on the court, nothing matters except the quality of your game. As in most pickup games, play is serious, especially when the losing team must leave the court. The established rules of courts often just exist, like a joke you hear going around. No one quite knows how it originated, but there it is. And on this court, the first five guys to arrive have the next game, no matter who they are.

At some courts the next guy waiting can pick any four he

wishes, including four who were on the losing team. I prefer the way it is at NYU because everyone gets an opportunity to play right away, and more guys play sooner. Also, when you play with younger, faster, and stronger players, they tend to pick other young, fast, and strong players.

There have also been occasions, though, when a urologist, an anesthesiologist, and a cardiologist have come to my apartment building, which is about a block from the courts, and have called up for me to go over to the courts with them and play as a team.

If I can finish my writing by four o'clock or so—and have no other duties, from either my newspaper or my spouse—I try to get over to the court. You never know what to expect. Sometimes the court is empty. And I shoot alone, giving myself a good workout for about forty-five minutes. Sometimes one guy shows up, and we have a one-on-one. Or we get a two-on-two, or more. Sometimes the place is crawling with players, and, as on this day, full-court games may follow one another into the night.

I always bring my ball—I buy a new Spalding NBA indoor/outdoor ball every few months—since I like to make sure that there will be a ball there with a good grip.

On this October afternoon the game is tied at 11 and is on the line. My teammate Mike Attubato, a dark-haired cardiologist, a friend, and an excellent player, takes a spill. He grabs his right knee, moaning on the concrete.

"Mike," I say, bending over, "are you hurt?"

"No," he says, "just mad."

"Mad? Why?"

"Because," he says, "that was my last healthy joint."

Several other doctors and med students, those in the game and those watching, hurry over to take a look at Mike. They ask about fibulas and tibias.

"I'm OK," he says. He gets up and is able to continue. I've seen guys sprain their ankles, and the doctors and students will gather round and diagnose: half will say keep the shoe on, the other half will say take it off. It doesn't always inspire me with confidence in the medical profession. In Mike's case, though, it is universally agreed that he will survive nicely.

I had hit a few outside shots early—one on a crossover dribble that I hadn't made, or attempted, in quite a while—but I had not contributed as the other team caught up from 10–7 deficit. In fact, I had thrown a bad pass that resulted in a basket for the other team and had dribbled the ball off my foot, which also resulted in another score for the opposition. It is now 11–11. One more basket wins—there is no deuce, or win by two, as on some courts.

I have the ball again, and I'm dribbling at the top of the key when I see that our husky black guy with cornrows, Tyrone Flowers, a clerk in radiology at NYU, has the inside under the basket on the man guarding him. I am to the right of the key, Tyrone just to the left of the basket. I loft a pass that goes over the outstretched hand of the center defender. Tyrone catches the ball, turns without even taking a step, and lays the ball in for the winning basket. There are high fives and congratulations all around. Nice to help win a game with an assist. We hold the court, win two more games, and then lose the third.

I also try a couple of drives, as I begin my quest to amplify my game. Driving is primarily faking, quickness, and strength. And mind-set. You look for the defender leaning, and then go. Or you try to split the seam between two guys. Easier said than done, at least for me, and at this stage.

I see an opening and drive across the lane, but the ball is slapped away. Another time I dribble hard along the baseline, but there are too many defenders to enable me to go straight up for the shot, especially since I don't quite spring like a jack-in-the-box. I give a couple of pump fakes and lay the ball in off the backboard for a score. It's not the great drive I had in mind, but it is a step in the right direction.

And in our four games my winning team shows a nice little cohesiveness to it. At some moments, with our passing and movement, there is even a sense of a jazz quintet, all of us playing together and combining improvisation with harmony.

"Life is beautiful," I inform Dolly as I come into our apartment, swinging my gym bag.

I had played four full-court games, and, feeling achy but happy, took a long hot bath. I rested the next day. When I was younger, I needed no bath—just a shower—and could have played another round of full-court games the next day. Not anymore.

The calendar was getting late into fall, and the weather was getting cooler, so the games went indoors, to a nearby gym. In one game, with the score tied at 7–7 in an 8-points-wins game, I hit a jumper at the top of the key to win. But in games a few days after that, my shots were off. Not only that, but the guys I was guarding seemed to be hitting all their shots. It was frustrating. One afternoon the gym was particularly crowded with players, looking like rush hour at Grand Central. The pressure was on to win, because losing meant sitting for about a week. I hit a couple of shots, and the game went to 7–7. I got the ball on the side. Two guys were on me, and they realized that there had been a mix-up. So both went for the un-guarded man, leaving me alone!

I measured my shot, a one-handed push—we've all seen Scottie Pippen do this many times—and missed! The other team went down and scored to win the game. "C'mon, man," one of my teammates said to me as we walked off the court. "You gotta make those shots." This wasn't news to me, even without his unnecessary remark. I felt like a bad citizen, like a jerk. I had let my team down.

I left the gym discouraged and came through the apartment door with what must have been a transparently hangdog expression. Dolly was in the kitchen preparing dinner. She looked up, brushing her hair from her face, and saw me. She knew immediately. "Basketball is supposed to be fun," she said. "You'll do better the next time."

"If there is a next time," I said. "I'm prepared to quit."

"Again?" she said.

And that night I had a dream: a rottweiler was biting my ear. He and the owner were on the sidelines of a game at Sullivan High School in Chicago, where I had played as a teenager. I was without sneakers and in stocking feet. The owner said, "My dog will stop biting your ear if you promise not to play anymore."

I said, "OK, who wants a rottweiler biting your ear?"

End of dream.

Isaac Herschkopf, a Manhattan psychiatrist and fellow pickup basketball player, interpreted the dream for me:

"Your ears represent your testicles," Ike began. "You felt very emasculated on the basketball court. It was something you've been good at, and proud of, and you were playing with younger guys, and yet on this day were not able to compete to your satisfaction.

"Rottweilers and Doberman pinschers are known to go for the balls. The dream expresses your anxiety, but it does so in a such a manner that it doesn't wake you up because it disguises it.

"The only two pairs of organs that dangle from your body are your earlobes and your balls. The earlobes are wonderful symbolic representations of your testicles."

Ike was rather matter-of-fact about all this.

"It's classic," he said. "When playing poorly, you feel less of a man. When playing well, you not only feel immortal, you feel omnipotent. The owner of the dog obviously represents the guy on the court who you felt was insulting you. It's like saying, 'If you stop shooting I'll stop insulting you.' "

But for me to stop shooting would be the same as to stop breathing. It would be curtains.

I would try again. Rottweiler or no rottweiler.

At fifty-five, I was still seeking to prove that I belonged on the court and could meet the competition. But as I've gotten older, I've gotten slower, by degrees, and it was hardly noticeable until I discovered that the pickup in my engine needed an overhaul that I was now unable to give it. I tried to compensate, making careful passes, playing defense with deft feet, and of course sneaking the occasional tug on my opponent's shorts.

My slowing down had surely been happening over a period of years, but it struck me most forcibly about ten years ago, when I was invited back to Chicago one summer to participate in a charity basketball game in a suburban high school. I was forty-four years old at the time.

The game was played between a team made up of Chicago Bears football players, some of whom were high school and even college basketball aces, and a group of so-called former North Shore all-stars—while I was a starting guard on my high school team on the North Side of Chicago, I was something less than a varsity star, but I wasn't about to quibble. The Bears team featured such young and swift and hefty people as the linebacker Otis Wilson, the wide receiver Willie Gault (once an Olympic sprinter), and the cornerback Leslie Frazier. (They were among the standouts on the Bears' Super Bowl championship team the following year.) In the charity game, which was competitive, I started for the all-stars. My parents came to watch. I did reasonably well, particularly in the first half, when I sank five outside shots.

"I watched you and you played well," my dad said to me after the game. "But at one point I thought that you were running kind of slow. Then I reminded myself that you weren't a kid anymore, but a forty-four-year-old man."

"Anyone would run slow next to Willie Gault," I protested lamely. But I pictured what he had been seeing.

At one time I played in leagues and in tournaments. But my travel schedule as a journalist was so erratic that I missed games, lost a starting position, and began not to feel a part of the team. Better just to walk into a gym or onto an outdoor court and ask for next. I played an average of twice a week, if I could, sometimes taking my brace on the road if I knew I would be gone for an extended period. I wouldn't hazard playing without it.

I no longer have a regular indoor game in summer. I've tried a few in which guys rent out a school gym on a particular night once a week. Two problems with that: One is, at my age, late games jumble my nerves too much, and I can't settle down and get a good night's rest; for another, I like eating dinner at dinner-time, rather than before going to sleep. That jumbles up my digestive tract.

I first moved to Manhattan in the fall of 1967, and shortly after arriving I began playing regularly at the Vanderbilt YMCA on East 47th Street. I had left the *Minneapolis Tribune*, my first job in journalism, to be a sportswriter for the Newspaper Enterprise Association, a national feature syndicate, and the Vanderbilt Y was just a few blocks from my new office.

The Vanderbilt Y gym was a mecca for observing, in condensed fashion, the mind and quirks of much of New York, if not all of America, as players sometimes literally bounced off

the walls—the gym is a small full court, and the sidelines are
so close to the four walls that a normal-size person sitting on
the floor with knees bent and back against the wall will have
his feet on the court.

At one time or another people from the four corners of the
world seemed to come through the doors of that gym. "You
just missed Burt Bacharach," a guy told me, shortly after I
joined. "He gave up playing here a few months before you
came. Went in for a shot and got low-bridged while in the air.
He fell hard and hurt his hands. He makes his living with his
hands. He decided it was better to give up his career in basketball than risk his career in music."

I remember seeing a lawyer argue a call with a passion he
might have reserved for another court. He wore a torn T-shirt,
blue shorts, and sneakers. He was overruled, his brief rejected
not by a judge but by a knot of his peers.

He had been supported by a pal of his, both of whom frequently made outrageous calls that rankled most of the others. On this occasion both grew so mad that they quit the
game. Others looked on as they stalked off. "Well," someone
said, turning to me, "there goes flotsam and jetsam."

Some talented players were regulars through the years. Bill
Butler, who had been a standout forward at St. Bonaventure
with Bob Lanier at center in the late 1960s, wore rubber
sweatsuits in order to battle a weight problem. Dave Golden,
an all-American high school player in Illinois, captain of the
Duke team, and the last cut of the Indiana Pacers, was as
smooth and swift a player as ever entered that gym. And there
was Jeffrey Newman, a play-making guard with behind-the-
back moves who had been all–Ivy League at the University of
Pennsylvania—and who left the gym to make a fortune, I
learned, in the stock market. Newman had been at Penn the
same time Candice Bergen was going to school there. "One

day I decided I should call Candice for a date," Jeffrey told me, with the implication that he was a pretty important guy on campus. "I got her number and phoned. A woman answered. I said, 'Candice?' She said, 'Yes.' I said, 'This is Newman.' She said, 'Paul?' " In telling the story now, Jeffrey raised his eyebrows. "I shrunk to about three feet," he said, "and I gently hung up the phone."

The gym became a kind of oasis for me, or so I thought. And while we all imagined that we had left our lives behind us as we played, it wasn't true. We brought all of what we were and had become into the game. All the frustrations and anxieties, as well as the pleasures and experiences. The businessmen, the theater directors, the writers and actors, the architects, the doctors and lawyers showed up, cutting schedules, missing a rehearsal, changing a meeting.

Charlie Miron, one of the older players at the gym, believed he could tell by the way guys were playing—pushing, elbowing, arguing—that there was some kind of trouble at work or at home. "I bet that guy's having a problem with his marriage," Charlie said at one point. Turned out the guy was going through a nasty divorce.

I would slip away from the typewriter before 4:30 and for the next hour and fifteen minutes play frenetic full-court basketball games. A nucleus of about twenty guys—some regulars, some transients—generally made their appearance in this game between shirts and skins, as the teams on the court there were differentiated. It seemed we were all there for a purpose: to live a little for today. But also, perhaps, holding on to the past a little as well, and maybe more than many of us wished to admit.

Some of us never learned the full names or the actual names of the people we played with for years. This imparted a sense of being an auxiliary of the French Foreign Legion.

There was Green Pants, because he never changed his shorts. And Wristbands and Headband. There was Big Al and Little Al. A guy with a wide-eyed, gaunt look was called Orphan Annie. Diogenes got his name because he read a book while waiting for next. (It was obvious, however, that he never read a book about how to play basketball.) And Junior Jive was a young guy with a lot of fancy moves, his most consistent being a behind-the-back pass that routinely bounced off the wall or, once, the ceiling.

J.J., as he was generally called, was a teenager from the Bronx who had finished high school and was self-employed. That is, he was a ticket scalper. One evening I ran into him at Yankee Stadium, where I was taking part in a television production. A limousine had been made available for those in the project, and so I offered J.J. a ride home. He agreed, and he loved being ensconced in the limo. But when I asked his address, he said that we should drop him off about two blocks away from the apartment he shared with his mother and two sisters. "If people see me pull up in a limo," he said, "they'll be trying to break into our apartment to rob us."

On First Avenue one winter day someone hollered my name. It was a panhandler, in a black knit cap and frayed coat. I looked closer. He was jumping up and down in the snow and appeared to be imitating a jump shot. Mine! "You the man with the J," he called out. "Still got the J?"

It was Fuzz. He had played at the Y and had had a decent game. He also had charm.

"Fuzz," I said, genuinely happy to see him, "'S up? You haven't been to the gym in a couple years."

"Been away," he said.

"Anywhere I've been?"

"Coxsackie."

Coxsackie is a New York state penitentiary.

"For what?"

"A little break-in kinda thing," he said.

I nodded in understanding. "Still got a game?" I asked.

"Oh yeah," he said. "Played a lot. Was unstoppable in the joint!"

There was a guy in the gym named Animal for his aggressive style of play. I once brought a friend up for a late afternoon of basketball, and afterward he suggested that everyone up there be called Animal. Animal 1 through 20. My friend never returned.

Then there was Monster, whose style of play was not unlike Animal's. One time Monster and another player were discussing a transaction dealing with Knicks tickets. The other player's name was Sly. He always thought he was putting something over on everyone, and his very slyness made him appear suspicious and thus transparent. This time, though, there was nothing tricky, just a matter of a sale of tickets. Monster told Sly to call him at home.

"But I don't know your real name," said Sly.

"Oh, just ask for Monster," came the reply.

Sly called, and a boy answered.

"Can I speak to Monster?" asked Sly.

The boy shouted past the receiver, "Da-a-a-d!"

One problem I've had at that Y and in pickup games generally is that since I had played some organized ball, and since, as a sportswriter, I keep up with rules, I've argued too many calls. There are times when it hasn't been worth the trouble and the headache, trying to explain to someone who won't listen to the difference between a basketball right and a basketball wrong.

It's amazing the ignorance—and the adamant ignorance—of so many people, people one would think might at least admit to simply not having knowledge of something. All of the players considered themselves experts on every phase of the game, and at the top of the list was kicking the ball. What is kicking? "It's when the ball hits your foot," is commonly the answer.

Ah, but of course not. The rule book reads, "Kicking the ball or striking it with any part of the leg is a violation when it is intentional. The ball accidentally striking the foot, the leg or the fist is not a violation."

I once saw a guy I'll call Roach throw a pass downcourt that hit the sole of a sneaker of an opposing player running with his back to the passer. "Kicking," Roach called. I said, "It's not kicking." And I was on Roach's team! An argument ensued between him and me. The other team supported me, which was hardly a surprise since they retained the ball.

I have long concluded that the only thing dumber than arguing with an ignorant person is continuing the argument, which I've done on numerous occasions.

I try to control myself. But then someone calls the top of the backboard out—it's out only if the ball bounces over and *behind* the backboard—and I am trying to explain the error of his ways.

One time a guy called traveling when another player bobbled the ball without moving his feet. "How could he travel if he didn't move?" I asked. A few days later I generously brought a rule book to show the idiot who had called the bobble. Naturally, he refused to look at it.

Then came the notorious out-of-bounds play. A guy threw the ball and it hit an opponent who had tripped, and his body was out of bounds. The passer said it was his ball because it hit the guy on the other team. I said, "Impossible, you idiot. The guy was *out of bounds*."

Big argument. I don't remember who won it. But that night I went to the rule book. Oh, shit! The son-of-a-bitch was right! This time, I didn't bring the rule book into the gym. And I never mentioned it again, either.

I made several friends in the gym, and some of us had social functions and dinners with our wives and girlfriends. But after twenty years, my time at the Vanderbilt Y came to an end when I had embarrassed myself to an extent that made me feel uncomfortable. It is a story that remains painful for me, even nearly ten years after it happened.

In my two decades at the Y, I had the occasional altercation. Usually words. I had never come to blows with anyone, though others had, and fights were broken up when passions and bad calls got out of hand. Then one afternoon Roach seemed particularly out of sorts. Something happened—I don't remember exactly what it was—but it was an accumulation of things, to be sure. Maybe I had turned down his invitation to his Thanksgiving Day party. Or maybe—and this is hard to believe, even for me—but maybe I was somewhat at fault, as well. Roach had had other problems in the gym. He was very physical and when racing for a loose ball would throw a body block at his competing opponent. At one point several other players presented a written complaint about him to the Y's athletic director. Roach received a warning.

But on this afternoon there was a disputed play, and then I was to take the ball out of bounds. Roach held onto the ball. I asked for it. He was just a few feet from me and threw the ball at my face. He only grazed my head, which was the same kind of accuracy he showed in shooting for the basket, and I charged him. We scuffled and tumbled and threw punches and he bit my finger and drew blood. I was active in some other fashion, particularly around the area of his ear. Then we were pulled apart. Shortly after, one of the new players came over to me and asked if I was the same guy who wrote a column for *The New York Times*. I was taken aback, and felt abashed. "Yes," I said.

Later, I thought about what had happened. I was forty-seven years old and getting into a fistfight? It was the first fistfight I had engaged in since I was a teenager. And while sometimes one daydreams about punching someone out, the reality of it took on a different hue when I reflected on it.

I had been going up to the gym for two decades, or as long as I had been in New York, and old habits are hard to break. It took me several more months, but I decided to take a rest from that gym—it turned out to be a permanent rest. Some other players had left as well.

I found a place to play even closer to where I live, at the NYU courts, which does not seem to be as great a magnet for such a mad array of humanity as the Vanderbilt Y—perhaps because of the security guards who sit in the lobby nearby and who occasionally patrol the area.

While the games can be aggressive, and invariably there are antagonisms, I have seen no fistfights. I finally gave up the Vanderbilt Y because while playing basketball is something I've enjoyed all my life, I was now an adult. Or liked to believe I was. And the notion of me fighting like a punk didn't quit fit that self-image.

Over the course of this past summer, I played in the NYU school yard with a young, thin, dark-haired Puerto Rican kid named Kenny Garcia, who was close to six feet tall. I later learned that his parents were separated and that he lived sometimes with his mother and sometimes with his father. He was seventeen and going into his junior year at Seward Park High School on the Lower East Side of Manhattan. He traveled to NYU by bicycle, cap turned backward, and often with a black friend and classmate of his named George. Kenny had a cousin named Junior who worked in admitting at the hospital, and he and George played in the games as well. There were times when the four of us were on a full-court team together, and I enjoyed playing with them. They had a good attitude about the game—they passed when they should have, worked at defense and rebounding, and were skillful on offense as well. Kenny had a point guard's mentality and knew how to give me the ball in a way that I liked it for my shot—chest high, crisp, in my rhythm. One day we held the court for several games.

"You're in pretty good shape," Kenny said to me, "like my father."

"How old's your father?" I asked him.

"Thirty-nine," said Kenny.

"Kenny," I said, "your dad's a young man."

"How old are you?" he asked, his voice rising.

"I'm a hundred and sixty-seven years old," I said.

He looked at me closely. I thought he wasn't sure what to believe.

Every so often I talked with Kenny about his future. He asked me how hard college was, and I told him that it wasn't so hard that he couldn't do it. He seemed bright and polite and had a way about him that made him easy to be around. While his grades were not great, and he had failed a course that rendered him ineligible for the high school basketball team, he still had been chosen as one of the ten students in the school to have a conversation with Hillary Clinton when she visited Seward Park earlier in the year.

Kenny and George and I spoke about their future. I asked Kenny what he hoped to become. "I think I want to be a businessman," he said.

George looked at him. "What do you mean, 'businessman'?" he said. "There are all kinds of businessman. What *kind* of businessman?"

"I dunno," said Kenny, "maybe own a bodega, or a sneakers store."

Shortly after that Kenny approached me on the court, looking excited. "I saw you on television, on a sports show," Kenny said. "I almost fell off the chair. I didn't know you was a sportswriter."

I confessed. From then on, he and Junior and George would talk to me about the sports world, the Knicks, the Yankees, and the like. Then one day Kenny said, "Hey, Ira, can you get me a job at the *Times?*"

"We already have a publisher, Kenny," I said. "But what did you have in mind?"

"Mail room—anything to make some money," he said. "Jobs aren't easy to get."

I told him to send me a note about himself so that I could pass it on to the appropriate people. I told him to send it to me at the *Times*, but I didn't give him the address. I thought I'd let him use his ingenuity if he was truly interested.

Then we went back onto the court.

In November I traveled to Minneapolis for a story on Kevin Garnett, the nineteen-year-old, 6-foot-11, hugely talented forward for the Minnesota Timberwolves. Garnett had come right out of Farragut High School on Chicago's West Side the previous June as the fifth draft choice overall in the National Basketball Association draft. And almost immediately he was making a solid place for himself in the NBA, alongside Michael Jordan and Shaquille O'Neal and Charles Barkley. Fantastic. I pictured myself coming out of Sullivan High School in 1957, and then suddenly competing against Bob Cousy and Bill Russell and Bob Pettit and Dolph Schayes. Then I tried to picture this after I got out of college. Then I gave up.

In Minneapolis I stayed again at the Hyatt-Regency. I wanted to return to the scene of the accident and play again, a somewhat reconstituted basketball player. I went through the same routine as I did the last time. I changed into my basketball clothes in my room—this time, however, I added the brace—and I took the elevator down to the gym. It was Paradise Revisited, and I entered with some trepidation. It was like mounting a horse that had thrown you.

I felt fortunate that I was even able to try. Bud Armstrong couldn't. Armstrong lives in Minneapolis, and he and I began working at the *Minneapolis Tribune* within a month of each other in the summer of 1965. (I had received a master's degree from the Medill School of Journalism at Northwestern University and then applied to some twenty-five newspapers for a general-assignment job; the *Tribune* was the first—and only—newspaper to make me an offer, in the sports department.) Bud and I have stayed in touch—he has remained in Minneapolis and continues on the sports desk as a senior editor and also as a frequent reviewer on the Sunday book section. And I saw him, shaved head and goateed, on this visit. He had suffered a heart attack sixteen years earlier, and while he is allowed to bicycle, he can no longer play basketball, as he and I had done together when I lived there.

Three guys were in the gym at the Greenway Health Club when I entered. We organized sides and played two-on-two, games in which there was a certain degree of bouncing off one another and scrambling hard for rebounds and loose balls. I drove, with only modest success—but I was driving.

After two games, my teammate quit, excusing himself because he had a dinner engagement. Another player said he was going to the weight-lifting room. So I played a few games of one-on-one with the remaining guy, a stocky fellow in the blue shirt, and had my workout. My T-shirt was comfortably drenched. And the especially good news: my knee held up in this gym of mixed memories. Well, both knees held up, since I have occasional thoughts about my left one buckling, too.

The next morning I went downstairs for breakfast and by coincidence the player who had been my teammate was in the elevator. We introduced ourselves, and I asked him what he thought about the games we had played. "I said I had a dinner engagement," he said, "but I really didn't. I just didn't want to keep playing against the guy who was guarding me, that guy in the blue shirt. He was too rough. He did a lot of unnecessary banging. I've seen guys get hurt."

"Yeah," I said, "I know what you mean."

When the elevator stopped at the lobby level, we said good-bye, and he walked away with normal strides, as did I. It was nice, four years later, to go about my business in Minneapolis in one piece.

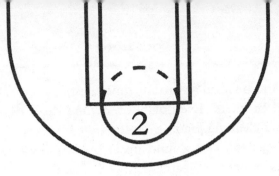

Chicago Style

On the way back to New York from Minneapolis, I stopped in Chicago, and, as I usually do when I return to my hometown, I stayed with my parents. They live in a first-floor apartment in West Rogers Park, on the far North Side. My mother is eighty, my father two years older, and both suffer from numerous physical ailments, particularly arthritis. My mother recently took to using an aluminum cane, which she sometimes forgets when she leaves home, and my father's pace has slowed; when he hurried several steps while recently crossing a street to beat the traffic, he recalled that "I felt like I was running like an old man."

Even so, they both get around reasonably well, leading an active life with friends and family. Both were born in Chicago—in the Maxwell Street area, the old-world marketplace—and were the children of immigrant parents who spoke little English: my mother's family is from Russia, my father's from Romania. My dad was an orphan by the time he was a teenager, and he lived at various times with his several married sisters and brothers. Eventually he owned three dry-cleaning stores and a cleaning plant, then left that for an aborted try at the steel business, and wound up in his last working years in politics, as a precinct captain and an administrator in the county health department. Through the patronage of Mayor Richard J. Daley's imperial reign, he got us all jobs: my mother was a bailiff in the Clerk of the Circuit Court's office; I was a garbage collector in summers during high school and college; and my brother, Steve, my only sibling and five years younger than I, had summer jobs in the park district, where he picked up litter and cut down dead trees.

One evening on this visit the phone rang in their apartment and I answered it. It was Steve. We said hello.

"Just a minute," I said, after an uncomfortable pause. "I'll get Ma or Dad."

"OK," he replied.

That was our entire conversation. We had hardly said much more than that to each other for the past three or four years. I wasn't sure why. He had stopped speaking to me, and he never told me the reason. I didn't ask him to explain. He's a man, not a boy, I thought, and if he has a gripe with me, he can tell me. In my view Steve had always been very sensitive, always a little too quick to take offense, and over the years he and I have had a fluctuating relationship. A separation of five years in age makes a big difference when young and contributed to a distance between us, but as we matured we did draw closer for long periods—though this, too, was difficult, since I had moved from Chicago in my early twenties, and he had stayed, eventually settling in Skokie, a suburb, and teaching in an inner-city public grade school in Chicago.

My parents were aware of this most recent distance between us, and they regularly urged us to reconcile. There have been problems with siblings from the beginning of time, from Cain and Abel to Joseph and his brothers to, well, to my mother's own brothers, a situation that pained her deeply. Now she had to suffer it being replayed between her only two sons.

I, too, was unhappy with this simmering conflict. As my parents had told me—and, I know, had told Steve—you only have one brother. You should be friends. And the fact is, I liked Steve. He was quirky, he was loving to his wife and daughter, and he had a sly wit. For my birthday several years ago, he and his wife, Judy, sent me an album, Paul Simon's *Still Crazy After All These Years*.

I called to thank them. They were on phone extensions at their home. "By the way," I said, "did the name of the album have any significance to me?"

"Oh no," Judy said, "we just thought you'd like the music."

There was silence from Steve's end. I could picture him sitting by the phone, blond hair, glasses, stocky.

"Steve?" I said.

"Maybe," he replied.

And one day about a year ago, when his teenage daughter, Shayne, broke her collarbone in a fall, I called his house on a Saturday morning to see how she was.

I think I woke him up.

"Steve," I said, "this is Ira."

"What do you want?" he said.

I don't know whether he meant to be as abrupt as he sounded, but I was silent for a moment, collecting myself.

"I called to see how Shayne was."

"She's getting better," he said. And then he explained what had happened and the prognosis, which was good. The some-what hostile tone had changed to one more businesslike, but still not too brotherly. We hung up. I felt uneasy and angry. I wasn't about to call him again—at that moment I never even wanted to speak to him again.

While in Chicago I always like to drive through the familiar residential streets, lined with white bungalows and red-brick three-story flats. In my mind I still see myself as a young yout', as a high school coach used to say, and I could still envision the time when I began playing basketball when I was around eight years old. The smoke from World War II had only recently cleared, and although baseball was really the major sport for me and my friends in the Lawndale section of the West Side of Chicago, I still played basketball in one form or another, in summer and in winter.

The neighborhood kids would choose up sides in the alley behind Springfield Avenue near 13th Street, and we'd toss a rubber ball over a drain pipe that hung out at an angle from a garage door. Lawndale was a predominately Jewish neighborhood, but there was a substantial mix of Irish, Italian, and Polish families. James Hunter and his younger cousin Willie Nero were two of the first blacks to move into the neighborhood, and they played with us. There was not yet the mystique of the black player, though the Harlem Globetrotters were an ideal of basketball slickness, if not, as they should have been, of basketball prowess. There were few black college players, and none yet in the NBA. And I would learn an important lesson: You can't judge a player by his race. James, lean and with an impressive poise, jumped well and made magnificent moves, even when going to the drainpipe with a rubber ball. Willie, shorter and chunkier than his cousin, was at best ordinary at this game. And while I was even younger than Willie, I was often picked ahead of him. Never even in my grandest dreams could I have been chosen over James.

Sometimes we had to stop the game in the alley because

the old fruit-and-vegetable peddler, Carl, in his floppy cap was coming by on his horse-drawn wagon. There was the creak of wagon wheels and the clop of passing hooves on the uneven cement. And sometimes we players had the unpleasant task of sweeping up our basketball court with leaves and twigs and the tops of garbage cans after the old horse had deposited his road apples.

Eventually my pals and I graduated to a hoop on an outdoor court and then indoors to Franklin Park or to something called the Nathaniel Institute, on Crawford Avenue, where kids from the neighborhood were allowed to play in the two-story red-brick building's small gym. Basketball was a kind of lure. For at what was a half-time break, we urchins were led into a classroom, where we were subjected to an attempt at proselytizing. A preacher in casual dress—if he wasn't a preacher, then he was surely a professional lay minister—was stationed at the front of the room. He played the piano and read the New Testament to the predominantly Jewish group, still sweating from the basketball game and, with wiggling legs, impatient to get back to it.

I believe the preacher man met with zero success in saving our souls for Christianity. I did learn the words to "Rock of Ages," however, but that is as far as my personal conversion went. In the several years I played ball at the Nathaniel Institute, I never gave Christ much of a chance, to be honest, and by the time I was bar mitzvahed and entering high school, I possessed somewhat improved basketball skills thanks to my efforts there.

It was a glorious feeling to be running down the basketball court in that golden world, wearing the white-and-blue home jersey of the high school team: the lights above shining on the yolk-yellow wooden floor, the spectators in the brown foldout bleachers, the bright orange ball, the white squeaky sneakers, and sinking shots, long rainbow-arcing shots, from the corners, from the top of the free-throw circle, the ball flicking through the net strings, and hearing the cheers. On some days everything seemed to fall right. I can still picture vividly pulling up with the ball on a fast break at the top of the key, some 20 feet from the basket. Normally the ball handler looks to pass to a teammate closer to the basket for a hoped-for step-in basket. I saw only the hoop and released the shot. As the ball looped toward the basket, sailing past the meshed-in lights on the low ceiling, I saw Coach Scher leap from the bench, white-haired and in blue cardigan, his mouth open and about to protest that that wasn't what we had practiced!

The ball snapped cleanly through the net, and the coach sat down quietly.

Fans cheered. I was fourteen years old, and the cheers made me feel like flying. I pretended I didn't hear, but I did—all of it. So nice. The other side, though, is that those sounds seep into one's ears and have a tendency, particularly to the young and inexperienced, to inflate the head. This happened to me, though at first I wasn't aware of it. Then one day a friend called me "King," and it brought me up short. It sounded more sour than kidding. I thought at first he was jealous, since he had been cut from the team in tryouts, and I remember him smashing his fist against the locker in anger and disappointment.

But there were other calls from the stands, from the friends and relatives and curiosity seekers who stayed beyond the varsity game: "Gunner." "Hog." "Hungry." It began when some of those pull-up shots on fast breaks did not drop into the basket. And cries of disgust weren't just from the fans of the other team. It was from some in the Sullivan crowd—people I had considered friends, some, I'd discover, who hadn't made the team themselves. And sometimes I'd hear little remarks, just within earshot, from my teammates as well. It all came as a surprise to me—the development of my basketball skills, and their resentment. It was a strange sensation, to feel both exalted and rejected. It would not be the last time I experienced it.

In my teenage years, I learned many of the most important lessons—or at least the most deeply felt and painful ones—not in the classroom but on the basketball court while playing for the Sullivan High School team. In that impressionable time of life the grading of the social world and my peers carried far greater significance than that of my formal education. The impact remains, some forty years later.

I had tried out and made the frosh-soph team in my sophomore year and became the team's leading scorer. This naturally led to my visions of greatness for a varsity career. Before frosh-soph, I hadn't played a great deal of team full-court basketball. It was mostly shooting alone or half-court games. But I soon discovered that I had at least a modest "touch," the ability to shoot the ball well, particularly from the perimeter, some 17 to 22 feet from the basket.

The coach, Art Scher, was a small, myopic man with a quiet smile who had once been in a serious car accident that apparently affected his memory. He frequently forgot the names of us players and peered over the tops of his glasses in an earnest effort to remember. You might be in his office talking to him about meaningful matters for ten minutes, and then when you were about to go, he'd call you John when you knew quite well that your name was Jim. This caused some confusion among the players. Some of them snickered at him behind his back because of the name problem, but also because he had some eccentric ways about him, related, to a great degree, to his passion for his work.

Scher also coached the varsity, and one of the outstanding players on the team was Barry Holt, who had a driving competitive spirit like few others. Barry was an honor student who rarely studied; he just absorbed material like a sponge takes in algae. And he took to challenges in a similar fashion. Though he was lean, he was a stunningly big eater. Someone on the team once bet Barry he couldn't eat twelve hot dogs at a single sitting. He said he could, but a negotiation ensued that presaged Barry's career as an attorney. "No buns," he said. "Buns," said the other guy. But Barry prevailed: no buns. And with several of us as witnesses at Little Louie's hot dog restaurant, Barry won the bet, though it briefly cost him, as would soon become obvious, a certain intestinal well-being.

And Barry was always looking for ways to improve. Somewhere or other he hit upon the idea of making his arms longer. He hung from the top of a door in his home. "I had a lot of explaining to do when the door came off the hinges," he confided to me.

Holt also had disagreements with Coach Scher over strategy. Holt read all these books, studied the games on television, and had a depth that I did not approach. Coach Scher listened and went his way. Despite his genial smile on most occasions, Scher was a profoundly serious man when it came to basketball. Before sending a player into a game, Coach Scher would summon him to his side on the bench. He had a habit of saying to the kneeling substitute, "We're counting on you" or "You can do it." Something that he hoped would make us soar. Once, with the team hopelessly behind and less than a minute to go in the game, he was about to send in Earl Pratt, a stone-faced but witty forward. "Think you can do it, son?" he asked.

Earl looked at the scoreboard, looked at the clock, and

then looked at the old man. "If I don't get tired, coach," he said, straight-faced.

Another good friend on the team was Dick Brandwein, a thickly built, red-haired transfer student from Von Steuben High School who taught me several facts of life, one of the most enterprising being the distinctions between winning and losing in our one-on-one games. I learned early. We played for money, maybe a dollar or two or five a game. He won the first game we ever played and said, "Paysies." That is, I had to pay up, of course. The next time we played I won. I asked for the money. He said, "Owesies." I said, "What?!" He eventually did pay.

Coach Scher was dedicated to coaching basketball, and I admired him. I ran into him one morning in the crowded high school corridor between classes. You couldn't miss him coming down the hall. He stood no more than 5 feet 5 inches tall. A lock of gray hair fell across his forehead, and wire-rim glasses rested on his thin nose. He wore his customary gray cardigan buttoned up, with a whistle dangling from a lanyard, and white canvas Converse sneakers.

We stopped to chat. I don't remember how we got into it, but he soon was demonstrating to me a pivot move without the ball. Amid all the students' movement and clatter, this little gray-haired man backed up a few steps and ran at me—I stood with books in hand—and he slammed down on his right foot, spun left and slipped behind me, arms outstretched, to catch the invisible pass from the nonexistent teammate. I had to bite my lip to keep from smiling.

The coach was a genuinely modest man. When the team had won a few games and a reporter from the school paper came by to interview him, he said, "The boys deserve all the credit, write about them." He imparted, or tried to impart, life lessons to his players. One that he told each group of basketball players was his story of when, in 1918 or 1919, he was a substitute on the Benton Harbor High School basketball team, which played in a gym that was built around a stove in a corner. Coach Scher told of how, as the shortest player on the team, he was unable to break into the starting lineup and played infrequently. But he yearned to play more and dreamed of his chance and continued to practice with diligence. Then it happened that a starting player got injured in a game in the last quarter and young Art Scher was inserted into the lineup. His team won, 17–16, and he scored the winning basket in the last seconds of the game.

Coach Scher told this story with humility but with surprising enthusiasm, considering the number of times he must have told it. But his point was that if you stay prepared and don't despair, one day you, too, will get your chance. Or, if we're having bad times, the tide may one day turn. It had happened before—he was a man of experience in this regard—and it could happen again.

His story of patience and triumph, though good to hear and remember, had its limits: in the end each of us would have to construct our own stories of winning and losing, patience and impatience, loving and leaving, falling and rising; it would take less of a toll if we could learn from others' mistakes or lessons, but it doesn't usually work that way, and one's own experiences remain the most reliable rule of thumb.

At Sullivan we played our games in a small gym—so small that the several radiators were affixed on the walls rather than on the floor—with foldout bleachers that filled up quickly with about four hundred students. Other spectators often were forced to stand along the pale, peeling walls behind the baskets to watch the varsity games, their toes on the end lines of the court. Fewer stayed for the frosh-soph games that followed. The games began in the daylight, and large yellow curtains were pulled across the windows to keep out the streaking sunlight. The games ended in darkness, under the glow of lightbulbs covered by small cages.

Though I could shoot well, in the early days I didn't fully understand or appreciate the rest of the strategy, how important, even artistic, passing was, or positioning for rebounds, or the nuances of defense. And, perhaps, with less mobility and speed than I would have wished for myself, I drove to the basket infrequently. I read an observation years later by the painter Paul Klee: "You adapt yourself to the contents of the paint box." I relied on a fake and a couple of dribbles, or a screen or pick from a teammate, to set me free for the jump shot. Not a winged elevation, since I was never a good jumper, but a slight jump, just enough, some friends joked, to get a newspaper under my feet. The accuracy of the shot was in the balance of the body, anyway, and the touch. But if you could shoot—oh, man!—that was a lot. Most of us in school wanted to be good shooters. It's where the action seemed to be, and, everyone knew, the glory.

I had some extraordinary games on the frosh-soph squad, good and bad. There were a few games in which I scored nearly as many points as the entire opposing team. Against the Schurz High School frosh-soph we won 40–33, and I scored 23 points. About a week later we beat Roosevelt, 46–36. I again scored 23 points.

It also happened that I wasn't quite as good a player as I had led myself to believe. Some days I scored considerably fewer points. I had 6 points in a losing game against Von Steuben, watching in anguish as the ball bounced off the rim time and again. Sometimes it was my rhythm on the shot— some imperceptible thing was off, or sometimes the problem was more visible, like the long, obtrusive arm of the defender. The day after the Von Steuben game, troubled, I sought out

Coach Scher. "Coach," I asked him in all seriousness, for I did not know, "will I ever hit again?"

I learned over the years that this is the fear of almost every athlete, regardless of his talents. It is true of young athletes, to be sure. But even older ones, after a bad day, will question their ability. Is this, they wonder, the end of the road? I don't remember exactly how Coach Scher answered my question, but I know his response was designed to build my confidence. He was like that. When we were about to graduate, another player, a senior on the team who hadn't played much and who had caused him particular grief, received the school letter, "S," from Coach Scher. About a week or so after the letter winners had been announced, I was curious to learn why Scher had given him the letter, knowing their history. I asked him. "Because," the coach said, "I don't want him to leave school with a bad taste in his mouth."

During my last three years at Sullivan, basketball grew in importance to me. I loved the game. Our team won more than we lost, but deep down it was really the personal challenge that made the game significant for me. I believe anyone on the team would have said the same. If you played well—not selfishly, but your best—then the day was not a disaster. Basketball gave me a sense of myself that I had never quite had before. As I wound deeper into my teenage years, the game helped me feel as though I had entered a new world.

But before my junior year, as I was about to join the varsity basketball team, I thought of quitting. I had suffered on the frosh-soph with calls from some of the students in the stands of "hog" and "hungry" and "gunner," and had got into a few scuffles over it. I wasn't sure it was worth it. I talked about this with my girlfriend at the time, Flora Estes. Somehow I found it easier to discuss this with a girlfriend than with some of the guys or with my father or mother. With a girl I felt less vulnerable than if I had shared this with any-one else. And Flora, sitting beside me on a couch in her home, was a good listener. She also had some good advice. "Don't be stupid, you like basketball," she said. "How can you quit?" Then I hit on a decision. I would stop shooting. And I did, to a large extent.

I started at guard on the varsity in the second half of the season, when three previous starters had graduated after the midyear semester. And though I had a few good shooting games, I still was reluctant to take many shots. And when I did, now, I seemed to be thinking about it. I felt myself tight-ening up. In sports, and in most other activities, the best per-formers are free of doubts, of inhibiting mental restraints. You practice the routines but in the game the subconscious takes over, the muscle memory, as dancers call it. There is an ease of confidence that is fundamental to success. I had lost that looseness. Once Yogi Berra was told by a coach not to swing at bad pitches at the plate, and to think up there. When he batted next time and struck out with his bat on his shoulder, the coach asked what happened. "I can't hit and think at the same time," Berra explained. I understood. I might score 8, or 11, or 12 points—in a game against our archrival, Senn High School, which had one of the best teams in the state, I hit six straight shots—but I'd also have games in which my line in our box score in the Chicago newspaper the next morning might read, "Berkow 0–0–2," for no field goals scored, no free throws, and two fouls committed. Not terrific.

I concentrated on defense. I had found in a sports maga-zine a quote from Honey Russell, the basketball coach at Se-ton Hall, who said that playing defense took guts and that basically only your coach and the players in the game would appreciate it. The girls in the stands probably wouldn't. I tore out that observation and carried the clipping in my wallet.

Under Coach Scher we practiced diligently, but in the way it is with many high school teams, all the good intentions of practice are lost in the welter and emotion of the game itself. A play is signaled and someone forgets to cut, or cuts to the wrong place, and two guys are whizzing past each other as the passed ball bounces off the head of a spectator in the first row. Meanwhile, the coach is shouting, "That's not the play!" Sometimes I was the passer, and sometimes I was the cutter heading for the wrong coast.

And something else was going on, too.

One of my best friends on the team was Stuart Menaker. Stuart was a semester behind me and had been the tenth man on the frosh-soph team. Suddenly, over the summer when I went from a sophomore to a junior, he improved spectacularly. We both played over the summer, but I worked on a garbage truck until late afternoon. He didn't have a day job, so instead he went to the YMCA with his lunch in a bag and spent the whole day working on his moves and his shooting.

I hadn't concerned myself with this. After all, I was not only a starter on the frosh-soph, while he sat on he bench, but I was also captain and high scorer. And we played the same position and were about the same height and build. Stuart had played only when the game was nearly out of hand—when we were losing or winning by a wide enough margin so it didn't matter if substitutes were called in.

I felt sorry for Stuart when his dad, a sign painter, and his mother, a cashier in a bank, took time off from work to watch our team play and Stuart wouldn't get into the game. My parents never came to the games since neither felt it important enough to relinquish a day's pay to see a basketball game, even one in which their son played. And I never expected them to come, though when I had had a good game, I would have loved to have them in the stands. When I wasn't playing well, or even playing much, I didn't miss them at all. I was happy not to have to explain my failings to them and was content to let them be blissfully ignorant of that part of my world.

Stuart and I lived about a mile from each other, traveled to and from school together on the city bus, and double-dated. One time we all got thrown out of a movie theater because we were laughing too loudly, and too much, and it had nothing to do with the movie, but with our own silliness. Stuart and I also ate at each other's homes. I'd go through his refrigerator, and he'd go through ours. Stuart came to our home for dinner three times in one month. And it happened that my mother, who usually cooked, had bought Chinese food for the sake of convenience on each of those occasions. Maybe the only three times in that period that she had. Upon arriving home she found Stuart sitting at the kitchen table with me, ready to eat.

My mother, who always wanted me to call ahead when bringing someone home, displayed only momentary dissatisfaction, then graciously split up the meal. Stuart and I wolfed down the fried rice and the egg foo young. And Stuart, ever polite, couldn't say now how good a cook my mother was, because she hadn't cooked. So he said, "Boy, Mrs. Berkow, you sure know where to buy your chop suey!"

Stuart and I once went with two other friends on a weekend trip to South Haven, Michigan, a resort town that was popular with people from Chicago. We were sitting on the porch of the small hotel and talking with one of the employees, a kid about our age. Stuart asked him what he made there.

"Aw, crap," he said.

"Oh," said Stuart, "you must be the cook."

Stuart was a delight to be around. He was good-natured and good-hearted. Stuart's house was always a place where our friends could comfortably gather. As we'd be walking up the walkway, we'd hear Stuart's mother, Fritzie, hollering at him and his two younger brothers, "Will you kids stop running around the house in your jockey shorts when we have guests coming? Put on pants!"

Stuart and I both made the varsity basketball team in our junior year, and while he was still was my replacement, he no longer entered the game during what we called "garbage time," late in the fourth quarter of a one-sided game. Now he was coming in late in the *first* quarter. He soon became a star. He was faster than I was, shiftier, and had better moves. He made spectacular shots. One time when he was knocked off his feet in a scramble and was parallel to the ground in a supine position, as though in levitation, he shot the ball, and it went in!

I was confused by Stuart's success. I was envious. I was angry. I was embarrassed. I cursed the coach under my breath. Possibly Stuart had felt the same way toward me when we were on the frosh-soph. In a one-on-one game one day we got into a brief scuffle. And it ended that game. But the next day we played together in practice, and then we'd share a joke, or a good pass, or someone would say something and we'd be in the conversation, and soon we were friends again, as tight as ever.

But in the first quarter of a varsity game, when the buzzer sounded to signal that time was called, Stuart would come off the bench, stepping toward me and pointing, which is the custom when informing a player that you're replacing him. And then a surge of anger would rise in me. Coming out? This is pure bullshit! But I wouldn't blurt it out. I'd just grab my warm-up jersey from the side of the bench and tug it on.

And of course to add to the indignities, the coach sometimes forgot my name because of his infirmity from the automobile accident. Though I believe I understood, it still hurt, especially now.

In the last game of my junior year, we played at Schurz High, the team with whom we were tied in the North Section standings, for the right to enter the Public League playoffs. I was playing one of my better varsity games, with eight points at the half. But I had also been called for four fouls. The third period had hardly begun when I got whistled for a fifth—and disqualifying—foul. I still believe I was about 25 feet away from where the infraction occurred, but nonetheless, in this important game for us, I wound up on the bench, again.

Stuart finished with 10 points, but he fouled out, too, and we lost 84–72. Schurz went on to play Dunbar, an all-black school, in the first round of the playoffs, and got wiped out, saving us, I guess, from the calamity. Dunbar continued on to win the city championship, and its ace guard, Alphra Saunders, who dribbled very low in the way Groucho Marx loped, became a standout for Bradley University—on a championship team with Chet (the Jet) Walker.

In my senior year Stuart and I started together as guards on the Sullivan varsity. By now I had developed an understanding of my limits—or grudgingly admitted them. There comes a time when reality finally lands with both feet on the brain. I had gained, painfully but inexorably, a heightened appreciation of Stuart's talents. His quickness on the court, his fakes that seemed so natural and could have his defender flying through the air as Stuart dribbled around him, and those odd-seeming shots from impossible angles that dropped through the hoop.

I also began to accept my role as a feeder for Stuart. I even began to take pleasure in setting him up with a pass for him to score. Stuart went on in our senior year to be the coscoring leader of the Chicago public high schools. But despite my little foray into maturity—rooting now for Stuart and marveling at his skills—I still would have changed places with him to see my name in the paper among those other stars who had made the coveted All-North Section team.

While New York has been my home for nearly thirty years, Chicago, my hometown, remains in my heart. Perhaps, as someone once said, a writer accumulates all the life experiences he needs by the time he is twenty years old. It's a neat phrase, but it's not true. The "first times" might be all that a writer needs, but the second and third times also shape that initial experience. And yet the first time may be the most memorable, or the most delicious, or the most painful. It does take hold.

For that reason I took a special interest in those college and NBA players who grew up in Chicago. I felt a certain bond with them—we had played in many of the same gyms, the same playgrounds, and shared, I imagined, a similar view of the game. It may have begun when I followed the careers of Ron Rubenstein and Hershey Carl, two of the best high school players in the North Section public league when I played. They both went on to play major-college ball: Rubenstein at Louisville and Carl at DePaul, with Carl even making it to the NBA.

In 1981, when I learned that Isiah Thomas, the 6-foot-1 star guard for Indiana University, was from the West Side of Chicago, I was eager to see him play in person. And so I drove down to Philadelphia on March 30 to see his team play North Carolina for the NCAA championship. With 12 seconds left in the first half, North Carolina led 26–25. Thomas coolly dribbled the ball downcourt, looking for his team to take a last shot. He was as unhurried as a waiter in a coffee shop, and I got edgy just watching him. But my inner clock and Isiah's were obviously not measuring time at the same speed. It was an application of Einstein's theory of relativity: there is truly a difference in time not only in different places, but in different heads, too.

With two seconds left in the half Isiah cleverly found an open man, Randy Wittman, and hit him with a sharp pass. Wittman sank the jump shot to give Indiana the lead and an emotional lift as the Hoosiers ran off to the locker room. At the start of the second half, Thomas stole two straight passes, and Indiana went up 31–26 en route to a 63–50 victory and the championship, with Thomas scoring a game-high 23 points.

About a week later, I traveled to Bloomington, Indiana, to write a story on Isiah. If I could find him, that is.

I had called his coach's office, but Bobby Knight wasn't speaking to the press about his great guard at this time. Rumors were circulating that Thomas, a sophomore, was thinking about leaving Indiana and turning pro. This, apparently, had put Bobby Knight into a funk, for he saw two possible championships slipping away. If Thomas chose to turn pro, he might make $1 million. If he stayed in school and if the team didn't do as well the next year, or if he sustained injury, his value would drop precipitously. The nineteen-year-old Thomas understood this, because he was a wise young man.

After asking questions around campus, I was led to an apartment building, and then to an apartment on the third floor. I knocked. Isiah Thomas, in sweatshirt and jeans, and with that deceptively boyish smile, answered. He was surprised to have been found, he said. "Not even Coach knows where I am." Thomas was in the midst of not just making his decision to turn pro, but also deciding how to tell his volatile coach. I thought back to the case of Al McGuire and Jim Chones. In 1970 McGuire was the coach of Marquette University, and Chones was his seven-foot star junior center who had been offered a huge contract with the New York Nets of

the American Basketball Association. "I looked into his refrigerator," recalled McGuire, about going to the home of
Chones's mother, "and I looked into my refrigerator, and I
said, 'Take the money.'"

Isiah did, and he went on to have an outstanding pro career, lasting thirteen years and helping Detroit win two NBA
titles. Three weeks after his playing career ended, at age
thirty-three, he leaped at another opportunity and became
vice president and general manager of the expansion Toronto
Raptors of the NBA. By the time the Raptors took the court in
1995, Thomas's front-office savvy had earned him renewed
respect around the league.

In that first conversation with Thomas, in Bloomington, I
asked where he was from.

"Chicago," he said.

"I know Chicago," I said, "but where in Chicago."

"The West Side."

"The West Side's a big place, Isiah. What street?"

"Congress Parkway."

I persisted. "But where? By Lawndale Avenue? By Millard?
By Central Park? By Trumbull? Where? What was your address?"

He looked at me curiously. "It was 3340 Congress Parkway."

"Oh, between Homan and Spaulding," I said.

"Why, uh, yes?"

"Did you go to Garfield Park?"

"Yeah, all the time." And then a broad smile creased his
face. "Wow. You really did your homework!"

"No, Isiah, I grew up in the neighborhood."

He couldn't believe it. I explained to him that the neighborhood had changed considerably from the time I had lived
there. But, as homeboys, more or less, we shared a back-

ground, a "first," for we both grew up in the area. This tie created what I have always felt was a particular bond between us.

The only player picked ahead of Thomas in the 1981 NBA draft was his friend and fellow Chicagoan and West Sider, Mark Aguirre of DePaul University. Aguirre's NBA career lasted exactly as long as Thomas's, thirteen years, and there was some similarity in my relationship with him. It began one afternoon in 1990 when I was in Boston to cover a playoff game between the Celtics and the Pistons—by this time Aguirre had been dealt to the Pistons, at Thomas's urging. I arrived in Boston Garden a few hours before the game and saw a solitary figure shooting baskets. It was Aguirre, in gray sweat clothes, looking a little chunky but with a smooth shot. I walked beside the court and stood and watched him. A ball bounced over and I caught it and motioned to shoot and he nodded OK. It was a shot of only ten or fifteen feet, and I sank it. As is the custom in school yards, if you make a shot you get another. Aguirre tossed the ball back to me. I sank that one, too. He looked at me with a kind of joking, disbelieving look.

"Bryant School, class of '53," I said.

"You went to Bryant School?!" he exclaimed.

"Of course," I said. "How else do you think I can make that shot?"

"You're kidding," he said.

"I'm not kidding. Remember the leather nets on the baskets in the gym?"

"The leather nets!" he said. "Sure!"

I knew that Aguirre had graduated from the same grammar school that I had—his class was twenty-one years later, '74—and it turned out that he had grown up only a few blocks from where I once lived.

"Yeah, Mark," I said, "you broke all of my records at Bryant except for one."

"Oh, what was that?" Aguirre asked.

Records, I'm sure he was thinking, there were no records kept in grammar school basketball, were there?

"I spent three years in the second grade," I said.

Aguirre half-smiled at the silly joke. "Thanks for the shots," I said. And we both went back to work.

About forty-five minutes later, I was in the Pistons' locker room and talking to Isiah. Aguirre had come in and was at the other end of the small room. I told Thomas about what happened—including the business about breaking my so-called records. "Isiah," I said, "if you wouldn't mind, why don't you ask him about the shots I took?"

I was thinking this was a kind of fraternal West Side thing. And I was feeling pretty good about it.

"Hey, Drawers," Isiah called out, using his nickname for the broad-beamed Aguirre, and nodding toward me. "What's he look like on the court?"

Aguirre was taking off his sweat shirt. "He's got this OK little shot," said Aguirre, somewhat distracted.

Thomas turned to me and raised his eyebrows. "Whattya gonna do?" he said sympathetically.

I shrugged. "Well," I said, "I guess I'll just have to go back to writing."

In December of 1995 I again returned to Chicago and went out to the new, sparkling, and cold-as-crystal United Center, home of the Bulls, to write a piece on Michael Jordan.

I had covered Jordan for a number of years. After all, to be a sportswriter and to not have written often on Jordan would be like a White House correspondent neglecting to mention the president. There are so many reasons to like Jordan, but the one closest to my heart is that he has always had a so-called "love of the game" clause written into his contracts. It

legally enabled him, essentially, to play in a pickup game any-
time he wished, anywhere.

When he broke his foot partway through the 1985–86 season, he returned first to play pickup games while the Bulls'
management screamed in protest, and then he returned to the
Bulls before even management thought it worth the risk. And
even when he announced his first retirement from pro basketball in 1993, he said he'd "probably become a pickup basketball player," that he still loved the game.

The 1995–96 season was Jordan's first full season since his
nineteen-month hiatus from the NBA, and he was having
some problems, despite scoring 55 points against the Knicks
in Madison Square Garden in one of his first games back. He
seemed to have lost a little quickness, and the word around
the league was that Jordan, who had been one of the greatest
defensive players, now was unable to handle some of the
younger, quicker guards in the league.

When I saw Jordan at the United Center, it was several
hours before a game against the Indiana Pacers. He would be
thirty-three years old in two months, and I asked him about
getting older, and about the difference it makes. He looked on
the positive side. "I'm wiser now," he said. "I don't get rattled
like I once might have."

"You, rattled?" I asked.

"Sure, sometimes you try to do too much to help the team.
I'm more relaxed now. I see things differently. And while I
might not be able to do all the things I once did, I think I
make up for it mentally. I understand the game in a way I
never did before."

Does this mean he can't jump as high as he once could?

"Hmmm," he mused playfully. "Maybe I've lost a quarter
of an inch." In fact, the team physician, John Hefferon, had
told me that he felt Jordan had lost some explosiveness in his

legs but was able to compensate in other ways. All of this is going into my personal basketball brain, wondering if I could use any of this insight for my game, how I could make some little compensations of my own. And Phil Jackson, the Bulls coach, told me that he believed Michael was not driving to the basket as often as he once did. Was he simply saving his legs for the playoffs? Or had he lost the bounce?

"But Michael, one thing you don't do as much as you once did," I continued, "is drive." And then, as a little aside, I added, "I don't drive as much as I used to, either."

Michael looked at me out of the corner of his eye, and passed over my remark. "The reason I don't drive as much now is because they're giving me the jump shot," he said, with just a hint of displeasure, since this was clearly not the first time he had heard this observation. "The defense is falling back. If they came up on me, I'd go to the basket more."

OK. Duly noted.

I watched the game that night from the press table, which, at the United Center, is placed directly behind one of the baskets. In the first quarter, the first time Jordan got the ball on offense he drove to the hoop, the one I happened to be sitting behind. He slashed right through the Indiana team. Slam dunk! The official play-by-play report that is distributed to the press after the game read: First period: "08:35 M. Jordan DRIVING DUNK." The very next time he tried a shot, it was on a fast break, and again he flew to the hoop: "05:53 M. Jordan FB layup." The third time he got the ball, he torpedoed in once more: "03:38 M. Jordan DRIVING LAYUP." After that third basket, as Jordan turned to run back downcourt, he looked in my direction and gave me the most subtle and fleeting of glances, as if to say, "Sure I can't drive!"

I didn't know how I was going to incorporate any of *that* into my game. But it certainly gave me food for thought.

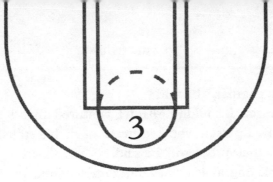

Legends

Over a professional career that spanned twenty years, Kareem Abdul-Jabbar and his stellar sky hook amassed 38,387 points in the National Basketball Association. It is the all-time professional scoring record, one that many believe may never be broken.

"It's nothing," Charlie Miron told me. "It's minor league."

Minor league? "Certainly," said Charlie. "I've scored close to 300,000 points, and I'm still playing. I'm the highest scorer in the history of half-court basketball."

I was walking up snow-covered Second Avenue with Charlie, a long-time friend with whom I used to play basketball at the Vanderbilt Y. His bald head was covered by a Tyrolean hat with a red feather, and he also wore a down jacket, dark slacks, and, of course, sneakers.

"Charlie," I said, "are you trying to tell me that in the one hundred years of basketball no one anywhere has ever scored more points than you?"

"Name another," he said.

I confessed I couldn't. And I ventured that I could not name another person who kept track of such a statistic.

"That's their problem," he said.

After playing at least several games of pickup basketball several days a week for about five decades, Charlie said his self-figured total comes to, in round numbers, about 280,000. And I don't ever remember him not wearing sneakers. "You never know when a ball game might break out," he said.

Charlie Miron is a Brooklyn-born New Yorker of an indeterminate age; that is, he won't determine for anyone how old he is. Sometimes when age is brought up, I ask him what his is. "What's the difference?" he asks.

"If it doesn't make a difference, then tell me," I said, on Second Avenue.

"Forty-two," he said.

"And last year?"

"Forty-one."

I know he was off by a couple of decades.

He says he was poppin' 'em in on the Rockaway Beach Courts in Queens in the 1940s with players like Tricky Dick McGuire and Bob Cousy, who "started as a center in the parks, and if he hadn't gone into full-court might have broken my record." Charlie smiled with a certain humility.

"Games were tough there," he went on. "In other places a defensive ace would be happy if he held his man to two shots. At Rockaway I've seen Tricky Dick hold his man to two *passes*."

As it happens, Charlie and I have drifted to separate basketball venues, but we have lunch occasionally and talk on the phone—that is, he calls me on the phone, since I have infrequently had a number for him, and he also kept vague where he lived.

One of his regular haunts in summer, however, remains the basketball courts in the beach area in Brooklyn. He told me about playing in Manhattan Beach with Chris Mullin, the high-scoring Golden State Warrior forward and Dream Team member who also hails from Brooklyn. "Mullin was scoring like crazy," said Charlie. "But yours truly had a few, too."

Charlie stands 6-foot-2, has added a few pounds around the middle, and his head is now clean-shaven in the Michael Jordan manner. "The hair was graying and starting to go," he said. "So I helped it along. After Michael, a lot of guys adopted that style. Makes you look ten years younger."

He plays basketball—generally half-court games—on various indoor and outdoor courts around New York, and at other points domestic as well as foreign.

"Played in Sweden some time back," he said, "and they're funny there. No one speaks. I play in New York, and no one shuts up."

Charlie's scoring record—he counts one point for a basket in his personal record if the half-court game counts one point for a hoop, and two points when full-court games count two points—has been achieved through an undiminished love for the basketball and a looping, left-handed set shot. Charlie never went much to his right or drove to the hoop or rebounded—all of which, he admits, has helped avoid wear and tear on the legs. Also: "I don't drink, don't smoke, avoid fried foods—except for potato latkes at holiday time—and have never done drugs." He laughed. "But of course that's not my complete dossier."

And Charlie's dossier, beyond intimate details such as being a lifelong bachelor with a weakness for leggy blondes, contains a variety of careers: art dealer, magazine writer, published novelist, screenwriter still looking to sell a script, and a devotee of animals. It is a life that allows ample time for hoops.

Over my own nearly half century of playing basketball, I have met a multitude of unusual, offbeat, and remarkable people. Charlie Miron ranks in the top percentile. Once he told me that a good friend of his was Marcel Marceau, the internationally renowned French mime. People often tell you a lot of things. Then one afternoon I had occasion to interview Marceau. He was staying at the Plaza Hotel. Marceau greeted me at the door, and when I walked in, I noticed someone sitting in a corner. "You know my friend Sharles Miron," Marceau said, in his French accent. Another time I received a note from Paris from Marceau. Could I find Charles and have Charles call him? I had no number for Charlie, of course, but I located him in a gym the next day.

Charlie once owned a pet ocelot—visitors were taken aback to find in his apartment a jungle beast that he had described as a pet cat. He once nurtured a greyhound he named Misty—"a bag of bones when I found her in a pet store"—into a show champion named Misty of Romin (Romin being Miron jumbled).

Charlie was also once a stage actor. In the late 1950s he sought a role in the road show of *Diamond Lil*, starring Mae West. He auditioned for the part of her Latin lover. "You know her line, 'Why don't you come up and see me sometime?'" said Charlie. "Well, I did."

"She held her auditions in her penthouse at the Wellington Hotel. I was young and nervous. She was lying on a couch in a green satin dressing gown. She was twirling her hair—golden blonde—with her finger. It was about a hundred degrees that day. She said in that sexy way, 'Most people's hair gets flat when it's hot. Mine gets cur-ly.' Oh, man! I got so weak in the knees I almost fell over." Charlie read, Mae West listened, and she hired him. Not as the lover, but for a smaller part.

Basketball, though, was never far from Charlie's heart, or

feet. "You never get your name in the paper playing half-court," he said, "and I've never seen a great half-courter who played for the girls, either, like a lot of guys do in college. You play for within yourself."

One day several years ago, he was about to board a plane when he noticed a fellow passenger who was particularly large. "Dipper!" said Charlie to Wilt Chamberlain. This was the first time he had ever met Chamberlain, but he knew that the retired NBA star liked the nickname "Big Dipper" and hated the better known "Wilt the Stilt."

Charlie told him that he looked in great shape. "I play a lot of volleyball," Wilt explained.

"I still play ball, too—hoops," said Charlie. "I'm the king of half-court basketball."

"No kidding," said Wilt.

"Over 170,000 points, Dip."

"Congratulations," said Wilt.

Chamberlain boarded and sat in two seats in first class, in order to spread his huge frame.

As Charlie walked up the aisle past Chamberlain, he said to him, "I'm sitting in half a seat."

"For half-court," said Wilt.

"Precisely," said Charlie.

Charlie had quit the Vanderbilt Y years ago for a variety of reasons, not all of which he shared with me. He was living too far away. He was no longer enamored of the games. He felt the laundry service was unsatisfactory. Maybe all of them, maybe none of them. The fact is, Charlie stopped coming. But I still would hear from him, and see him.

"I play in places where the guys are younger," said Charlie. "And they're not bad. I don't like to play with older guys." I asked why. "Because they always play dirty. Not that I'm afraid of it. But it's embarrassing. They grab your pants, they try to trip you. All kinds of nonsense. I tell those guys that they're embarrassing themselves. I tell 'em they should be off the court. I always said that if I ever got like that, I would just never play the game again.

"I've played the game for a long, long time, and I find that the guys never change, really. And I like to play with good players best of all. They know the game. They don't make phony calls. They aren't really dirty, though they might be physical. In all the years that I've played, I don't ever remember getting into a fight with a really good player. But I have gotten into fights with a lot of half-assed ballplayers."

Charlie once got into a fistfight with Roach, the same guy with whom I'd had a fistfight. "He started pulling my hair—I had a lot of hair then," said Charlie. "He was a truly horrible human being on the court. He always cheated on the scoring. Always. If the game was 6–4 and he was losing, suddenly it's 5–5. He had a habit of walking almost every time he got the ball. But he thought he was a player. And after awhile if you play with the guy all the time, you get tired of calling walking because that's his game. But one time he was out playing with a friend of mine in a Sunday morning game in the Hamptons. Pretty good game, pretty good players. And the players didn't know who he was but they called walking on him every time because it was so obvious. He had a long morning. On the way home from the game, he told my friend, 'You know, I never could play well outdoors.' "

Early in the season the Bulls were playing the Knicks in Madison Square Garden, and I had a conversation with the Bulls' guard Steve Kerr. If there is one professional player that I might now correlate my game with, it is Steve Kerr. He's white, about my height (in context, that is, because among the

NBA giants his 6-foot-3 looks shorter), and his specialty is shooting three-point shots. I have rarely seen him drive.

"I don't normally drive because, well, on this team, I really don't have to," said Kerr. "That's the beauty of being on the Bulls for me. I have three guys who create so much that I just try to give them a lot of space." He referred to Jordan, Pippen, and Toni Kukoc. "And when I have some room, I spot up for the jump shot. Everybody knows what I do. Usually the team runs me off picks to get me my shot. But we play so many games that eventually I get off a drive. When I'm inside I get leaners or runners—I rarely drive and bank one off the boards. And if someone like Alonzo Mourning or Shaq are in the game—real shot-blockers—I tend to keep my distance from him. But if I got it, I'll take it."

I thought, yes, leaners and runners. For the most part, he meant fadeaways as he approaches the basket. And the next day, in a pickup game, I tried it out.

The indoor basketball court near my home where I generally play in wintertime is connected to the medical center. And a similar group of players from the outdoor court plays there. It is an old court, and not especially well lit. Some of the lights from the ceiling in the gym don't work very well and intermittently flicker and go out. But if a ball hits the backboard hard, a ceiling light may flicker back on. The floor itself is uneven, and sometimes a floorboard pops out of place. A player has to stamp it with his foot back in its setting. Otherwise, it's a pleasure.

I got into a three-on-three game since only seven guys showed up, and one would wait for next, and get two losers. A quick but somewhat shorter black guy named Ron was guarding me, and I had some trouble practicing my leaners and runners because the first element in the move is to get around your man. And Ron seemed to be in two or three places at one time—that is, he was there when I went right, and he was there when I went left. So I went back to my jump shot, which I could get off either from a standing position or with a dribble or two, a go-and-stop, or pump fakes, and I took Ron low in the post. I remember overhearing Magic Johnson's advice to another tall point guard, Jalen Rose, then a University of Michigan player. "Keep giving back to the community," Johnson counseled, "and always take advantage of the smaller guards." But maybe the next time I played, I decided, I would succeed in driving like Steve Kerr.

Around this time I went for my annual physical checkup. While waiting in the doctor's office, I looked over the anatomy chart on the wall. The red-and-blue veined skeletal depiction seemed to bear no resemblance to me. Then again, I don't really see myself. Few of us do. For beneath the cover of the book is the book itself. The one made up of—scanning quickly from head to toe—the parietal and occipital bones, the trapezius, the latissisus dorsi, the adductor longus, the femur, the fibula, the tibia and, last but not least, the phalanges.

I stared at the skeleton who would be me and wondered, How could I orchestrate those bones into becoming a better basketball player?

My internist, Dr. Marcel Tuchman, came in and sat down behind his desk. He is a man of average height and build, but that is all that is average about him. The white-haired physician, his eyes keen behind his glasses, possesses a vitality and vigor that belie his seventy-five years. He continues to ski regularly and climb mountains, and he takes profound delight in hobbies such as photography and driving a team of huskies in a sled across the Antarctic. The vitality also belies the emotional and physical suffering he has endured. When his shirtsleeves are rolled up, one can see the number tattooed on his forearm that he received when he was twenty-two years old in the Auschwitz concentration camp during World War II—one of several camps in which he was held captive—places to which many members of his family accompanied him, but most did not survive.

I asked Dr. Tuchman about the changes in my body as I've aged, and what I can do about it.

"The best analogy I can give you—and talking about a well person, not a sick person—is to a splendid car you bought forty years ago," he said. "You maintained it well. You lubricated it, you prevented it from rusting, and so on. The car that you bought forty years ago is not the same car, in spite of all the maintenance, that it is now. It does not drive as well, the suspension is not as good, the cylinders and joints and axles are not as reliable. There is such a thing in the human body as wear and tear. Even though it's a splendid machine and it's conceived and put together remarkably well—probably better than any machine I know of—the components in this machine simply wear out over the course of time.

"Your joints are a little bit creaky. They're not as limber. Your muscles—even though strong—are not *as* strong. And that's really the reason why certain athletic endeavors—I'm talking now not about amateurs, but professionals—end at a certain point. You develop to a certain point, and then you reach a plateau and then you begin to decline.

"Now, that is not to say that you cannot do the same things or reasonably the same things at an advanced age. People run marathons in their seventies, or people like myself ski in their seventies, or climb mountains. But we have limitations.

"There is another component," he continued. "It's the total abandon with which you do things as a young person. When I rode a motorcycle or schussed down a mountain, I didn't think twice about breaking anything or hurting myself. I wasn't smart enough to think about that. And my investment in life was not that great. It's kind of a carelessness or callousness of youth. When you become a father, a professional, a breadwinner, you don't want to hurt yourself because you know that if you're disabled for a month, that hurts not only you, but it hurts others. And it interferes with your responsibilities."

"You lose the killer instinct?" I suggested.

"To a degree," said Dr. Tuchman.

"I think I still have it to some degree," I said.

"I don't doubt it. My colleague in this office, my partner, who is now sixty-three years old, he still has the killer instincts on the tennis court. So you don't lose it completely. But you see, for example, a John McEnroe lose that instinct enough so that he could no longer compete on the highest levels, even though technically he was still very good."

I wanted to know about jumping. Is the lift different as we age? Is it as different for me as it is for Michael Jordan?

"Jumping is a complex activity," he said. "First of all, the activity has to have strength. That implies strength in the muscles. Then it has to have elasticity, which is a complete range of motion of the joints, as well as the supporting structure. Then you have to have balance, which people with age begin to lose. And then the springiness that we had when young begins to flatten out. We amble through life. When we get into our fifties, we have to make an effort that we ambled through before.

"In the cardiovascular system," he went on, "you have reserves of oxygen, but they decrease as you get older, which results in earlier fatigue. But developing your muscles properly and by developing your stamina, if you exercise regularly, the heart is able to work at a slower rate, therefore not demanding so much oxygen. And not tiring so fast. This accommodation through training helps the person who's aging."

My eye wandered again to the anatomy chart, and then back to the hearty doctor. I knew he loved skiing the way some of us love tennis, or golf, or, well, basketball.

"This may seem like a frivolous question, doctor," I said, "but when you were in the concentration camps, did you ever think of your participation in sports? In skiing, for example?"

"Your question isn't frivolous at all," he said. "I think that such thoughts of idyllic times past—I think they sustained many of us. It was precisely thoughts of the good days, when we skied, when we swam, when we played soccer, when we had meals, when we did all those things, that were so important to us. And perhaps because of the wonderful childhood that many of us had—that I had—we hoped that we would survive this horror. Not hoped. But even *believed* that we would survive it. This was very much a part of our sustaining spirit."

I had an image of snow and barbed wire. And yearning.

"Every day I have the mental images of my experiences in those camps," he said. "And because of it I have a great capacity to appreciate that I can do things like ski again."

In the end Dr. Tuchman pronounced me fit. The laboratory tests showed that everything was "within normal limits."

The idea of the appreciation of participating in sports, especially hoops, and at an advanced age, got me to thinking. And so I decided to call someone whose views I was curious to hear. This was Mario Cuomo. He may no longer be the governor of the state of New York, having lost his bid for a fourth term in 1994, but I heard that he was still an avid pickup basketball player at age sixty-three.

When I called Cuomo on the telephone to set up an interview and explained the subject, he said, "By all means. This'll be fun. And, hey, one day we'll play some one-on-one together."

"I'd look forward to it," I said.

When I met him at his new law office at the pinstriped Manhattan firm of Willkie Farr & Gallagher, we shook hands—his was a firm grip—and, as we did, he gave me the once-over.

"You don't look fifty-five," he said gravely. "I might have to conduct an investigation into this."

Then he laughed. "And you're bigger than I thought. You wouldn't be easy to push around under the boards."

"Well," I said, returning the favor and checking him out, "it may be easier than it appears."

Cuomo told me he plays about once a week—and would like to play more to keep up his skills—but work and travel are obstacles. He looks as if he can play about as often as he wants. He stands a shade under six feet, weighs what appears to be a solid 200 pounds, and has that wanna-go-one-on-one? look in his dark eyes. His dark hair is only now turning gray, his hands are broad, and his laugh is rich.

Cuomo has a reputation as a rugged player, even at his age. Nicky Dawidoff, a *Sports Illustrated* writer with whom I have often played, went one-on-one against Cuomo for an article a few years ago. The governor beat him in a one-point game. "He's a strong, burly guy," Nicky had told me. "Lot of elbows, lot of body. He muscles you. He's an old pro." As for his shooting, Dawidoff said, "Not a deft outside shooter, but good." I asked if he went left or right. "As I remember," said Dawidoff, "rather than go left or right, the governor goes right through you."

"Nicky said you were pretty rugged," I said.

"I hope he wasn't passing himself off as a little angel," said Cuomo. "I took a few belts from him."

But it was apparently nothing like the belt he took in a game shortly before making his stirring nominating speech for Bill Clinton at the 1992 Democratic National Convention in Madison Square Garden, which left him fortunate not to spit out his teeth in the process. If it had been otherwise, Clinton might never have made it to the White House. Such are the vagaries of fate. Such are the whimsies of history. Such are the effects of a rough pickup basketball game.

Cuomo is one of the nation's great orators, but had his teeth flown into the audience when he came to the fricative part about "the next president of the—," the country might have split its sides laughing. And *then* where would Clinton have been?

"My mistake the day of that game when I got clobbered in the mouth was that I had told the guys I was playing with that I'd just had dental surgery," the former governor recalled. "I told them that I had packing in my mouth, that until the incision healed, the dentist did not want me to do anything strenuous, especially play basketball. But basketball is important to me. That was my mistake, telling these guys about my vulnerability. Three guys I'm certain aimed deliberately not just for my head but for that side of my head where the putty was, and one of them connected and all the putty was spat onto the court along with much of my blood. My two front teeth were loose. I went home feeling very foolish. Fortunately Matilda was in Los Angeles, which was a very big break for me because there is no telling what she would have done to me if she knew the whole scenario."

Cuomo's wife knew only that he was to give one of the important speeches of his life in a few days.

"Now that I didn't mind because I have been through this before," said Cuomo. "And I know that, all right, if you leave it alone and don't bite down on anything too hard, it will take six, seven, eight months but they will tighten up. The problem was, I had to give this speech the following Wednesday at the convention.

"So I go to the dentist. I'm the governor and I said, Can't you at least rig something so I don't spit the goddamn thing while I'm giving the speech? He said, Well, you know you shouldn't be giving a speech. He tried and couldn't help. So he sent me to another dentist. I said, Do anything at all just so that my mind stays secure. He looked and poked and checked and shook his head. He couldn't do anything, either.

"You know what it's like when your teeth are loose. It's a sickening feeling. I gave the whole damn speech with both teeth loose. Now somehow the adrenaline took over with all the people and all the lights and I got into it and nobody noticed except my son, Andrew, who had played in the game."

The governor smiled, and his front teeth seemed solidly in place. "But now," he said, "when I play I wear a mouth guard."

I turned to the photographs on his wall, Cuomo with Supreme Court Justice Harry Blackmun, Cuomo with President Clinton, Cuomo with Mickey Mantle. The photo with Mantle was taken in 1994, about a year before Mantle's death. "It looked like he had shrunk," said Cuomo. "A very nice guy."

Cuomo enjoys telling the story of how he and Mantle were signed to major-league contracts in the same year, 1950. Cuomo, a standout center fielder for St. John's University, got $2,000 from the Pittsburgh Pirates, while Mantle, a high school kid out of Commerce, Oklahoma, got $500 from the Yankees. Playing Class D ball in Visalia, Georgia, Cuomo was hit in the head with a pitch, ending his baseball career. He returned home to Queens, New York, where he went to law school at St. John's and finished first in his class. He also played tournament basketball games in leagues around the city, once scoring 36 points in a game. And basketball, he said, was the game he loved most of all.

"Basketball was always more fun than playing center field because as soon as you got on the court you were in the game," Cuomo recalled. "Even if you didn't have the ball, you were in the game and even if you weren't scoring, you were in the game. You could defend, you could steal the ball, you could make yourself useful as long as the game was on. That was not true of center field. It's a great diversion for me. You get so absorbed in the game that you don't think of anything but basketball."

"You were saying on the phone the other day that the problem with America is golf," I said to him.

"No, now come on, Ira, now you sound like a political opponent."

"I didn't mean to bait you," I said, "but you did say that what it takes to be a good golfer is not what it takes to make a great society—and that playing team basketball does."

"That is absolutely right," he said, warming to his subject. "Golf is a lot of fun, tennis is a lot of fun, track is a lot of fun, but these individual sports that stress your ability to take on the elements, to take on a single opponent, to take on the ball are very important to the human psyche, especially the American psyche because for a hundred and fifty years that's all we were, were individuals. But not anymore. Since we've been industrialized, we have to compete with the rest of the world. We cannot make it as two hundred fifty million disassociated individuals. It's the only way for us to win. If you play as a team, you know the strong player will have to compensate for the weak players, and we have to lend ourselves to the whole."

I told the governor that, while I like the team aspect of basketball, I also enjoy playing one-on-one because you don't have to rely on anyone else, and any mistake you make is your mistake. Which may be the difference between a writer who often works alone and a politician who must work amid multitudes.

"The idea of playing on a team is very important to me," Cuomo replied. "One-on-one is fun, but I found the team game much more satisfying, and to participate in a team victory. I'm a politician. I was the leader of the political unit in this state for twelve years as governor, and the one point that I tried to make over and over is that we have to do this thing as a team. We are all in this together—the rich people and the poor people and the people in the middle. And unless we play together we will not get maximum results."

He recalled that Michael Jordan didn't win a championship until he was in his seventh season in the NBA, "when he learned to use his other players effectively," said Cuomo. "But let me give you an example in my own experience.

"We had a very good team in the Long Island Daily Press League, and some of the best college players in the Northeast played in it. When school was out, you could play against Ray Felix, who played with the Knicks, and Bob Cousy and Sid Tannenbaum. Donnie Forman and Ray Lumpp from NYU. One night our team had only four guys show up. I wasn't supposed to be there because I was supposed to be playing in school, but I was playing under a pseudonym—Matt Dente. I also played under the names Lavar Labrette and Glendie LaDue. I always preferred Italian names. Anyway, we were playing the first-place team, the Baisley Park Civics. I'll never forget it.

"The ref came to me and said, Mario, we have to start this game. The Civics were in their sweatsuits and doing their figure eights and warming up and we had four guys—the Austin Celtics, in green and white. I said, They're coming in a car. They must've had a flat tire or something. I had no expectation that anyone else was coming, but I said, Let's start the game. The ref said, You have only four guys. You can't start the game. I said, Why not?

"And we played. We went into a zone defense—how else can you play four against five? We had some small guys, and we were all over the place. In the beginning it was a kind of joke, but it got serious when the score was 16–16. The Baisley Civics started getting aggravated, and we beat them 38–36. A headline in the *Long Island Press* the next day told of our victory and said that Matt Dente scored 14 points. Now to me that was one of the great experiences of my youth. It was astounding.

"Two things happened in that game: first, the players on the other team lost their orientation. They couldn't handle it mentally. They could have beaten us easily. All they had to do was get their composure. Say, hey look, somebody's got to be free—let's get rid of these clowns. We were scurrying around after balls, cursing, banging, and the adrenaline and the inspiration we got from being the underdogs and knowing they were losing their composure. I tell you, I have never gotten over it because it says to me how capable we are of doing wonderful things. If you don't quit. If you play like a team."

Cuomo plays basketball every Sunday morning—"No matter what," he said. "I play with a lot of young people, one of whom was the former captain of the Yale rugby team. And he plays basketball like he was still playing rugby."

"This is your son," I venture.

"He is my son," said Cuomo.

"You have to wear earmuffs when you play against him because rugby players bite ears."

"Is that so?"

"You don't know anything about rugby. They bite your ear. Oh, sure. But playing basketball with younger guys is a lot of fun, because they play an entirely different game from the one I grew up with. They're racehorses. They get the ball and everybody runs down the other end of the court as fast as they can. There is some fun to that, and excitement, and I try to run with them but they are not as much fun in half-court games. They are great athletes, probably much better than we were. But once you get into a half-court game, they don't pick well, they don't position themselves well, they don't use players well, and they don't defend well."

How much longer will he play?

"Until I can't do it anymore, until it's not fun anymore. Then you do something else. Then you coach, but you can keep the competitive fire alive until God blows it out, as long as your mind is working and you keep yourself prime and being competitive."

He paused and gazed out the window. "I understand that guys seventy years old, seventy-five years old, play three-on-three games in some leagues in Florida," he mused. "I probably won't make it as a player that long, but you do it the way you do all the rest of life, until you absolutely can't do it anymore. Until absolutely you can't do it anymore."

Governor Cuomo is nothing if not competitive. In June of 1992, Vice President Dan Quayle visited Hempstead, Long Island, to promote his "family values" theme and shot some barbs at Governor Cuomo. Then Quayle, in shirtsleeves and tassled shoes, took to a basketball court with some kids and policemen and shot around, making some baskets and missing some.

Cuomo responded, sending this message to Quayle in a television interview: "If you really want to come and make a fool of yourself, bring your jock and a pair of sneakers and let's play ball."

Quayle retorted that "You better tell Mario before he takes me on he'd better have his scouts out there."

The game never came off. I believe that it was Quayle who quailed in the face of the hoop competition. But perhaps the Governor was too busy playing in the basketball league that he organized in Albany, near the Governor's Mansion, or just in a variety of one-on-one games.

In a November 1993 story on Cuomo and basketball, my *New York Times* colleague Kevin Sack wrote, "In one-on-one grudge matches against legislators and state agency heads, the Governor is not above demanding points to compensate for his age or bad back. In pregame negotiations, he often wins the right to appoint the referee."

As I left Cuomo's law office, he didn't say any more about our playing one-on-one, as he had suggested on the telephone. Curious, I thought, but I let it pass.

Charlie Miron repeated a story to me that he had heard. He didn't know how true it was, but it represented for him some of the wonder, some of the mystery of basketball. This is how it went:

It was around 1970. Billy Cunningham, then a star with the Philadelphia 76ers, was in Chicago and he went up to a YMCA court to work out. There was only one other guy in the gym—a very tall, rather elderly fellow. Rather wide, too. And the older guy said to Cunningham, "Do you want to play some one-on-one?"

"Do you know who I am?" Cunningham said.

"Yeah, you're Billy Cunningham."

"Well, do you still want to play me?"

"Sure, let's go."

They started to play. Cunningham was all-NBA at the time and was called the Kangaroo Kid because of his great jumping ability. Well, the Kangaroo Kid wasn't getting very far with this guy because he was so wide. He was blocking Cunningham out, and Cunningham had trouble containing the guy's hook shot. As the story goes, Cunningham barely won the game from the old guy, something like 10 baskets to 8. After the game, they shook hands and the guy said, "Oh, I'm George Mikan."

Mikan, as most basketball fans know, was the dominant center and dominant player of his era, from around 1946 to 1956. In a poll taken by the Associated Press in 1950, he was named the best basketball player of the first half century. Babe Ruth got the honor for baseball, Jim Thorpe for football.

"Mikan was so big and strong and tough," said Charlie. "And he would have developed more than that hook. One of the few guys of that era who would have made it in today's game and been outstanding."

I loved the story about Mikan and Cunningham. It's one of those irresistible tales of young and old, and old hanging in there while young gave him little credence and then was shocked to find out how good he was. It reminded me of the story Mark Twain allegedly told about leaving home when he was fourteen because his father was so ignorant he couldn't stand it. "But when I got to be twenty-one," Twain said, "I was astonished at how much the old man had learned in seven years."

George Mikan lives today in Minneapolis and practices law. He is now seventy-two years old and played his last NBA game, with the Lakers, in 1956, when he was thirty-one. In 1970 he would have been forty-five or forty-six years old and retired for fourteen years. So in a game of that nature, Mikan, who stood 6-foot-10 and weighed around 250 pounds in his playing days, might well have been able to hold his own with Cunningham. Or so I imagined—or perhaps wished to. But Cunningham, in his prime at the time, was himself 6-foot-7, 210 pounds, and supremely springy.

I called George Mikan to confirm the story.

I didn't know Mikan, and he didn't know me, but I know he gets a lot of calls to talk about the old days. And when I did get him on the phone, he sounded impatient.

I asked Mikan if he still plays basketball. "I quit about fifteen years ago," he said. Which, I immediately calculated, would have made him fifty-seven years old, about my age. "I used to go down to a gym here in town," he said, "but it got to a point that every time I played there was someone trying to prove himself against me, and they'd try to beat up on me. And if I hit 'em back I was a jerk, and if I didn't, I was a coward. I didn't want to go on with that business."

I sensed that he wanted to get off the phone. I cleared my throat. "George," I said, "I heard this story about Billy Cunningham and you in a gym in Chicago—possibly Chicago." I related the story, with the end being, "Oh, I'm George Mikan."

Mikan laughed. "That's a good story," he said.

"Is it true?" I asked.

"Not a word," he said.

I thanked him and hung up the phone. I got another phone number and dialed it. A woman answered.

"Is Billy Cunningham home?" I asked.

"No, he's not," she said. It was his wife. "He went to the gym."

"To play basketball?" I ventured.

"No, darling," she said, with a little laugh. "Squash." I had covered Cunningham as a sports columnist when he was an NBA all-star and also when he coached the 76ers. Cunningham and I had had a cordial relationship. And he returned my call later that day.

I asked Cunningham when he had last played basketball. "Not really since I tore up my ACL in 1975, when I was thirty-two," he said. "Oh, I've gone out and fooled around a little—I mean, I wasn't putting an all-out effort, but my knees still started to puff up. I would love to play, but the game is too demanding. It's still the best workout. The running, the jumping, the reactions, and the time goes by so fast, and you've got a great sweat. The beauty part of playing basketball is that your mind is occupied with basketball and nothing else, and you're having fun. But when I tore my ACL, they didn't have any of the procedures they do now to correct it." I silently gave thanks for Dr. Hershon and for my trusty brace.

Cunningham said surgery for his knee is out of the question, however. "I wouldn't go under the knife now," he said. "You never know what the outcome would be, and especially at my age. Besides, I have enough fun playing squash. I play mostly doubles, so it's less wear and tear on the knee. Actually, I can do almost any sport *but* basketball. If I tried— What? Are you an idiot? Boom! Can't walk. Or maybe it's the way I play now that does it." He laughed.

I was curious to know if he had heard that story about Mikan, and was there some fire where there was some smoke? Did Mikan just conveniently forget about it—after all, he supposedly lost, and legend has it he was a fierce competitor—or did it really happen?

I related the story to Billy just as I had heard it from Charlie Miron, just as I had passed it along to George Mikan.

Cunningham laughed, too. "Mikan was a great player," said Cunningham. "My goodness—how many championships did he win? A dominant player for his time. And you know, it's scary. I just turned fifty-three. Oh my God, and we're talking about some old man."

"Billy," I said. "Did it happen? Did you play one-on-one with George Mikan?"

"No," he said. "I don't know how a story like that got around."

As Charlie had told me, that one-on-one game between Cunningham and Mikan had presumably occurred in Chicago. I had pictured it in the Lawson YMCA on Chicago Avenue, perhaps because I had a one-on-one incident there that I won't forget. And this one actually happened.

It was the fall of 1974. I went up to the Lawson Y for a basketball workout at noontime. It happened that just as I entered the gym, the full-court game in progress was nearing its conclusion. I waited for next. But when it was over, everyone on the court left. I decided not to take it personally and simply assumed that people had to return to work. One guy stayed, however. We shot at a basket for a few minutes, and then I suggested a game of one-on-one, "for the sweat." He said sure. He was a black guy about my age, somewhat taller than I, around 6–2, and athletically built. I had been up that gym a few times before, but I didn't recall having seen him.

We threw fingers for first out. I won. I took an outside shot that hit the back rim and bounced away. My opponent got the rebound. In this game the ball had to be taken past the free-throw line on every change of possession. He did, and scored on maybe a seventeen-foot jump shot. A very nice shot, very good form. I moved him back, and this time he hit a jump shot from the top of the key. I moved him still farther back and, my God!, he hit that one, too! Now I got in his face. And he drove around me for another basket. And that was how the game went. I might have made a few baskets, and we might have played more than one game. But I honestly don't remember, since I was so stunned by his performance.

Afterward, I extended my hand. "Nice game," I said. I introduced myself.

He was genial. "Good to meet you," he said. "My name is Flynn Robinson."

"Flynn Robinson?" I said. I looked closer. "Flingin' Flynn Robinson?"

He laughed. "Yes," he said.

"Of course!" *Now* I recognized him. Robinson had been an all-American at Wyoming and had had an eight-year career in the NBA. He had been a feared long-range shooter, averaging more than 20 points a game with the Hawks and the Cincinnati Royals, and a prominent player on the Lakers' 1972 championship team. Bill Russell used to say of Robinson, "He's shooting even before he's off the bench." When Flynn and I played, he had only recently been cut by his last team, the San Diego Clippers.

Flynn told me he was in Chicago to try to hook on with the Bulls. He was then thirty-three, a year younger than I was.

"I'd sign you," I said. Not only could he shoot from the next county with deadly accuracy, but he could also play defense. On me, anyway. Maybe against Tiny Archibald and Walt Frazier, it would have been a different story.

Robinson never did catch on with another NBA team. And the levels of the game, as steep as they are, became apparent to me, first hand.

Charlie Miron liked this story, too, I know. He told me he has repeated it on numerous occasions. "But it doesn't have quite the appeal of Mikan versus Cunningham."

"Yeah, Charlie," I said, "but mine is true."

"Doesn't make it any better," he said.

I couldn't disagree.

• • •

Another classic mystery-man pickup game story I heard has to do with football, not basketball. The story was told to me by Cass Jackson, who used to be the head coach of the Oberlin College football team, in Oberlin, Ohio. In 1974 Jackson hired his friend George Sauer as an assistant coach in charge of the offensive line. Sauer had been an all-pro wide receiver with the Super Bowl champion New York Jets, but he had grown disenchanted with the National Football League and had retired. When Sauer arrived at Oberlin, he was only twenty-nine years old—a prime age for many athletes, and Jackson observed that his friend was still in great shape.

"I knew George still liked to play," Jackson later told me, "and I thought I'd take him out to play in the local sandlot pickup game. It was funny. You had to see this to believe it.

"The local hotshots, all of us black, play every Sunday evening in summer. This is serious stuff, although we have fun. A lot of us were high school or college heroes. And I even played defensive back in the Canadian League.

"The week before I had brought an Oberlin philosophy teacher, who is white. It was embarrassing, he was so bad. He had been chosen on the team opposing mine, and after the game one of the guys whispered that I shouldn't bring back any more white dudes like that.

"During the next week, George arrives. I suggest he play on Sunday. He says OK. I bring him out to the field, and guys are giving me dirty looks. You know, like, what, another white dude like that other guy? And George doesn't look like much of a player. He's wearing a sweatshirt and black shorts and he's tossing the ball real loose. And he's wearing glasses the way he does down on his nose.

"Nobody realizes this is George Sauer. I keep quiet just to see what happens.

"There are about twenty players. Sides are chosen and George isn't picked. But one of the guys on the other team tells me that if I want my friend to play he's got to be on my side. I say, 'Well, OK.'

"I throw the first pass of the game to George. It's an 80-yard touchdown. Nobody can believe what they've just seen, especially this guy Joe, who is a star defensive player.

"Joe figures there was a slipup somewhere. He says, 'I got this new cat.' The next play we run, George puts this fantastic move on Joe. George gets behind him, fakes toward the goalpost. Joe lowers his head and starts chugging. George spins around and breaks for the sideline. I put the ball right on the money. Meanwhile, Joe is on the other side of the field. The crowd goes berserk.

"Now guys are on Joe. 'Hey, man, this cat's burnin' you up. Two TD's. I figure now it's time. I got to fill 'em all in. 'This is George Sauer,' I say.

"The guys say, 'Who?' I say. 'George Sauer.' And someone says, 'Joe Namath's receiver?' I say, 'Yeah.' And Joe pipes up, 'I got him!'

"So George scores four more touchdowns. We win 60–0. It became the biggest story of the season in the black neighborhood in Oberlin. Joe's a great athlete, and he can laugh about it, too. He can even laugh at his new nickname. Everyone now calls Joe, 'I Got Him.' "

Charlie Miron added that story to his repertoire, too.

But the story that is unmatched for me was the most unexpected—even to the mystery man himself. It happened on Magic Johnson's barnstorming team tour through Europe in October of 1994. I had a freelance assignment from *Esquire* magazine to do a piece on Magic and his life at that point. Magic had by then retired from the NBA twice, first when he had learned of having tested positive for HIV, and then when he decided to return to the league only to see the fearful looks on players' faces when he got cut. But players on other continents didn't seem to be nearly as concerned about the very remote possibility that Johnson could infect them, and Johnson loved basketball so much he couldn't stay away. He began playing again, in exhibition games.

He gathered a team that included retired NBA players—among them Mark Aguirre, Kurt Rambis, John Long, and Lester (The Molester) Conner—as well as some younger players just out of college or the Continental Basketball League.

I met the team in Barcelona, after they had played in London and Amsterdam, and continued on with it to Paris. I attended their practice, watched their game, rode on the players' bus, ate with them in the restaurants.

In the course of my reporting, I spoke with several of Magic's teammates and took two of them to lunch on my second day on the story. The two players were Kurt Rambis, who had been a bruising forward and teammate of Magic's with the Lakers, and John Long, who had been a superb shooting guard on a few NBA teams, including the Detroit Pistons' 1989 championship team. In fact, I had only asked Rambis for lunch, since he had known Magic for nearly ten years, but Long showed up, too. The players liked to kid Long about being tight with the dollar, but I was happy to have him along. The more possibility for background, the better, and he was a pleasure.

During lunch I brought up the practice session I had observed the day before in a school gym in Barcelona. And I talked about how seriously Magic took this, how he seemed to want to give the fans their money's worth, and how he was going to do that by having his team well conditioned and well prepared. They agreed. I added that he plays as hard in practice as he does in a game and illustrated this by recalling a pass to Lester Conner, a former New Jersey Nets' player, that had impressed me in the practice.

"That pass to Conner in the corner was perfect," I said, "easy to handle but crisp, and right at the chest. And just as he got to his spot."

I made this observation in part to impart to my lunch mates that I knew something about basketball, to let them know that I could catch a nuance of the game and appreciate it.

The pass that I recalled came at a small and virtually unimportant moment in the practice, but I thought it pointed up Magic's professionalism and virtuosity. Somewhere it is written that genius is an infinite capacity for taking pains. Magic had it.

At some point I also mentioned that I still play pickup basketball games—again, to try further to gain their confidence about my basketball acumen. It wasn't just ego on my part; I knew that if they trusted my knowledge of the game, they might give me better stuff. They nodded when I mentioned my basketball playing, and nothing more about that was said.

The following day, while waiting to board the plane for Paris, I was sitting with Magic, and I again recalled that pass he made to Conner.

"Shooters like to get the ball in their rhythm," said Magic.

"I know," I said. "I'm a shooter."

I smiled. He smiled. I had interviewed Magic on several occasions over the years, and I had never mentioned anything to him about my playing basketball. They are, after all, two different worlds, his ball and mine.

The next day I had breakfast with Magic, and we had a long, intimate interview. He told me how he first broke the news to his wife, Cookie, that he had tested positive for HIV. "I said to her, 'Cookie, I can understand you wantin' to leave me,'" Magic recalled. "Right then, she smacked me in the face. She said, 'I married you because I love you.'"

Although Magic answered my questions directly, I still felt that he was somewhat reluctant to talk to me about the layers of his personal life. Like any writer, I hoped my subject would trust me, and I wanted to do what I could to build that trust.

Later that morning the team had a shoot-around in the Palais des Sports Marcel Cerdan, where they were scheduled to play a game that night. I walked into the gym and stood courtside. At the basket near me, Magic and Long and another player—it may have been Rambis, but I'm not sure—happened to be warming up. Magic noticed me standing there and motioned to throw me the ball. I was carrying a notebook, but put it into my back pocket and raised my hands. Magic passed me the ball. Now I stood at the corner of the court in my street shoes.

Obviously Magic was curious, as were the rest of the players. Could I in fact shoot a basketball? I was a middle-aged sportswriter, after all. But Magic would be able to tell, of course, whether I was "a shooter" by how I took the shot. This seemed a test—lighthearted, but a test nonetheless. And something wholly unexpected. The players stopped to watch, as did Lon Rosen, Magic's business manager, and a few others in the entourage seated at courtside.

I stepped onto the court in my sweater and street shoes and stood at the three-point line just in from the corner—about 22 feet from the basket. I turned to Magic and Long.

"You want to put big bucks on this shot?" I said to the players. Somehow I thought the moment called for a bit of goofy bravado. Locker room stuff, I guess. Magic laughed.

"I'll bet two thousand dollars that you don't make the shot," said Long.

A look of concern flashed across Magic's face. "Why don't you move in for a warmup?" he suggested kindly.

"I don't need to move in," I said. Magic's eyes widened. I knew that I just had to show good form—and hit the rim. An air ball would have been embarrassing. I did know that even for great players this was a long shot in every way. Not only was it from three-point range, but the players knew I hadn't picked up a ball at any time with them, and that I had to be stiff from traveling.

I looked up at the basket. I reminded myself to get a good arc on the shot to assure distance. And I let the ball go. It felt good as it left my fingertips, lofted nicely and dropped right through the hoop. All net!

Magic shrieked. He ran over and threw me a high five. "I trust you now!" he exclaimed. "I trust anything you say!" He turned to John Long. "You owe the man two thousand dollars, J. Long," said Magic.

"Hey, I was only kidding," said Long. "He told me he still works out. You think I'd make a bet like that?"

"Let the money slide," I said. "No problem." I played it cool as could be. Like I make this shot in my sleep. But I couldn't resist asking, "Magic, how was the release?"

"The release? I liked the follow-through!" he said, flicking his wrist.

I absently took the notebook out of my pocket—it remained unopened—and sat down in a chair beside Lon Rosen, who still looked surprised.

No one suggested I try another shot, and I wouldn't have. Not for all the money in the world.

Back to Basics

I first saw the basketball court one afternoon a few years ago. I happened to be driving south on the Pacific Coast Highway through Laguna Beach, California, that little dream town built on a hill overlooking the ocean. I had never been there before. On my left art stores and boutiques leaned against one another as the hill rose and fell, and beyond them pastel homes, glistening in the sunshine. Coming into view on my right, meanwhile, was a sight that I found equally spectacular, and more improbable.

As I turned a bend, I noticed a park along the beach. And beside a walkway that separated sand from grass was a basketball court. I slowed the car, despite the burp of horns behind me, and leaned across the wheel to check it out.

Now a pickup basketball player's requirements for a sweet outdoor basketball court are minimal. What you want are among the simple pleasures: a flat backboard; an even, 10-foot-high rim; a level playing surface; and that feature only occasionally seen in public courts, that dollop of whipped cream on the Danish: a net hanging on the basket, preferably not ripped.

The wind on the beach seemed inconsequential, unusual given the location. The nearby palm trees swayed only slightly. The colorful sails atop the boats in the diamond-glittering water hardly fluttered. The nets on the baskets hung virtually straight, and the shots in the half-court game in progress appeared on line. The players themselves looked as if they knew the game; a bounce pass to a cutter immediately suggested as much to me, the way a physician can plunge a tongue depressor down a patient's throat and know the story at a glance.

When a pickup player spies such a basketball vision, it makes the mouth water and the fingertips itch. The Laguna Beach court had that immediate effect on me. I have, to be sure, seen beautiful settings before—the Amalfi Coast, the Alps, the Grand Tetons—but I have rarely seen anything of a basketball nature to rival this.

I parked the car and looked to see if the court at Laguna Beach was as remarkable as it had seemed from the highway. It was. I wanted to slip on my brace and get into a game. I was on my way to an interview in San Diego, though, and reluctantly returned to my car. But I deliciously filed all this away in my mental archive.

I later mentioned the court to Rod Carew, the Hall of Fame baseball player, who lives in nearby Anaheim. He said he had never played there but told me that there were legends concerning the court. "Like the story I heard that Reggie Miller and his sister, Cheryl, and their brother went there one afternoon," said Carew, "and wiped out everybody. But I don't know if it's true."

One day, I told myself, I'd go back there.

And one gentle Sunday morning in December, I did.

The setting of what is called Main Beach in Laguna remained the same, its blue and yellow and red and green hues
as vibrant as a Dufy watercolor: the seagulls and the bathers
and strollers, the lovers arm-in-arm on the benches and the
lazy dogs at their feet, the palm trees, and the sailboats. And
the basketball court, just as I remembered it, down to the
good players. Though none of the Miller clan was in evidence.

It was a warm day, but not hot. It was, after all, southern
California wintertime, with a bright bold sun in a cloudless
pale sky. I wore a sweatshirt but saw that those in the game
were in T-shirts patched with sweat. There were two baskets,
one about 40 feet in front of the other, but no full court, since
both baskets faced north. There was even padding tied
around the steel poles of the backboards, a salient detail that
had eluded me the first time I drove past. It is a rare outdoor
court indeed that contains a padded pole, a true convenience
in helping to prevent bones from breaking like twigs on a hard
drive to the hoop.

When I arrived at the court, two games were going on, but
as I approached the northernmost court, I noticed that it had
the clearly better game, and this was the one that interested
me. The lesser game ended, and some guys on the sidelines
stepped on the court to take a few shots. I took a couple myself and then walked over to the guy who looked like he had
next on the other court—you can usually tell the guy who has
next because there is a kind of calm in his eyes, like the man
who has a reserved seat on a crowded train.

"You got next?" I asked.

"Yeah."

"Got room on your squad?"

"I'm one down," he said, which meant that in a game of
four-on-a-side, he had only three players. There was room for

me on his team, but he also could pick any of the other players on the sidelines or even one of the four players on the losing team in the game in progress. Still, I noticed that he had
seen me shoot, so I was hopeful.

My potential new teammate—the captain, you'd have to
say—was short and stocky with close-cropped hair and a tattoo on his left arm. He happened to be white, in this racial
melange of players, and appeared to be in his early or midtwenties, about the average age of most of the guys at the
court. I heard someone call him "Cooley High," which was a
hip way of saying he was hip, I think. He introduced himself
to me as Jude.

It turned out that Jude didn't have next because four black
guys, who had presumably arrived together earlier as a team,
had called next before Jude. So Jude and I leaned against a
bench and watched the end of one game and then the following one, lasting a total of nearly an hour, given interruptions
for arguments, recuperations from pokes, and then, once, to
gawk at two young women coming down the sidewalk. They
both had on sunglasses and heels. One wore a pink T-shirt
and jeans, but the other, the blonde, was easily the more eye-
catching: she wore a short white knit dress that clung so
tightly to her curves she might have been packed into it with
an ice cream scoop.

"Oh mama!" cried one of the players.

"Stop the presses!" shouted someone else.

"C'mon, knock off the shit and play the game," said another. "It's only celluloid."

I believe he was referring to her breasts. And I believe he
meant silicone. Anyway, the girl blew a kiss and waved in that
friendly California style—delighted, I thought, in the fuss she
inspired.

And as she receded, with what appeared to me a little more

wiggle than necessary for ambulation, the game resumed.

Jude told me that he comes regularly to the courts and that the games here attract players from all over the area, including some past and present high school and college players. I told him I could understand why, meaning the caliber of play and the setting—which didn't quite include the passersby.

The skill of the players was uneven in the games we watched. But the intensity level was high. One player, who had red hair, got hit in the mouth with an elbow under the basket and began to bleed.

"You OK?" asked the guy who hit him. The redheaded guy mumbled an answer and, holding his mouth, walked to the nearby water fountain to wash the cut.

Another player looked at the drops of fresh blood on the gray concrete court and seemed to resent the interruption of the game.

"It's kinda fierce out there," said Jude. "You don't wanna lose. Otherwise you can wait two hours for next."

The game resumed without the redheaded player, who departed with a handkerchief covering his face, like a Wild West bandit. He was replaced by a player with dark hair and an earring in his left ear who appeared to be a regular, and a good one, because he was chosen from the sidelines without hesitation. He hit a scoop drive and a jump shot at the free-throw line to help his team win a close game, 12 baskets to 10. He was instrumental in their winning the next game, too, against the team of four young black guys, all pretty decent players.

Now it was Jude's game. He nodded to me, which, to my satisfaction, meant I was on his team. Jude also chose a black guy from the sidelines and another white guy who looked like one of the older players, perhaps in his early thirties. I was old enough to have been his father, I thought. It's a reflex with me to check out how old guys look on the court. Maybe it's self-conscious because I suspect they might be thinking that of me. Yet I'm aware that they'd probably not guess I was fifty-five—that's because they rarely see ten years past themselves. Bernard Baruch once said that "old is anyone fifteen years older than you are." For people the age of these basketball players, I'd say it was closer to ten years. So to them I might be thirty-five, which is still pretty old in their book, but not impossibly ancient.

Before the game began, I was able to get in a few shots to get a feel of the ball in my hands. The game ball was well used but still had enough pebble for an adequate grip. I also wanted to get a sense of the rim and backboard and to stretch my muscles that had stiffened during the long wait. The older I get, the more warm-up I need; I like to be sweating before I play in a game. But there was no time for that now.

Jude made the defensive assignments. The man I was to guard was the guy who had replaced the redheaded player in the earlier game and had done so well. I still like the challenge of guarding good players—stirs the juices. After all these years, I like to think I know the nuances of the game. And while my crablike moves on defense aren't quite what they once were—or what I imagined they once were—I do understand positioning, which can often neutralize an opponent.

I observe a player's habits, how he brings the ball up to shoot, the places on the court he favors. My guy was right-handed, but he could use his left. He liked to drive and go hard to the hoop, though he could also pull up from around 15 feet and shoot the jumper.

"We gotta win," Jude reminded me quietly, as we took our defensive positions, since the winning team gets the ball out first.

"I know," I said.

As always when a game is about to begin, there was just a

little tension in my body, a nervousness that anticipates the test.

Our opponents missed their opening shot. We got the ball and scored, and scored again and again, quickly taking a 3–0 lead. One of our guys got the ball in the post, faked, and tossed the ball to me on the side. My man had double-teamed him, and I was free for a shot and hit it clean—about a 15-footer. On the next possession we missed, they got the ball, my man drove, and I made slight body contact with him, though not enough to throw his shot off. He missed it on merit. He called a foul.

"This shit's gotta stop," he said to no one in particular. Was this meant for his teammates or for me? The other team made a comeback, as I painfully missed two shots. I didn't feel comfortable—I wasn't really warmed up, and to be a first-time player with guys who know one another made me feel like a stranger. I wanted to meld into the team. But that wasn't to be.

My man hit a long jump shot from what in the pros would be three-point range. He got the ball on the next position from about the same distance. I moved up on him, hunkered low but with arms up, and he fired in a second straight shot. He shot it nicely, with excellent form, and that accomplished snap of the wrist and backspin on the ball that tells you he's done this before. I still had to play him for a drive but tried to give him more attention from outside. He then bombed in a third straight long shot!

"Switch!" Jude hollered from somewhere behind me. This is insulting: the meaning here is that you have failed on your defensive assignment and someone—anyone—could probably do better. It was humiliating as well.

"It's OK," said the black guy on our team, who was our best player. Perhaps he understood that I was in a learning mode, though it might be too late by the time I absorbed my lesson. "Get tight," he said. I appreciated his sensitivity, and I remained with my man.

I now got so close to the jump shooter that I could smell his sweat and see hairs on the tip of his nose. He tried another jump shot, but forced it and missed.

"Good D," said the black guy.

Not good enough at this point, however, since we were down 7–4 in a game of 10 baskets. I drove left and, instead of powering to the hoop, attempted a left-handed hook. I missed.

"Go strong!" advised the other white guy. I should have! For some strange reason Reggie Miller came to mind. He would've gone strong, I thought.

An exchange of baskets followed—I got a rebound, I dished off for a basket, but the other team was even more active—and it was 9–6 when we got the ball again. We had to score four to their one to hold the court.

I cut for the hoop, and the white guy threw me a pass that was over my head and slightly behind me.

"C'mon!" I heard Jude holler, in a tone of near desperation that seemed to echo through the park.

And suddenly everything was in slow motion, including the echo. I tried to stop in order to jump and twist and fling my arm up to catch the ball, like an outfielder, and keep it in play. We needed to keep the ball in play! I saw the ball clearly arcing like a small moon about three feet over my head. It was a bad pass, but I knew I could snare it—after all, the ball was traveling in slow motion. The problem was, my body was unwinding in even slower motion.

My fingertips had been only inches from the ball, which now bounced toward the highway. I jogged after it and retrieved it. When I tossed the ball back to the court—and felt a twinge in my back from the awkward twisting for the ball—I didn't make eye contact with any of my teammates. They said nothing. I could imagine what Jude was thinking—that he had been a fool to pick this bird in the first place.

The other team got the ball and scored again, to end the game. At least it wasn't my man who hit the winning shot, I thought. But it wasn't much consolation. I had done little on offense and even less on defense, and had contributed to a one-game-and-out run. I picked up my sweatshirt without saying a word to anyone. I didn't say "Nice game" or slap a palm or give a shrug that, well, next time it'll be different, as is often done. I felt stupid, and still not quite warmed up. Was I too old for this particular game—that is, with these particular players? Or too old for the game, period?

As I walked toward my car and past the bikers and strollers, who seemed like people in a dream, I replayed the game in my head as though in a videotape. I took no notice of the splendor of the surroundings, as I had earlier. The palm trees, the ocean, the seagulls—nothing else existed except that miserable game.

I thought about the shots I missed and felt mortified at not having guarded my man closer and sooner. And then I stopped the mental tape at the ball soaring over my head, the pass I came so close to getting. Would a younger body have stopped it? Maybe. Probably. Thoughts crept into my mind, thoughts of inadequacy. Well, I reasoned, I'm probably still a better writer than the guy I had been trying to guard. I knew nothing of him, other than from this little game. I didn't know if he ever wrote a sentence in his life or knew a pronoun from a compound verb. No matter: when you're low, you're low. And I slunk back to the car, though not slinking half as fast as I wished. The strain in my back from twisting for that high pass didn't help my mobility, either.

I returned to the hotel, where Dolly was sitting on the terrace reading the Sunday newspaper.

"How was the game?" she asked, her eyes still on the paper.

"OK," I lied.

I didn't say much more as I undressed. I showered. I poked my head into the minibar in the room and downed a soda and chomped an apple. Dolly and I then took a walk on the gorgeous beach. We talked about this or that, the seagulls, the huge tableware store she had visited while I was out and had a compulsion to return to—she called it Dish Heaven. I listened somewhat to her, to the waves breaking, to the seagulls cawing.

After a few minutes of silence, and looking out at the ocean, she said, "You'll get over it. You and John Starks."

John Starks? He was her favorite Knick player, an erratic, sometimes lovable shooting guard who wears his emotions on the shoulder strap of his jersey. Once again she had nailed my mood.

"It wasn't that bad," I said, attempting to salvage a little machismo.

"You always get over it," she added. "You have your good days. You have your bad days."

I grunted. I was disappointed with myself. I knew now I should have gotten to the court earlier and warmed up properly. Would that have made a difference? Well, it couldn't have hurt. I should have been more aggressive and less like some dewy-eyed newcomer. But had I given myself a signal that only now I was comprehending—the signal that perhaps I really was at the end of my basketball life? Bad days on the court seemed to come more often than was comfortable for me now, and the game that morning made me wonder if I had gone downhill so far that there was absolutely no way to make a return climb.

Perhaps now it was time to hang up my knee brace and sneakers and bid the game farewell, the game that no longer seemed to return my love. My game that morning gnawed at me. How, I wondered, could something so beautiful as that basketball setting be so exasperating?

"I'm going back there," I told Dolly, with an emphatic nod.

"There?" she asked incredulously, following my gaze to the ocean.

"No," I said. "The basketball court."

"Now?" she asked.

"No," I said, "not now."

"Good," she said, "then we can have lunch."

"But one day," I said, with conviction. "One day."

When I returned home to New York, I went back to basics. That is, I thumbed through Red Auerbach's instructional book, *Basketball for the Player, the Fan, and the Coach*, retained from my boyhood, and now dog-eared. As a writer I frequently reread those who deeply impressed me, like Dylan Thomas, E. B. White, Virginia Woolf, Red Smith. Just as I sought to incorporate their textures, their tones, their élan into my writing, now I hoped to reenergize my hoop life with an infusion of Arnold (Red) Auerbach.

In guarding the dribbler, Auerbach says, "Keep slapping around his knees to worry him. Give him the impression that you may stab for the ball. This will tend to make him more cautious."

On shooting the jump shot: "Don't release the ball until you have reached your highest point." Aha. Maybe I've been shooting too quickly.

And: "Avoid reading too much about basketball. Do not let the game get too complicated." In other words, stay loose, stay cool. OK. And of course, following instruction, I put the book down.

I also recalled something Coach Scher at Sullivan High School had told me. "One of the best fakes is the eye fake," he said. "Look one way and go the other, either with a pass or dribble. And this is for defense, too. So don't watch a guy's eyes. Watch his belt buckle. He doesn't necessarily have to go where his eyes are looking, but he can't move without his belly button." Yes. In basketball, the belly button is the mirror of the soul.

And I hearkened back to lessons learned from playing with Walt Frazier while we were working on his book *Rockin' Steady*.

About the drive Frazier said, "The first move is explosive. You have to go hard for the basket. Driving isn't easy."

On defense he was aware that "everyone has a weakness. Study your man to find his." And: "What hand is he? That's the first thing I know about the guy I'm guarding. I try to force a guy to the right if he's lefty, and left if he's righty." This may seem obvious, but it is the obvious that we often miss. I was reminded of this when I read Winston Churchill's small book *Painting as a Pastime*, in which he described his passion for painting and observed how it brought certain aspects of everyday life suddenly into focus. Like the shadows on buildings. He wrote that he had never taken notice of how dramatic they looked until he began painting. A more acute visual awareness cannot hurt the writer or, for that matter, the basketball player.

Working out with weights is something I have avoided, since it seemed that it would require—well, work. And one of the several reasons I have found writing an appealing vocation is that I don't have to lift things. But I know that weight training has helped a lot of people get stronger, including big-time athletes. I thought I'd look into it.

In the New York Knicks' locker room after a practice one day, I spoke with the team's conditioning coach, Greg Brittenham.

"It's more of a physical game today than it used to be," said Brittenham. He is a young man with a T-shirt bulging with muscles. "Weight training can enhance flexibility. We lift to increase speed, agility, quickness, coordination, and balance."

All of that sounded impressive, and I liked the vision of myself being faster, more agile, quicker, and better coordinated, with the balance of a ballerina. But it also sounded like a lot of work.

"Take a guy like Derek Harper," said Brittenham. "On days he's not playing, he comes into the weight room at nine-thirty in the morning and leaves at two or three in the afternoon. He lifts heavy weights, he lifts light weights. He does a bunch of repetitions, then he goes to shoot for half an hour, and then comes back for the Stairmaster. And then more weights. He's my best worker."

Now I was feeling discouraged. I went over to talk to Harper, who was dressing in front of his cubicle.

He told me that he had done very little weight training in college, at the University of Illinois, which he had left some twelve years earlier. He began "fooling around" with weights about six years ago and got serious about it some three years ago.

"Yeah, I think weight training has definitely added a few years to my career," he said. "People talk about me being thirty-four, but I've piled up a lot of minutes." He indeed looked in terrific shape, and on the court seemed capable of playing as hard and as long as younger players in the NBA.

I also spoke with Hubert Davis, then the Knicks' shooting guard along with John Starks. He was a weight lifter, too. Since his game was primarily outside shooting, I felt I could relate to him to some degree. Had the weights helped his game?

"It's been tremendous," he said. "It's made me stronger, and I think it has increased my range. But I don't do it to bulk up. I have no interest in looking like Schwarzenegger."

I didn't either. But I decided to give weights some more thought. And yet I felt weighted down just thinking about it.

I also had occasion to think about one of the greatest basketball coaches of all time, courtesy of my editors at *The New York Times*.

The year-end issue of *The New York Times Magazine* was devoted to prominent people who had died in 1995, and I had been asked to write a short article on Nat Holman, who had died in February at the age of ninety-eight. Holman was the last great living link to the origins of basketball. Holman was born on the Lower East Side of Manhattan in 1896, just five years after basketball was invented, and in the 1920s he became to basketball what Babe Ruth was to baseball, Louis Armstrong to jazz, Darrow to defense, and Houdini to handcuffs.

Nat Holman was the star of some of the great barnstorming teams of the era, including two of the finest, The Original Celtics and The Cleveland Rosenblooms. He was billed as "The Greatest Player in the Game" and "Mr. Basketball." Holman stood 5-foot-11, was well-built, and his black, slicked back hair gave him a matinee-idol appearance.

In most respects the game that Holman grew up with was a slow-down, one-on-one affair. But he saw a different way and began to instill his notions as a coach. He coached the City

College of New York teams for thirty-seven years, retiring in 1959 with a lifetime record of 421 wins against 190 losses. During those years he always insisted on one thing: ball movement.

Holman demanded that his players move without the ball, hit the open man with a pass, play a well-patterned offense, help teammates on defense—the whole concept of team basketball, in fact, became Holman's trademark. And that style of play that he urged and taught so successfully became known and copied throughout the nation as "New York–style" basketball.

His 1950 CCNY team achieved unprecedented glory as well as unprecedented infamy. It won both the NCAA championship and the NIT. But shortly afterward it was learned that several players had been paid by gamblers to shave points in games during that season. It was a scandal in which numerous other teams, including Kentucky, Bradley, and Long Island University were involved, and it took years before college basketball overcame the ignominy. Even though Holman himself was cleared of any wrongdoing, he suffered from his disappointment in the players, his agony at not having been more aware of the gamblers in their midst, and the terrible humiliation. He was briefly suspended by the New York City Board of Higher Education but soon returned to coaching in his innovative basketball style.

That style could be seen in the best teams in basketball history: the great Boston Celtic teams of the Bill Russell and Larry Bird eras, the Lakers of Magic Johnson, the Knicks of the early 1970s, and Michael Jordan's Chicago Bulls. The legendary Knick coach, William (Red) Holzman learned his game directly from Holman as a playmaking guard for CCNY in the early 1940s and passed it on to the two championship teams he coached.

The seventy-six-year-old Holzman now stays fit by playing tennis—"doubles with a friend, against the women, who usually beat us," he says, perhaps only half kidding. In addition to his outstanding record as a coach, Holzman had been a crafty, 5-foot-10½-inch guard who went from being an all-American college player under Holman to enjoying a respectable playing career in the NBA. Among his achievements on the court, he was an important playmaker and captain of the 1950–51 NBA champion Rochester Royals.

Red's style of coaching can be gleaned from the way he handles situations in his personal life. He uses an indirect, humorous approach that gets the point across. I was with him once in a restaurant that he frequented in Madison Square Garden. When the waiter, whom he knew, came to take the order, Red asked, "Is your soup hot tonight?" The waiter smiled and said, "Of course, Mr. Holzman." Three things about this: (1) Red surely had had soup here that wasn't hot, (2) he wanted to make sure the soup this time was hot, and (3) he didn't want to embarrass the waiter by having him take back the soup to heat up. When the soup arrived, it was steaming hot.

Phil Jackson, the coach of the four-time NBA champion Chicago Bulls, had played for Holzman, making him a second-generation coaching descendent of Nat Holman. Jackson says he learned much of his coaching style from Red, both in terms of play and in handling of players. His ability not to take too seriously the antics of a player like Dennis Rodman—earrings, chartreuse-dyed hair, a madcap aggressiveness—has helped him get the most out of his team. Jackson recalled to me an indelible moment that taught him a lesson about handling a situation.

Holzman had replaced Dick McGuire as the Knick coach in December of 1967. The Knicks were an undisciplined team, and Holzman thought they needed some tightening up. "One of the rules Red introduced was that everyone must ride the team bus," said Jackson. "But shortly after Red took over, Cazzie Russell decided to drive his car to a game in Philadelphia. When he came into the locker room, Red said, 'Cazzie, those highway tolls must be expensive.' 'Oh, yeah, Coach,' Cazzie said. Red said, 'How much were they, Cazzie?' Cazzie said, 'Eight dollars.' Red said, 'Well, Cazzie, I'll take that off the hundred-dollar fine.' Cazzie thanked him. I never saw a guy get fined and thank the coach for it."

Like Phil Jackson, I've tried to incorporate a move or two of Red's style myself. I once was playing with a guy in a pickup game who shot every time he touched the ball. After awhile, I said, in what I supposed was a gentle manner, "Aren't we playing passing today?" Without hesitation the guy retorted: "You weren't, so I thought we aren't." I wondered what Red would have said to *that*. I just shook my head and moseyed back downcourt.

Red could be no-nonsense when the situation called for it. I was in the Knicks locker room in 1972 when Sargent Shriver, the Democratic candidate for vice president, came in to solicit some attention, followed by a battery of photographers, cameramen, reporters and assorted assistants. Holzman was in his office, just off the locker room. He heard a commotion and could see a bunch of civilians bursting in. Holzman said to Frankie Blauschild, an administrative assistant, "Throw them out. You know we have a rule about visitors in the locker room before a game."

"But Coach," said Blauschild, "it's Sargent Shriver."

"I don't care if it's General Shriver," said Holzman, "get them outta there."

Red had given up playing pickup basketball years ago because when he went onto a court he felt like a marked man.

"Guys were out to prove that they could have played in the NBA instead of you," he said. "And it became dangerous, and no longer any fun." But Red would sometimes shoot with the Knicks teams he coached.

Red recalled shooting with Marvin Webster, a Knick center, after a practice. Webster and Holzman each put down a $10 bill on the floor for a shootout from the top of the free-throw circle. "Marvin went first and made nine out of ten," said Holzman. "He went to pick up the money. I said, 'Just a minute.' Then I shot. I still shoot the old two-hand set. I made nine out of ten. He couldn't believe it. I don't know if Marvin had ever seen a two-hander before.

"People talk about the game changing," said Holzman. "It doesn't change as much as it might seem. The basics are still there. You've got to play good defense. You've got to hit the open man. You've got to pass and think. And the players still take pride in winning, no matter how much money they make. You try to tap that pride. Coaching today is as simple—and as difficult—as that.

"When I see teams today that play smart, that play with a lot of movement, that play unselfishly, I see the legacy of Nat Holman. He was always preaching to us to hit the open man, to be unselfish, throw more fakes, pick, screen, to be in constant movement. Sometimes I'd hold the ball too much, and he'd say to me, 'Beel, you're letting the air out of the ball.'

"Some of us on the team were a little hardheaded—including me—and we couldn't believe a lot of the things he was saying could be done. Now, at this time, Coach Holman was about forty-five years old and always in good shape. He was one of the top-ranked squash players in the country then. And of course he had been a basketball legend with the Original Celtics years before.

"Well, this one time he put himself on the second team in a practice session, and the guys on the first team decided we'd show him. It turned out that he showed us. He was fantastic and made us all look bad. He was a great teacher, and still a pretty damn good player."

Holman and Holzman have both been inducted into the Basketball Hall of Fame in Springfield, Massachusetts. It was at the YMCA in Springfield that Dr. James Naismith invented the game of basketball in 1891, and one hundred years later I found myself on assignment in Springfield. I brought along my sneakers and basketball clothes and went to play basketball in the Springfield Y. It was my first trip to the modest mecca. I paid a $10 fee at the gym entrance and asked for a basketball. The woman behind the counter handed me a rubber ball with a bump in it. I asked for a ball without a bump, preferably a leather one. She had about six other balls. "They're all rubber, except for this one," she said, holding a worn leather ball in both hands. "But this has a flap on it." Indeed, there was a loose tear in one of the strips on the ball.

"I'll take the one with the flap," I said, with a shrug.

How nice, I thought, that after a hundred years the Springfield Y still has all the same balls that Naismith had used to invent the game.

Some things had changed, however. For one, this was a new building. And Naismith, with his sumptuous mustache, would never recognize the gym. No peach baskets hung from a balcony facade. Instead, the large, well-lighted facility featured glass backboards and a corn-yellow wood floor. Two young men were shooting at one basket. They invited me to play. I said yes. "Hey," said another guy who had just come in, "can I run wichyoo." Sure, I said.

We played with the best ball we had, which was the one with the flap. We picked, we screened, we tried to hit the open man, we took a bad shot, we made a surprising one—and heard the welcome snap of the net—we stole the ball, we lost one. There was a dispute. It was resolved. Play resumed. I enjoyed the game—all except for the ball, that is. Anyone who plays basketball with any kind of regularity knows that the best indoor ball is a leather one without a flap, and with grooves and a good grainy feel.

When I returned home to New York, I decided to do something in commemoration of basketball's centennial and to express my gratitude to Dr. Naismith. I bought an official NBA Spalding leather ball, wrapped it up, and sent it with a note of explanation to the director of the Springfield Y, basketball's Garden of Eden.

It was Christmas time, and I wasn't exactly Kris Kringle, but I felt that that was the least I could do for the history of hoops.

I don't know what happened to the ball, or whether it was ever used. I can only assume and hope that it was. But I never heard back from the Y.

As I thought about the special basketball coaches I have known, I recalled a particularly significant one for me, Edwin Turner, my college coach. I imagined that Coach Turner now would be more than eighty years old, if, in fact, he was still alive.

I had not seen or been in touch with Turner since my playing days at Roosevelt University, a commuter school in downtown Chicago. I wrote to him in care of the school, and about a week later I received a response, with a return address of Highland Park, Illinois, an exclusive northern suburb of Chicago, which I knew to be decidedly white and primarily

Jewish. But Edwin Turner, a black man, was always difficult to categorize and always his own man.

I had asked Coach Turner if I could come for a visit. He responded that he was pleased to hear from me and would look forward to my stopping by. He signed the letter, "Edwin Turner, Coach." He underlined "Coach" twice.

He could have underlined it a third time, and he would have been justified in my view, as I thought back on the year I had played for him at Roosevelt University. It was the season of 1958–59, my sophomore year at Roosevelt, the year I turned nineteen.

Edwin Turner was then in his forties, tall—about 6-foot-3—with a wiry, athletic build. He had a mustache and gentle but aware eyes. His wife, Gladys, was the head of the school library. I imagined that Coach Turner could have worked there, too, for he had a quiet way about him and was one of those people whom others either don't quite take notice of the first time around or, if they do, may underestimate. He was not blustery, like some coaches, and not given to pronouncements, either. But when challenged, his eyes blazed.

Once, when a player gave him back talk in practice, Turner stopped practice and walked onto the court with a stride so determined that everyone was rooted in his place. He stopped in front of the player. "If there is going to be any dictator here," he said, "I'm the dictator. We don't do what you want to do—you do what I want you to do." He did not raise his voice, but he said this so firmly that it ended discussion.

Edwin Turner was the first black coach I had ever had. And with black players on the team, I didn't know how that was going to work out. How would I be treated? How would he treat them? Would he give me playing time? There was something else occurring that didn't dawn on me at that time—I imagine I was just too self-involved to consider it. But

Edwin Turner was possibly the only black head basketball coach of an integrated college team in the country.

Not only was he the head coach, he was the only coach we had. He had no assistants. He was also the coach of the bowling, tennis, soccer, track, and golf teams. He was the entire athletic department of Roosevelt University. He even taught a physical education class. I suppose he also found time to eat a meal once every few weeks or so.

I had enrolled at Roosevelt after flunking out of the University of Illinois in Chicago—by a fraction, I hasten to add, after just one semester. I would have been given another semester to prove myself at Illinois if I hadn't entered the school on probation, but I had finished in the bottom quarter of my high school graduating class, and this made me suspect, in the eyes of university authorities, as college material.

On the placement exams for Illinois-Chicago, I had scored exceptionally high in English and so had been placed into a class for gifted English students. I am pretty sure I was the only one in the class who had been in the lowest quarter of his high school graduating class. But on the same placement exam I scored miserably in math, a class I rarely bothered to attend. To compound matters, I had decided to major in accounting because other friends of mine had, because I thought I would go into business one day, and because I had no real direction. After the first week at Illinois, I knew accounting was a mistake, but my school adviser wouldn't let me get out of it. That—combined with math—all but sealed my fate at that school.

I was embarrassed about flunking out, but I was determined to try again. I applied to Roosevelt and was accepted. Roosevelt was a school known for giving people a second, and a third, chance at a college education. It was a liberal arts school with open admission at a time when open admission in

America was barely heard of. If you could come up with the modest tuition, then you would be admitted. If you came to class, you would learn. If you didn't, you wouldn't. It was all up to you. It was a college for adults or for those who looked at education in an adult way.

I wasn't sure how I looked at it. I just didn't want to be a college flunk-out. I wanted another chance. My parents were busy working, and since I was also working and helping to pay the rent while in high school and college, they didn't trouble themselves much with my schooling.

In fact, it wasn't until years later that I told anyone, including my parents, that I had flunked out. I just said I had decided to transfer. That was all.

"Dad," I told my father one day, "I'm going to Roosevelt, and I'm going to major in English."

"English?" he said. "What can you do with it?"

"I don't know, but I like it."

He tried to be helpful. "Do you think you can take another accounting course?"

"I don't think so."

And that was the end of it.

Roosevelt University was hardly a typical college. It was located in the heart of the city, in the old Auditorium Hotel on Michigan Avenue. Hotel rooms and suites had become classrooms. The dining room became the library reading room, and the kitchen and pantries were converted into stacks. As years went on, renovations and reconstructions made it feel like a busy, nicely appointed college that happened to be vertical instead of the more commonplace ivy horizontal.

And most of the students had jobs before or after their classes, as I did. On Sundays, I ran my own belt stand on Maxwell Street, the teeming old-world marketplace where my parents had been born, and on Saturdays and some evenings I sold door-to-door religious pictures and sometimes lamps on commission for a clothing, furniture, and jewelry store on the West Side. But all that took a shared place in my life with my new interest in formal education. I hadn't been sure what to expect from the instruction at Roosevelt, but the professors were of a high level, and stimulating. I took four liberal arts courses and made the Dean's List, which allowed me to receive a modest academic scholarship the following semester. I was breathing easier.

During this time I was still playing basketball in pickup games in Loyola Park, where I had played since the beginning of my high school days, and in a league. But my high school basketball career still bothered me. I thought I could have done better, and that had left me with a sense of unrealized promise. I felt I had bowed to the criticism of my shooting too much and that that sensitivity had handcuffed me. Only later did I learn that developing a hard shell to ward off insecurities is essential to success in sports and writing alike.

When I came across an item in the Roosevelt University school newspaper that Coach Turner was holding tryouts for the Roosevelt basketball team, I thought, Why not? I hadn't even been aware that Roosevelt had a team. I tried out, made the squad, and to my great satisfaction was named to the starting lineup.

Roosevelt played on a Division III level, with no athletic scholarships (though, a few years later, it moved up to Division II and did offer scholarships to players). It also didn't have a gym. The team used a well-worn recreational facility named Olivet Institute, about four miles from the school building. There were exposed pipes on the ceiling and walls, and not all of the lights were always working, so we sometimes practiced and played games in circumstances that seemed to require miner's helmets.

There were stands in a balcony that could seat several hundred, though for games they were usually more than half empty. We had no band, no cheerleaders, no pom-pom girls, no conference. We just had a basketball team and Coach Turner.

The purpose of the team was to play basketball, and not for any other reason than that it was fun or, perhaps, to prove something or other to ourselves or both. There were no illusions of glory. We could quit the team any time we chose to without financial jeopardy. And some did.

Coach Turner scheduled games against schools like the University of Chicago, teacher's colleges, other small liberal arts colleges, junior colleges, as well as the DePaul University freshman team. (This was at a time when freshmen were still not eligible for Division I varsity play.) Our starting five were Jim Malone at center, Louis Campbell and Peter Lutterbeck at forward, and Jim Pazeatopolis and I at guard. It was a proper city mélange: two blacks, a German, a Greek, and a Jew. And a guy named Kelly was sixth man.

Malone and Campbell—who we hoped would dominate the front court—were our most imposing players. Both had been good high school players in Chicago, and I could never figure out why they were playing at Roosevelt instead of at a college on scholarship. It just wasn't something I ever found the opportunity to ask either of them.

In our first game Wilson Junior College beat us by a wide margin. We lacked cohesion, and I scored eight points. I had played cautiously and had several turnovers. At the next practice Coach Turner took me aside. "You had shots and you didn't take them," he said. "I know we can win games, but if we are, you are going to have to help with the scoring."

In our second game, against a team from the Great Lakes Naval training base, we lost by one point, and again I played tentatively. I still felt a constraint about shooting. "If you don't shoot more," said Turner, "I'm going to put you on the bench. But I'd rather you helped the team. And I know you have the shot." There was a decency in the man, and it came out even when he had possible bad news. But his approach was encouraging, emphasizing my potential.

Looking back, I can see that Turner was obviously sensitive to inhibitions, self-inflicted or otherwise, even those of an eighteen-year-old white boy. He had grown up in the segregated South, in the small town of Gilmer, in northeast Texas, where he was allowed to sit only in the balcony of the local theater; where he was not allowed to attend the grade school a block from his home but had to travel a mile to the black school. Despite this and other forms of discrimination, his family—his father and his uncles—owned five funeral homes in the area, and he was raised with a sense of independence and dignity.

He attended nearby Texas College, an all-black school, where he was a standout in basketball, track, and football, making the Negro Colleges' all-American team as a running back and end in 1934 and 1935. He graduated with honors. He taught school and then, when war broke out, became an infantry officer in the U.S. Army—one of only three blacks in his Officer Candidate School class of 257 at Fort Benning, Georgia, and ranked third in the class. He served two years in Europe, primarily in Italy, during World War II. I once asked if he had ever been shot at. "Not to my knowledge," he replied.

In the time I played for Coach Turner, I never saw an opposing coach show any kind of disrespect to him. He was just another coach on the other bench, as I perceived it. It was only later that I learned of what had happened with his golf team.

The Roosevelt golf team was in a conference with eleven other area schools that included Aurora College, Illinois Tech, DePaul, and Loyola. They played on courses primarily in the suburbs. Turner was the only black coach in the conference and the only coach not allowed on the golf courses. Every one of the dozen courses they played on had restrictions against blacks—or, in the terminology of the 1950s, "negroes." He first learned about it when he walked onto a course in Mt. Prospect. An official of the club told Turner, "You may sit in the clubhouse, but you can't go on the course. Sorry. It's the rules."

So Turner had to sit in the clubhouse and wait for his team to make the turn at the tenth hole. "I'd have to ask them how they were doing," Turner recalled, "where the other coaches could follow their players around and *see* how they were doing."

And either before matches or after matches, other coaches could play on those courses. All but Turner, who also wanted to play. He liked golf, which he had learned to play as a boy when he caddied at golf clubs in Texas, and caddies were allowed to play on occasion. He decided that for the sake of his team he would not make a protest. "And sometimes you have to pick your spots about when to make a fuss," he said. "Under the circumstances I felt that this just wasn't one of them. Was I angry? Sure. But I know anger isn't good for you. You can't think clearly when you're angry. If you took all of these things seriously, you'd go batty, go crazy. It's very, very frustrating."

After a couple of years, the sense of unfairness on the golf courses in suburban Chicago began to eat at the other college coaches in Turner's conference. I would imagine, too, that, knowing Turner, they had to feel pretty stupid to be involved in something that shameful. And while Turner tried not to get angry, the racism took its toll. Turner, a young, healthy man, suffered ulcers.

"I don't remember how it happened, but one day I found myself playing one of the courses with the other coaches," Turner recalled, "and then I was being allowed to follow my team. And pretty soon, one by one, all the other courses allowed me to do the same."

In our third basketball game, with the bench looming for me, I was concerned and anxious. I had now the same question I'd had for Coach Scher four years earlier after a bad game for the Sullivan frosh-soph: Will I ever hit again?

I opened the game by missing a jump shot. I missed a second. But I glanced over to see Coach Turner on the bench clapping his hands with encouragement.

I scored on my third shot and went on to have my best scoring game in school ball since the frosh-soph. We beat Elgin College 56–53, and I had 18 points—or about a third of my team's points—to lead all scorers in the game.

"Nice job," he said with a smile after the game. That was all. That was enough.

In the previous two games I had hustled on defense, I had tried to look for the open man in passing, but I had not gotten the most out of my abilities because I hadn't trusted myself to shoot the ball. And the problem had come from within, a reluctance to throw off the shackles of insecurity. Turner helped me to do so.

In my next game, against the University of Illinois Professional Schools, I did even better, scoring 26 points in a 97–70 victory, hitting 11 baskets, and was 4-for-5 from the free-throw line. The team and I were riding a wave. After we defeated the Chicago Teachers College 86–65, the *Chicago Sun-Times* noted, "Ira Berkow paced the Roosevelt attack with 24 points on 10 baskets and four free throws."

After so many paltry lines in the box scores from my high school days, it was gratifying to see a fat bunch of numbers following my name.

Lou Campbell, our 6-foot-4 forward, had 23 points in that game against Chicago Teachers. Campbell was a soft-spoken guy who often let his wardrobe do the talking for him. He had a big mustache and a knowing wink, and he invariably showed up for games in a black evening cape. He wore a variety of hats, most black and wide-brimmed, like a gaucho. And when he played, he had a slicing, swooping, birdlike aspect to his moves to the basket—in his cape he also seemed to swoop into the gym. We called him Gull, for seagull.

Our center, Jim Malone, was a broad-shouldered 6-foot-6 senior who worked a full-time job in a factory, as I recall, in addition to going to school, playing ball, and caring for his family, which included a couple of kids. I never remember him looking tired, though he would have had justification. He was an ace rebounder, and what I remember most is people bouncing off him.

But my closest friends on the team were two sometime starters—they started when one of the regulars couldn't make a game. One was a Greek named Mike Simos. He was practical, and he was admiring, in a humorous way. Admiring of himself, that is. The practical: he taught me that when you get into a car on a snowy day, you kick your feet to get off the snow, so you don't create a puddle in the car. The admiring: he would sing a song, "I'm the greatest, I'm too much for words. I'm the greatest, haven't you heard." Usually he would sing it in his car to the rearview mirror.

My other good friend was a black guy named Raymond Tanter. He taught me the best way to win an argument, which was to agree in the gentlest manner with the one you're arguing with. When I heated up on a topic, he would smile and say, "Right again, Ira." Put me at a loss for words.

The Roosevelt team was not exactly one big happy family, however. Not for me, anyway. There was a black substitute player on the team—someone I'll call Baxter—who felt he wasn't playing as much as he should have. I wasn't sure if he resented me or the coach or the world in general. But he was grim and distant. There was a militancy in his eyes before militancy had grown as strong as it would in this country. The Little Rock school-integration crisis had taken place less than a year earlier, and Martin Luther King was still known primarily as a preacher in Birmingham—and then only to those who followed events closely.

I remember one game we won and I scored 17 points and Baxter 5, and by the look on his face, I wasn't sure it was safe for me to leave the gym alone. It was. Baxter had gone his separate way. We said little to each other the rest of the season. He has since disappeared into the mists of my history.

Coach Turner continued to be encouraging, and he suggested I drive more to be more effective. "Go in there and get those fouls," he said. "And you can get open more for your outside shot because they start to lay off of you." He was right, but I still found it more comfortable to settle for the jump shot.

For our team, meanwhile, there was no more important game than the one against the DePaul freshmen team. These were the scholarship guys, the future hotshots of America. We felt we could best test our skills against them.

I was assigned to guard John Incardone, who had been a widely publicized all-Catholic League high school player in Chicago and became a starter on the DePaul varsity. He was about my height and looked as solidly built as a steel cabinet. On the very first play of the game, he brought the ball downcourt toward me and then suddenly went left. That is, his left shoulder went left, and I followed it. The rest of him went right. Right by me for an easy layup. What a great fake! He didn't make that move off me again and had to settle for a variety of other great moves. The DePaul freshmen beat us, 82–51, but I had my moments. Although we lost, we gave them a battle until they pulled away at the end. It was especially gratifying to me because I scored 15 points and was Roosevelt's high scorer.

I wound up the season with a 15-point average, which I believe was the best on the team. I had come out of my shell as a basketball player—and proved that I could score consistently in interscholastic competition. And in large part I had Coach Turner to thank for it.

That season turned out to be the only one I would play for Roosevelt and for Coach Turner. I had signed up for the six-month National Guard program in order to avoid being drafted for a two-year hitch, and I knew that one day I would be called for active duty for six months. That day came in the spring of 1959.

While in the Army that summer, I met Ron Hamilton, who had recently been a star guard on the basketball team at Tennessee State, a black university. Hamilton and I and others played on grounds at Fort Gordon, Georgia, and one day someone told us about an American Legion hall in nearby Augusta that had a great basketball court. Six of us, including Ron, the lone black, piled into a car to play there. Turned out it was closed. As we were driving back to the camp in the dusk, deep in disappointment, I saw a handsome outdoor court—with nets!—at the side of the road.

In my nineteen-year-old enthusiasm I shouted to the driver, "Stop the car! We've got a place to play!" The guy driving was several years older than I and quicker to comprehend the situation. "I don't think so," he said, and continued driving.

Hamilton was silent. Then I realized: if some rednecks had seen the white guys playing with a black guy in Georgia in the fifties, we might have been shot. This was the South of separate drinking fountains, separate public toilet facilities, and state-mandated segregated schools. But this was the first time I had felt personally affected by irrational racial attitudes. Though it was a minor episode, I now had some inkling—as trivial as it was—of what it was like for blacks facing discrimination. My game, my pleasure, a kind of liberty, had been taken from me, and there was nothing I could do about it. I was furious about such intolerance and have remained so to this day.

Not long ago I tracked down Ron Hamilton, who now lives in a Chicago suburb and is a sales representative for an educational book company. After he left the army, he played for the Cleveland Pipers of the now-defunct American Basketball League—a team that starred Jerry Lucas and was owned by the young scion of a Cleveland shipping company, George Steinbrenner. Ron never made it to the NBA. He and I talked about going to the American Legion gym to play basketball that summer night, and he went on to tell me how it tough it had been for him to serve on an army base in the South.

"On the base, I remember that when I was on the chow line, I'd always be picked out to be a server, so I stayed in the barracks until almost everybody had gone in," he said. "And when I'd go off campus, I'd be wearing my black soldier shoes, and people tried to take advantage of me. I felt like a marked man, like they saw me as a trick. I mean the black folks. They thought because I was in the army that I had money, which was kind of funny because I was only making something like $97 a month. And since the area outside the base was highly segregated, I naturally didn't feel comfortable with whites, either. So I stayed on the base, essentially. It was very hot down there. I remember I just tried to stay out of the way and in the shade."

After the army I returned to Roosevelt for one semester and then transferred to Miami of Ohio, wanting a new experience at a college away from home. But my days at Roosevelt University and playing for Coach Turner were memorable for me. Now, nearly forty years later, I looked forward to visiting him in Highland Park. As I drove there, I saw that the house was in a woodsy, all-white area—Turner told me that he had gotten a good deal from a realtor who was one of his former students.

When Coach Turner opened the door, he hugged me. I embraced him back. He still looked fit and not at all his age, eighty-two. He said he still played golf, though he had considered giving it up.

"I had arthritis in my back and shoulders so bad that I couldn't follow through on my swing," he said. "And where once I had a 12 handicap, I now was shooting 98, 99, 102, 105—and I'd never shot over 85 or 86. Once you've done reasonably well in certain sports and you begin to falter, you get a little discouraged, disenchanted, and you lose interest. I told my wife that I was going to quit playing golf. She said, 'No, you don't quit playing golf. You like the game. Just go out there and enjoy yourself.' "

And what happened? I asked.

"I went back out," he said, "and I made adjustments. And then the arthritis got a little better. And I played a little better. Not where I was before, but better than I had been playing."

In the hundreds?

"Oh no," he said. He smiled. "In the high nineties."

When he and Gladys were considering moving into this

neighborhood, Coach Turner told me, a vote was taken of the residents in the thirty-nine houses in their development. All but one person voted yes. And that was the family that would be living next door. "Well, we moved in and they didn't speak to us for about three years," said Turner. "And then one day I had picked crab apples from our tree, and I saw the woman and offered her some of our crab apples. She looked hesitant but accepted. A few days later she came over with some tomatoes she had grown. We became friends after that."

He said that they had a fright when they first moved in. "We heard something pinging against our picture window in the living room," he said. "We didn't know what it was, but it sounded like somebody was throwing a rock or something at our window. We wondered if it was, you know, some kind of welcoming committee. Like, get out of here. Well, what happened was, a lot of birds fly around here. And they hit the windows. Sometimes you go out and find them lying on the lawn, their necks broken."

I told Coach Turner that I still play basketball and asked whether he thought I should still be at it.

"If you feel you can do it," he replied. "I don't put any limit on doing things. That's my philosophy of life. About ten years ago I told a friend of mine that I was going to buy a car and that it was going to be my last car. He said to me, 'I won't ever buy anything and call it my last. Even if I want something and I'm almost on my deathbed, I'm going to buy it if I want it. And going to buy top of the line, too.' I thought that made a lot of sense. What are you saving for at this age? So I went out and bought a Cadillac."

"Is it your last?" I asked.

"Oh no," he said, "but ours now is five years old. We're going out shopping for a new one."

Labors of Love

My birthday arrived on January 7, and I turned fifty-six. Another year older, another year slower.

Oddly enough, as each birthday passes, I seem to take each one more and more in stride. Fighting the inevitable is, at bottom, futile. When I turned thirty, I wrote a column about how anguishing that one was. I said that to contemplate turning thirty was very much like contemplating a bad accident: you think it can never happen to you. But now I think about a conversation I once had with Red Smith about aging. He mentioned his old friend, the legendary sportswriter Grantland Rice. "To Granny," Smith told me, "every World Series was his first, every championship fight was his first. He saw everything through fresh eyes. He never grew old."

But another great sportswriter, Jimmy Cannon, once said that sportswriters lead lives of arrested development because they are always involved in games. Some of us even go out and try to emulate some of the athletes' moves. I was doing it when I was thirty, too.

At the time I wrote that column, I talked to Stan Isaacs, then a sports columnist with *Newsday*, about this particular birthday. "If you think it's bad now," he said, "wait 'til you turn forty." And now sixty is just around the corner.

Mortality was on my mind this birthday because of a phone call I had received from my parents two weeks earlier. My mother spoke first, and I could hear trouble in her voice. My brother, Steve, she said, was to begin chemotherapy.

"Chemotherapy?" I said, taken aback. "Why?"

I had known that three years earlier Steve had been diagnosed as having chronic lymphocytic leukemia. The disease was supposed to be nonaggressive, and he had been told that he would most likely live to seventy and that by then new cures surely would have been discovered. He had also been told that his was an illness in which his blood and bone marrow had to be monitored regularly but that he did not require treatment. Somewhere along the line, however, the doctors either missed something or my brother's internal mechanisms had changed so dramatically that they were taken by surprise.

Now the doctors said they were optimistic about this treatment—one hour of chemo five days a week, once a month for six months—but my mother expressed great concern. "Oh, what *tsuris*," she said, using the Yiddish word for "grave trouble." My father, as he often does, tried to temper that. "The doctors believe they can control it," he said.

I asked how Steve and Judy and Shayne were taking this.

"They're worried," my mother said, "like you'd expect."

My father, on the other extension, was silent. This meant he agreed.

"Are you going to call Steve?" my mother asked.

"He's not talking to me," I replied, a bit defensively. "I'm not sure he'd want me to call. To tell you the truth, he wasn't that receptive the last time I called."

"This is different," my father said.

"I know," I said. "I'll see."

I called my internist, Dr. Tuchman, and asked his opinion. "Everybody responds differently," he said. "You never know. It's serious, but the chemotherapy might arrest it."

I sat by the telephone. Should I call Steve? I felt that if I didn't call, I'd be uncomfortable, and if I did call, I'd be uncomfortable, making yet another overture that Steve might not appreciate.

Steve had always been reserved, or, as Judy once described him, "not assertive." Which is not to say he was any kind of pushover. He wasn't. He could stand up for himself, and nicely. But I was less reserved, to be sure, and not unassertive. We grew up that way. I'm not sure whether he resented the way I went about things, and I had often told him that he shouldn't expect people—family, friends, even teachers—to always make approaches to him, that he has to meet them partway. Maybe he resented my telling him that, too. But on the other side of the coin, I liked that he was always independent, always did things honestly, was never phony, and never called attention to himself. In the end he was always my little brother, always the little kid who wore glasses from the time he was two years old after a devastating bout with measles, toward whom I often felt protective. The attachment to my brother, no matter how distant at times, was still there, still real. I felt it in my bones.

But I decided not to call him. I called my parents back. "I'd like you to tell Steve and Judy that you spoke to me," I said, "and that if there is anything they want me to do at any time, I would gladly do it."

•   •   •

At the office I received an envelope with Kenny Garcia's return address. Apparently the kid was truly interested in getting a job at *The Times*. He had enclosed a handwritten note, carefully scripted on lined notebook paper. It read:

> Ira, I am 17 years old. I am courteous respectful and punctuous [sic] young man who is eager to go out and dip into the real world. I consider myself a people person and someone with the ability to comprehend what's going on around him. I feel I am smart enough and responsible enough to handle anything that comes my way.
>
>   Sincerely,
>   Kenny Garcia

His address and phone number were written below the signature.

Kenny's description of himself was pretty much as I had observed him to be, too. Charlie Miron had always contended that you can tell a great deal about someone when you see him play basketball: ego, desire, even upbringing. I agreed. A player doesn't reveal everything, certainly, but he displays a lot, often unconsciously.

But sometimes even the most astute observer can miss, too. I once ran across an article about Dr. Joseph Bell, a professor who taught Sir Arthur Conan Doyle in medical school in Edinburgh, Scotland. Dr. Bell was the model for Doyle's inimitable sleuth, Sherlock Holmes, for he was a wizard at deduction, being able to tell merely at a glance from the mud on a man's shoe, for example, if and when he had served in the military, where he had been born, probably even what he had eaten for lunch. Dr. Bell also had a sense of humor and told this story on himself: He was making the rounds of patients with a cluster of students behind him. He stopped to visit a bedridden man. "Aren't you a bandsman?" Dr. Bell asked, standing over the patient. "Aye," admitted the sick man. Dr. Bell cockily turned to his students. "You see, gentlemen, I am right. It is quite simple. This man had a paralysis of the cheek muscles, the result of too much blowing at wind instruments. We need only inquire to confirm. What instrument do you play, my man?"

The man raised up on his elbows. "The big drum, Doctor!"

But I felt I had seen and talked enough with Kenny Garcia to feel comfortable about passing his note on to Marie Davitt, who was in charge of hiring noneditorial and nonexecutive people at the *Times*.

"All I know about him, Marie," I told her, "is that I like the way he plays ball, his mentality on the court, and that he did follow up about the job." Marie said there were very few job openings at the *Times*, but that the paper did try hard to accommodate minorities. I felt that Kenny had a long shot facing him—very long.

A few weeks later, I ran into Marie by an elevator at the *Times*. I asked her about Kenny. She said she had just placed a call to him and had left a message for him to come in for an interview. She added, again, that she is inundated with requests for jobs and that this was a formality. I said I understood. "I know you'll do what you can," I said.

About a month after that, I saw Kenny's cousin, Junior, at the NYU indoor basketball court. Junior is a spirited player, with good driving moves to the basket and some impressive hang time. That evening I played on the same team with Junior, and he was instrumental in getting me a good workout, because we won several games. I played more or less quietly, riding the coattails of Junior and a couple other talented players on the team.

I asked Junior after we had finished whether he had heard from Kenny, who doesn't play at this gym during the school year. Junior said he had seen him recently but reported that he hadn't said anything about the *New York Times*. "Next time I see him, I'll ask him," Junior assured me.

It was when I was seventeen—Kenny's age—that I first fell in love, or collapsed in love. And basketball played a part in it. Because the girl of my dreams at that moment had no interest in basketball, or any sports for that matter, I wasn't sure how to scale that barrier.

Laura Kogan was in my class at Sullivan High School, and it is a mystery to me today why I had taken such little notice of her during my first three years there. Earlier, I had been aware that she was smart—one of the best students in the class—but she was also reserved and rather run-of-the-mill pretty. One day early in our senior year I turned around and she had become gorgeous. She took my breath away. How this happened overnight, I'll never know.

I looked at Laura one afternoon in the crowded lunchroom and suddenly discovered the most appealing girl on the face of the earth. That day she wore a dark blue sweater, a tight gray skirt, bobby socks, and loafers. She moved with a sense of unstudied confidence, and with just enough of a womanly sway to give some emphasis to the lines below her waist. She had a somewhat tanned complexion, like the color of butterscotch, and wore her dark hair fairly short and with a wave in front. Her eyebrows had a slight arch to them. Her mouth was a little small, but her lips were full, and with just a hint of an overbite, which seemed more pronounced when she bit into her sandwich, giving her an odd but, to my gaze, irresistible sensuality. Her dark eyes seemed to understand everything I was thinking. At different moments she could be flirtatious and warm, or distant and indifferent. All of it unpredictable and disconcerting.

One morning I ran into her in a second-floor hallway, at a place we called "The T" because the corridors met and formed such a letter, and I stopped to talk to her. As we spoke, a strange thing happened. My knees got shaky. I also think I heard a buzzing in my ear. My heart beat like a jungle drum. My mouth was forming words, but I wasn't saying the things that were in my brain. My tongue was moving, but my head was turned off. I seemed far away at the very moment I was nearly stepping on her toes.

I realized for the first time in my life: This was Music. This was Torture. This was Love.

Laura lived on Lake Shore Drive in a ritzy apartment building with large chandeliers and a doorman. Her family had moved to the drive a few years earlier from an apartment in our neighborhood, and though she now lived outside the district, she was allowed to finish Sullivan. I lived on the other side of town, on a tree-lined street, but hardly Lake Shore Drive.

I tried to interest Laura in the basketball team, and in the baseball team, for whom I was a pitcher and first baseman, but she couldn't be bothered. Laura did read books, however, which is something I didn't do much of then. No time.

We dated off and on. She had an easy smile, and we laughed, but I always felt an indefinable distance. One night during our senior year we were driving in my father's red-and-white Impala—it was one of our family's great material possessions, and getting that car from my father always took clever diplomatic skills, and begging—and Laura idly said to me, "Have you read *Of Human Bondage?*"

"Oh," I replied, in my most literate manner, "you mean the book about the Civil War?"

"No," she said, and stared out the window at the night.

I don't remember what I said to her after that, but it had nothing do with Somerset Maugham's novel. The whole thing was a struggle with Laura: getting a date with her, and then the date itself. I'd take her miniature golfing: "Oh, I don't know," she'd say, "couldn't we try something a little less *earthy*?" When I'd have rock-'n'-roll on the car radio—bouncing to Jerry Lee Lewis or the Platters—she'd ask to switch to something like Montovani, a musical middle ground that I took at the time for classical. To my ear, then, Montovani was Beethoven, and neither, singly or together, added up to the Everly Brothers.

And then there was the ultimate struggle with Laura. On occasion, we'd pull off to a parking spot along the lake, where it was dark and romantic and tree-shaded, with stars reflecting on the water, and the smell of fall in the air. I would move over a little bit, and she would move over a little bit. But in the other direction. When she could go no farther—there was only so far she could travel in the front seat of a car—she would prepare for the next step. Laura was warm, she was soft, but her clothing, and sometimes even her lips, had the effect of a moat—that is, designed primarily to ward off invasion. Nothing much happened.

After one of these dates, I escorted her up the elevator of her apartment building, walked down the hallway to her door, then, after a short time of hemming and hawing, mentally and verbally, I put my arms around her and twisted to kiss her. I twisted in such a way that I thought I had broken something in my neck. She jumped back from my onslaught. "I have to go," she said, inserting her key in the door, swinging open the door, and vanishing inside the apartment, all at the speed of light. I was so alone so suddenly that it seemed as if there had never been another person with me.

Laura and I soon broke up, which came as no surprise to me. She had become exceedingly busy. Busier even than the mayor, it seemed. So it wasn't that we actually broke up. It was more that each day of her life had become so filled that she didn't have a day for me, or a night, or even six seconds.

I began seeing Joyce Abrams, an ash-blond, pony-tailed cheerleader, who was a junior, a class below mine. Joyce was a pretty girl, a sweet girl, a girl who generously filled out a white sweater with two faint but achingly appealing dark spots at peak points, a girl with whom I parked and necked at night-time in such an out-of-the-way place as the alley beside a cemetery a few blocks from her home. We'd climb into the backseat of my father's car, and in those rare moments when we glanced up, we were able to see only the tops of tall crypts, lighted by the moon.

And when I took her home, we often didn't part right away. Her mother used to call from another room, "Joyce, do you know what time it is?" I considered buying Mrs. Abrams a clock, but decided she might not appreciate the gesture.

After basketball games Joyce would wait for me, with my hair still wet from the shower. I might still be anguishing over a game as she handed me the orange that I had given her to safeguard in her purse. This was so I could presumably get back my depleted energy. I peeled the orange with my thumbs and ate the sticky fruit, and we walked and I spoke about my conflicted friendship with Stuart, whose game had overtaken mine. I'm not sure how aware of this Joyce had been since she had been busy jumping and twirling, in her blue cheerleader sweater and pleated blue skirt. I also didn't mention the occasional distraction of Joyce and her fellow cheerleaders, and the players' sneak peeks at exposed thighs when the skirts billowed with their leaps and twirls.

It was around this time that I started reading a few books,

by accident. In grade school I had been a good student and an avid reader, but in high school I was too busy for books. That changed in the last semester of my senior year, when I tore ligaments in my right ankle while playing in a pickup basketball game at Loyola Park and was unable to play for the school team in the last semester of my senior year. For about a month I was relegated to crutches and hobbling around our apartment.

My father seized an opportunity in my misfortune. "He's vulnerable," he must have thought. "He's bored stiff. He needs a book!" My father had always tried to steer me to read, and I had resisted over the last four years. Now he handed me a paperback titled *30 Days to a More Powerful Vocabulary*. I flipped through it. "Thanks, Dad," I said. I doubt if I mustered a convincing enthusiasm. I do know that when my father left the room I tossed the book aside.

I didn't open it until I picked it up absentmindedly several days later and suddenly became absorbed in the world of words. It changed my life. I felt like Alice tumbling into Wonderland. The words were exotic and hypnotic: *antediluvian, pedantic, meretricious, enervated, opprobrium, Brobdingnagian.*

And they weren't just great objects to roll around in your mouth. They were weapons. My father had always told me that words were power, and now I began to wonder about this, the ability to use words to fashion one's thoughts. Thought could be power, too. The smarter you are, the stronger you are. The more tools you have, the better chance you have. My father used to tell me that, too. Now I decided that, yes, maybe words could be power for me, too. And I was going to use that power to bring Laura to her knees.

One day in the hall at Sullivan I passed Laura, who I wasn't speaking to, though I got the feeling she hadn't noticed. I had heard that Laura was dating an older guy, someone in college. Someone, I was sure, who couldn't get enough of Montovani. She was carrying several books. I had planned this for some time, and now broke my silence and said casually, "Oh, I see you have a paucity of books."

Without breaking stride, she said, "You mean 'plethora,' don't you?"

I did! Shit! I had confused the two words!

"I meant what I meant," I said to Laura, defiantly, and probably lamely. I'm not sure she heard me, as her heels clicked down the tan-tiled hallway. And back I went to *30 Days to a More Powerful Vocabulary*, and to Joyce.

Meanwhile, Joyce was plethora to Laura's paucity, at least in terms of human and physical affection. Joyce's charms were bountiful, not the least of which was her delight in the electric touching of skin to skin. And she possessed a lust for life that seemed to elude Laura.

I liked Joyce very much, and one day in casual conversation I threw in a few of the sesquipedalian nuggets gleaned only a short time before from *30 Days to a More Powerful Vocabulary*.

She turned and looked at me. "Swallowed a dictionary?" she asked.

I decided to stop trying to impress her and told her about the book, and some of the words. I remember she liked the word *loquacious* for some reason. But talk of words didn't always hold her interest. We'd be walking down a street, and I'd be expounding about something—possibly basketball—and I'd turn and there was Joyce across the street, petting a dog. She loved dogs more, I'm certain, than she did verbiage. But it was distracting, especially when I had my earthshaking matters to discuss.

The senior prom was approaching, and I assumed that Joyce would be my date.

It was now the middle of May, about four weeks before the Prom, and the doors and windows of Sullivan had opened, and the smell and feel of springtime was everywhere—in the classrooms, in the halls, in the blood. I was placing books in my locker in the corridor on one of those warmly embracing days when I heard a warm voice say, "Hello."

I turned. It was Laura, looking sensational in a spring dress with a bow in her hair. Her eyes were soft and beautiful, and she smelled of springtime. She smiled.

"I'd like to talk to you," she said.

"OK," I said in my best distant voice. "Talk." I was, after all, a pretty tough guy.

"Not here. Could you give me a jingle tonight?"

"When?"

"Well, tonight."

"I'll think about it," I said.

She shrugged and walked off. I caught a glimpse of her walk, of her tight skirt, of those smooth brown legs tapering to her neatly folded bobby socks and brown loafers, and that distinctive, alluring ankle roll. I turned back to the locker. I was having trouble breathing. What did she want? What was going on? What should I do?

When I called her that night, Laura said she was interested in seeing me again. And I had no choice. The fly had wandered into the web.

I stopped seeing Joyce. I wasn't proud of myself, but I felt I would be living a fiction if I had continued dating her as if nothing in my head and abdomen had changed.

And I took Laura to the senior prom.

I'm not sure why Laura took a renewed interest in me, though I have wondered if she simply wanted a date for the prom and if her boyfriend in college wasn't interested in returning to a high school affair. Of course, there was an outside chance that she liked me, and I mulled that over awhile until the thought evaporated.

I still have a black-and-white photograph of the two of us, taken at Stuart Menaker's house. We double-dated that night. Laura looked dazzling in a white-and-red candy-striped dress that accentuated her bare, tanned shoulders. I was in a tuxedo with white jacket and black bow tie. Laura smiled brightly. I have a kind of peculiar, Edgar Allen Poe glaze in my eyes. The picture, appropriately, was taken on a slant, and it appeared that at any moment we, or I, would fall out of the room.

Prom night was uneventful, but as we sat beside each other at a downtown nightclub, I felt a growing distance from Laura, as if she really didn't want to be with me. But the next morning, as was the custom, I also took her to the annual prom picnic. I was playing softball with some of my classmates when, for some reason, my attention was called to an area where some of the girls stood. I noticed that Laura was holding a small sign in her hands, the kind that coffee shops have on the wall, such as "In God We Trust / All Others Pay Cash." This one read: "Don't Go Away Mad / Just Go Away."

I don't know where Laura had got the sign, or even why she was holding it. The fact is, she held the sign, and I held a softball, and I threw that ball at her.

All of my pent-up frustrations and disappointments and, yes, unrequited love, went into that throw that now flew toward her. As soon as I let the ball go, I realized that this was not quite the most mature thing a high school senior could do, and yet despite this, there was an irrepressible joy in my heart.

My aim wasn't too good—opposing batters, when I pitched for the Sullivan baseball team, had learned this some time ago—and the ball sailed over Laura's head and cracked into the tree behind her. She screamed, as splinters of wood broke from the tree and flecked onto her head.

Looking back, I'm glad I didn't hit her, and maybe somewhere in my unconscious I really didn't want to. Regardless, that errant missile—I can still hear the echoes of her frightened cries as the bark of the tree exploded—signaled the end of the picnic, the end of our date, the end of our romance. And I knew that I would love her forever. Or for what passed for forever when I was seventeen years old.

My dating life over the next several years was active. The women and the experiences varied widely, but the first time that I went out with an appreciably older woman—I was nineteen, she was about twenty-four—was when I was in college at Roosevelt. Raymond Tanter, a black friend and basketball teammate, fixed me up for a date one night with a friend of his wife's—both women were also black. They drove in Raymond's yellow convertible from their home on the South Side to my home in an all-white neighborhood on the North Side to pick me up. As we drove off, I saw neighbors looking out of their windows in wonderment.

We went to a basketball game at McGaw Hall on the Northwestern University campus. It was a primarily white crowd, including a number of people I knew. I got greetings and a lot of looks. Afterward, the four of us went to a South Side restaurant in which I was the only white person. Again, I got greetings and a lot of looks. I had heard of people saying that they could feel the hot stares of others on the back of their necks. I learned that it is true. It was especially so in the 1950s, and it mattered not whether the viewers were white or black. If it's out of custom, you're perceived as suspicious and maybe a little dangerous, too.

The best part of the night—except for Raymond's ebullient wit—was Renee, my date. She wore a black blouse, black slacks, black heels, and a string of white pearls. She was an elegant, lovely woman. She had a pleasant laugh and offered thoughtful views.

Later in the evening I said to her, "Can you take a compliment?"

She looked at me evenly. "I think so." she said.

"You are a *woman*," I said.

"Thank you," she said.

It was indeed a perfect way to accept a compliment.

I never went out with her again. It may simply have been that the inconvenience of traveling all the way across town for a date was just too difficult. I don't think race was a factor because I occasionally went out with black women after that. But I sometimes thought about Renee and her grace and sense of self remained for a long time a standard for me.

Through the years basketball has inevitably played some part in my relationships with women. And on occasion a woman has been jealous of it. When I was in my late twenties, I was seeing a woman named Cindy who hated the idea of our making love and then my leaving to go play basketball. There were times when, unfortunately, I was running late. I had to get to the gym because the basketball period was starting at a certain time, and it would end at a certain time, and if I didn't get there early and play, I might not get a workout. I admit that this was not the height of romance—well, for a woman it wasn't, for basketball it was. But one day Cindy came up with a ploy to keep me from the game.

As I pulled on my clothes in her bedroom, she stood partly nude in front of a mirror, casually brushing her shoulder-length auburn hair. I looked up, entranced by the languorous strokes, the loveliness of her skin and breasts as reflected in the mirror, and her tight backside veiled in sheer black panties. This was simply too much eroticism for a young man to resist. I missed the workout. The score that day: Cindy 1, basketball 0.

But in time I got married. And then I got married again. And a third time, at age thirty-eight, to Dolly, who has stuck with me for nearly twenty years.

My father had said that I was like a Hollywood actor, getting married so often. He and my mother, after all, have been married since 1938. But sometimes things aren't working, even between well-meaning people, and both have to have the sense to understand that. I consider it a good sign that I have remained friends with both of my ex-wives. In fact, when Dolly and I got married, my first wife, Willee, and her new husband took us to dinner at a French restaurant, and my second wife, Nancy, sent us a dozen roses. I have contended that they were so happy to be rid of me that they went the extra mile.

I believe my marriage to Dolly has worked because we were at an age to give each other the room we needed. It may have also helped that I was more settled in my life, having made a modest assault on a career. Our personalities meshed in a way they didn't with the others. And circumstances changed, too. When my first wife wanted children, I didn't, since I was a struggling young journalist and didn't want to be tied down to children. My second wife had two young boys, and I tried to be a devoted stepfather, but it was difficult. I took them to games, played ball with them, sought to help them with their studies and with their problems. But even so, a new husband for their mother—no matter who that man was—made for complications and some uneasy times.

But there were gentler moments, to be sure, in both marriages, and all three wives have been understanding of my work and life, including basketball. And so is Dolly. Dolly has a son, Allen, from a previous marriage, who lived with his father and never with us. But he was very much a part of our lives, often staying with us. He is grown up now, an electrician with his own company. Allen is a good softball player, a low-handicap golfer, and an occasional basketball player, and from time to time we go out and shoot around. He's also a Michael Jordan fan, and once I introduced him to Jordan. Allen told me later that he was hyperventilating, but it was hard to see. "Michael," he said, "everyone wants to talk about your basketball, but I saw your golf video, and you have a great swing."

Jordan looked at him with widened eyes. "You think so?"

"Yeah, I really do," said Allen. "And I think you could have a career on the pro tour."

"No kidding?"

"Sure. I can see the headlines now: 'Jordan Brings U.S. Open to its knees!'" Jordan laughed and they talked some more.

When Allen has had problems—work, girls, the suicide of a close friend—he seems not to have hesitated in seeking advice and comfort from Dolly and me. I am happy for his trust, and though I have never had children of my own, I like having young people in my life. On occasion, I feel that I have something to offer from my experience and that I couldn't hurt them by sharing it. And on occasion they listen, and have even agreed.

Just as Red Smith took an interest in me, however casual, when I was a college student and would-be writer, so I have returned the favor to others. I imagine that that was part of the reason I was rooting for Kenny Garcia to make it at the *Times*, too.

I know, too, that Dolly appreciates the interest I take in

Allen. And she reciprocates with my family, my work—and, yes, my hoops.

For a pickup basketball player she is the most understanding of wives. When, for example, I was suddenly called away on assignment, she was kind enough to take my knee brace in for a rehab in which all the joints were tightened, the Velcro straps replaced, and the medial and lateral pads realigned. A husband could hardly ask for more.

For my entire life the constants, of course, have been my parents. Our family has had the normal run of arguments over the years, but my brother and I have remained close to them.

Having lost his parents early in life, my father learned how to scramble for survival. And while I never knew him to be very religious—I don't remember him even mentioning God—he did have faith in certain sayings. When I graduated from grammar school, for example, I asked my father to sign my autograph book. He wrote, "Dear Ira: Always know that the person who said, 'Opportunity knocks but once' was either lazy or stupid. Good luck. I know you'll do well. Daddy."

My father understood the importance of sports for me. When we moved from the West Side to the North Side after I graduated from grammar school, I knew no one in my new neighborhood. I kept returning to the West Side to play ball and hang out with my old friends. Then, one Saturday afternoon, he took me to nearby Green Briar Park, and we shot baskets. This was the first time I had ever done this with him, for he had played basketball only a few times in his life and had this funny, old-fashioned underhand shot. And when he saw kids my age arriving at the park to play basketball, he suggested I try to get in the game. I did. He left. And soon I became a regular there, making numerous friends—some of whom have lasted a lifetime. And I found I no longer had a need to return regularly to the West Side.

In our home there was always music. My father had dreamed of being a singer. He began as a boy singing Yiddish songs for pennies that were tossed to him when he went with his father to Romanian steak houses, those festive restaurants that I remember from my own boyhood, places that were bursting with singing and violin playing and dancing and the sizzle of steaks. My father learned when he was a boy of maybe five or six that he had a good singing voice, but he never really followed it up. It was too chancy. He needed hard cash in order to eat.

My father also sang as a young man in the vestibule of the apartment house where he lived with my Aunt Rose. He liked singing in the hallway because the acoustics were so good, with the sound of the words bouncing off the walls in the circular stairwell and rising and reverberating up to the ceiling.

My Aunt Rose, a woman of flaming red hair, lived on the second floor, and she had a neighbor, Anna Harris, who lived on the first floor. Anna reported to Rose one day that she had heard my father singing and that it sounded, she said, "like he was in love."

It turned out to be true.

My father had met my mother and sometimes sang to her in the vestibule of that apartment building, even when she wasn't there.

But in listening to him sing through the years and seeing his interest in it—his passion—I sensed in him an unfulfilled longing, and I resolved early on, first in a vague way and later definitively, that if I had a dream, a goal, I'd try to reach it. For my father survival was the goal, earning a good living was the dream, and supporting his wife and family the necessity. For me, with the luxury he didn't have of parents who could provide financial and emotional security, there would have to be more—rather, there could be more. For me, unlike him, no matter how difficult times were, there was always food. My mother, always aware that another Depression could be looming on the horizon, loaded our pantry with so many canned goods that when you took one down, thirty more might tumble after.

My mother, like my father, had been born on Maxwell Street, the center for Jewish immigration in Chicago at the turn of the century. Her mother, Mollie, a Russian immigrant, had owned a chicken store on the street, and my mother sometimes helped there, though she was never able to crack the necks of the live chickens as her mother could. After her marriage my mother worked with my father in the cleaning store, and in later years, through politics, in the office of the clerk of the circuit court.

I had always found my mother a woman with firm opinions, though sometimes not based on a great deal of research. But she had good business instincts and an uncanny insight into people. My father, considerably better read than she, often relied on her views.

My father had fallen in love with her the first time he saw her, when he had crashed a party, and though I had seen photographs of my mother when she was a young woman, it wasn't until a cousin, Errol Halperin, uncovered a long-lost home movie of his parents' wedding that I saw how beautiful she was. As a sister of the groom, she was a maid of honor at the wedding, twenty-two years old, and recently married to my father. She had high cheekbones and was shapely in her light-colored dress.

I watched the film with my parents.

"What do you think of yourself?" I asked her.

"I don't like it," she said.

"You don't?" I asked, "Why not?"

"It doesn't look like me," she said.

But I delighted in the film, as did Steve. "It was like discovering a dinosaur egg with the dinosaur inside," he told my father. "And didn't ma look great?"

With illnesses, my mother, who was slim for much of her life, has grown heavier in the last decade or so, bloated from taking a steroid for her painful arthritis.

And, as mothers are, she was protective of her sons.

When I was in high school, she and my father were eating in Ashkenaz, a popular restaurant-delicatessen near our home, when they happened to overhear a conversation among some guys my age in an adjoining booth.

My mother heard my name spoken, and she listened to what was being said.

When she heard, "That Ira Berkow, he's really overrated—" she got out of her seat and walked in front of the adjoining table.

"You should be careful who you talk about," she said. "Because Ira Berkow is my son!"

My mother, with gray hair and standing 5-feet-2, is not necessarily the most intimidating person, but she later recalled to me, "Those boys looked scared. And they apologized."

My mother had no idea, of course, whether the boys were correct in their assessment, because neither she nor my father ever attended a game of mine in school. The games were in the afternoons, and they were always working. I never urged them or my brother, for that matter, to come to a game. They had their lives, and I had mine.

But I knew they were aware of what I was doing. When I was about eleven years old, I was playing baseball with friends when I happened to notice a car standing beside a curb across the street from the park. The driver's window was rolled partly down, and behind his spectacles, the driver watched the game. I saw that it was my father. He didn't want to assert himself and come and stand and watch. Perhaps he didn't want to embarrass me in front of my friends. But in one way or another he had always kept an eye out for me. As did my mother. I knew it. I felt it. They didn't have to come to my games.

Levels of the Game

*O*ne evening in early February the phone rang in my parents' apartment. I was in town and answered the phone. It was Steve. I said hello—not curt, but not overly cordial, either.

"Just a minute," I said, "I'll get Mom or Dad."

"No," he said, "I want to talk to you."

"Me?"

"Yes." He paused. "Don't you think it's about time we stopped this nonsense?"

"I've tried," I said. "And then I stopped trying. I mean, you were the one who stopped talking to me."

"But you never asked me what was wrong," he said.

"I felt you were pouting, and you're a fifty-year-old man," I said. "If you have a problem with me, then I felt you should tell me what it is. I had no idea what it was. I still don't."

"Maybe I was wrong in not coming to you, then," he said, "but maybe you've been wrong, too."

"I accept that," I said.

I knew that I had injured his feelings in some way—my parents had passed on a vague complaint, and they were often after me to patch things up—but I thought that Steve was too quick to feel slighted, and there was no substance that I could make out that should hold me accountable. And I knew that I had not done anything of a major nature to hurt him, like stealing from his bank account or wheedling him out of something that was his or being a jerk to his wife or daughter, since they remained friendly with me. But Steve was clearly reaching out to me now, perhaps to take me up on the offer I had made a month earlier when I heard about his condition.

I asked how he was feeling.

He told me that it was a pain to get that chemotherapy and that it sapped him of energy. Sometimes he could hardly get out of bed. And it made him nauseated. "But if it's going to do good," he said, "then good."

"Are you scared?" I asked him.

"A little, yeah," he said.

"And Judy? How's she holding up?"

"It's kinda tough," he said.

"If there's ever anything—" I began.

"I know," he said. "I know that."

The ice broken, we started talking about day-to-day concerns. Steve taught eighth-grade classes at Yates Elementary School in the Humboldt Park section on the Northwest Side of Chicago. The school was located in a kind of no-man's land between the black gangs to the west and the Latino gangs to the east. A few years ago I had visited him there, and he had pointed out the bullet holes in the doors at the school entrance.

Steve cared about these kids. He visited their homes, talked with their parents, made sure they had had something to eat before the school day began, took them en masse to places he loved and that they otherwise might never visit, like the Botanic Gardens located in a north Chicago suburb, or the Planetarium, or a roller-skating rink (he had to justify this with the Board of Education and submitted a request for a science project on time-motion study). He told me of times he was shocked to learn of the abuse and neglect and fears that these kids suffered at home or in their neighborhoods, and it pained him. But despite the conditions, he had an impact. Kids would often come back to the school after graduating and tell him how much he had meant in their lives, how he had urged them to go on with their education, how to deal with problems in the streets, and with their families. I was proud of my brother. And I told him so, though sometimes I'm not sure I convinced him.

I assumed, too, that for Steve there were difficulties in being the less visible brother, because of my name in the newspaper. My father and mother told me of times when stupid people would ask them, "How's your son?" And my parents would invariably ask, "Which one, Steve or Ira?" And Steve might be standing right there.

In fact, while growing up Steve had had to live in my narrow shadow, the way younger brothers often must. Not only was he five years younger and short, but he was very shy and a childhood case of measles had left him nearly blind in one eye. I know the problems with his eyes made playing sports harder. His glasses were often falling off, getting fogged up, breaking.

He was, though, strongly independent, and his response when I asked him to help me with something was invariably "Get lost." Despite that, he did sometimes help.

His attitude may have derived from my teasing him at home, which, I had intuited, was the divine right of older brothers. I would do things that I knew would annoy him, and which amused me. When we lived on the West Side we shared a bed, and I used to tease him at night by throwing my leg over his and past the imaginary line down the middle that he had drawn. When we moved to the North Side, we still shared a bedroom, but my parents bought us twin beds, which made both of us happier.

When my parents insisted that I take Steve with me and my friends when we went to watch the Cubs at Wrigley Field, I was dragging him, I admit. My friends and I would sneak into the park, sneak down to the box seats, chase balls hit in the stands, and run after the players for autographs after the game. But take my brother I did, generally pulling him by the hand as we rushed around. I showed him how to throw a baseball, how to wind up and pitch, how to hit with the bat not on his shoulder. Sometimes he'd listen, sometimes he'd throw the bat down in frustration. "Get lost," he'd say as he disappeared.

Through the growing-up years, I took on what I considered the obligation of advising him. Often, I'm sure, in a heavy-handed manner. Television was the big thing. He watched it endlessly. I'd holler at him about that, to little avail.

As we got a little older, the five years that separated us in age seemed to widen, especially when I entered high school, and was not about to lug him around on a date. But he was a funny kid with an oddball sense of humor. In later years I'd catch him wearing my army poncho and boots that were much too big for him. Or he'd spread on my shaving cream to look like a handlebar mustache, and shave it with a bladeless razor. On the wall above his bed, he had taped a photograph he had cut out from a sports magazine of Paavo Nurmi—"the Flying Finn," as he was known. No pictures of baseball or football players, but a Finnish track star of the 1920s and 30s. He admired Nurmi, he once told me, because "he tried real, real hard."

Nurmi was a kind of loner, or didn't seem to mind being by himself. My brother admired that, too, and sometimes the fewer people in his life, the happier he was. He also liked Nurmi's professionalism, how he'd carry a stopwatch with him when running to mark his time, and then, as he turned into the last lap, he'd throw the stopwatch away and run like hell to the finish line. I'm sure I kidded him about the old track star, but don't remember quite how. I'm sure it didn't thrill him.

Then came a Saturday afternoon during my senior year in high school when I was home on crutches, after tearing up my ankle in a basketball game. I asked him to go over to Little Louie's red-hot emporium two blocks away, to get me a hot dog for lunch. He refused. He sat there while I lay immobilized, and he wouldn't budge. His friend Barry Ansell was visiting, and I had to pay the kid a quarter to get me the hot dog.

About seven years later, when Steve was a freshman at Southern Illinois University, he called my parents to tell them he was homesick, hated school, and wanted to leave. My parents were worried and asked me to call him. I talked with Steve on the phone for quite a while. He told me that he would sometimes go to the train station in Carbondale and stand in the middle of the tracks, watching a train heading north for Chicago and wishing he was on it. I thought it was best for him to stay in school and told him why. At the end of the conversation, he said he'd think about what I had said. I followed it up with a letter.

A few days later, I received a typed letter from him, which I have kept. He wrote,

Dear Ira,

Thank you very much for writing me that letter.
Everything you said was absolutely true (I'll put it next
to my picture of Paavo Nurmi). I really appreciate your
advice because the more I realize quitting school this
one semester could have started a whole chain of quitting in what ever I do.

Again, you were right when you said we have con-
flicting personalities. I know you like me and I like you
and respect you but I can't act friendly to someone who
jumps me every time I do something. It is equally my
fault for the way I treat you; I hope this will change.

It is the most wonderful feeling in the world when
you have someone to turn to when you need help and I
thank God that Dad, Mom and you were there to help
me this time. Thank you. Any time you want a hot dog
I'll run out to get it.

Love,
Steve

Over the years I came to appreciate and seek out Steve's opinions. His views were candid and insightful, especially regard-
ing my writing. He had been an English major in college, as I
had been, and his strong suit in academics remained literature. Steve could be critical of me, even when we were on
good terms, but he was usually gentle in his criticism, and he
was always supportive. I never remember coming away from a
conversation with him about my work and not feeling better
about it.

On occasion, I would remind him how he began his interest in literature. He was fifteen, and he and my parents had
visited me at Miami University in Oxford, Ohio. I still knew
he was a television addict, and gave him a book that I thought

a nonconformist like him would enjoy: J. D. Salinger's *The Catcher in the Rye*. If there was one fictional character with whom I would associate my brother, it is Holden Caulfield, with his sensitivity, his introspection, his quirkiness, his low-keyed rebelliousness.

And of course if there was one nonfiction character I would associate with my brother, it was his old hero, Paavo Nurmi. "He was seventy-five or eighty years old," Steve once told me, "and he was still running. Still trying. Still determined."

And now, talking to Steve on that February night, I realized that there was in his voice a determination to patch things up between us.

What had he been upset about? He told me that at a sports affair in Chicago about two years earlier that we had all attended, I had neglected to introduce him to an old White Sox pitcher, Saul Rogovin. I didn't remember the incident at all, but he said our father was standing there, and I had introduced him to Rogovin while ignoring Steve. I told him that I remembered introducing him to others there, and if I hadn't done so with Rogovin, it was merely an oversight. He hadn't mentioned anything to me at the time, and I now apologized.

We discussed other matters of our long relationship—and the fact that that incident with Rogovin might have been simply a culmination of slights he had perceived, slights I did not realize I was making, because none were intentional. I believe that Steve understood that, though he still didn't like it. "I don't think you gave as much of yourself to me as I was prepared to give to you," he said. "I felt you didn't give a lot of yourself."

He analyzed our personalities. "You're a lot more aggressive than I am," he said. "But I never envied and was never jealous about any of that in you, or anything else you had or did. I never felt I was competitive with you. I guess that's because I've always liked myself."

It was a sad conversation for me, because he may have been right about my failure to get closer to him, and what I had missed—what we had both missed. I thought I discerned a certain Holden Caulfield quality, too, of seeing things as clearly as you wish to see them.

We talked about sports, and he said that he had once considered going out for the baseball team when he was at Mather High School, but decided not to. "I believe I could've made the team, even if I couldn't see too good," he said. "There was room on the team. But I wanted to live with the idea that I *could've* made it. Maybe it was a way to save face for myself if I hadn't made the team."

Just the day before, curiously enough, I'd had a conversation with Michael Jordan about getting older. He said something similar to what my brother told me. I asked Jordan if he could still take off from the free-throw line and dunk the ball, once a signature move of his. "I don't know if I can anymore," he said, "but I'm not going to try. I'd rather believe I can do something and not prove I can't." Even for the very best, it is better in some cases to live with a maybe than to risk a flop.

But both accepted challenges in other areas. Jordan in baseball and then a return to basketball, my brother every day trying to open up the possibilities for a better life for his kids at Yates.

As I was hanging up the phone my mother came into the kitchen.

"Was that Steve?" she asked.

"Yeah," I said.

"Did he want to talk to us?"

"No, just to me, ma," I said.

"Oh," she said, her face brightening. "That's good." I thought I heard her voice crack just a bit. "That's nice."

The next night, I met an old friend for dinner.

I have known Hershey Carl for close to forty years, and we have been friends for much of that time. We met playing basketball on the North Side, in the parks and school yards, and we played against each other in high school. Of all the players I played with and against in the extended neighborhood Hershey Carl was the most gifted in basketball and went the furthest in the sport.

He rose from a two-time all-city player at Von Steuben High School and the leading scorer in the Public League to an all-American at DePaul University—he broke George Mikan's single-season sophomore scoring record—all the way to playing guard in the NBA, for one bumpy season. In *Playing Tall: The 10 Shortest Players in N.B.A. History* by Bill Heller, the 5-foot-9½ Hershey Carl is profiled along with Calvin Murphy, Spud Webb, and Muggsy Bogues. Murphy, Webb, and Bogues dunked a basketball with ease. Carl's spring barely allowed him to touch bottom of the net. Nor was he fast. But he was quick with the ball, had exceptional reflexes, an uncanny shot, an outstanding basketball mind, and great will.

The first time I played against Hershey Carl, in the outdoor concrete court at Eugene Field Park, was in a half-court pickup game one summer evening, and I was impressed by a pass he threw me as I cut for the basket. I was fifteen years old, he was sixteen, and the pass, which he threaded sweetly past the ears and through the outstretched hands of the opponents, led me perfectly. It was high enough and sharp enough and soft enough that all I had to do was give the ball a little push and it banked off the backboard and dropped through the hoop. It was a casual pass but artistic, a pro's pass, and one I had never experienced before. It was an awakening, and while I maintained my outward cool-cat manner, I remember feeling a tingle of excitement.

When the teams switched and I guarded Hershey, I found his moves so slick, his fakes so clever, that he had me first back on my heels and then turned me into the Road Runner trying to catch up. He either drove around me or faded back for his jump shot, a shot released from the hip, but as quickly as a gifted gunslinger draws. I felt as if I were playing in stockinged feet on a varnished wooden floor while he had total traction. This became a familiar feeling. That winter, in a public-league game between our schools, I tried to guard him again, and I still felt as if I were playing in stockinged feet. I held him, as it were, along with two or three of my teammates, to 33 points, including a bunch of free throws, in his team's 72–62 victory.

Carl had a knack of drawing fouls because he was so shifty with the ball. When he was at DePaul and broke the Alumni Hall scoring record of 43 points—second best later belonged to Mark Aguirre, with 41 points—Carl had 26 free throws, of which he made 23. In fact, in 1961, his senior year, he finished second in the nation in free-throw percentage, at .875.

But perhaps the most stunning move I saw Carl make was in the NBA. It was November 1961. I was seated in the stands at the Philadelphia Convention Arena watching the Chicago Packers, a first-year expansion team, play the Philadelphia Warriors. Carl, in the game as a substitute guard, drove to the hoop on a fast break. Hurrying back to defend the goal for the Warriors was Wilt Chamberlain, the Big Dipper himself. Chamberlain stood about 7-foot-1, and his long, bony strides covered the court in a seeming instant. It appeared inevitable that Chamberlain would swat Carl's shot into the mezzanine.

As Carl went up and began to float toward the basket, Chamberlain crouched to time his jump and block. Carl suddenly twisted his body in midair to pass the ball to a teammate at the free-throw line, which seemed the wise choice. Chamberlain immediately shifted his body in that direction, in order to stop that other shot. Except there was no Packer at the free-throw line. And Carl turned back—in midair!—and laid the ball cleanly off the backboard and into the basket, as Chamberlain stood several feet away, rendered flat-footed by the fake.

I've never forgotten that shot and other startling moves, and I've thought, ah yes, there but for the grace of God—and substantially more talent—go I. For those of us in our neighborhood in our teens and young manhood who loved basketball, Hershey Carl was who we would have been if we didn't happen to be us.

His moves were the moves we, too, would have made if we could have. Though, to be sure, some of us tried. After all, what's a standard for if not to be emulated? Beethoven imitated some of Mozart's techniques, Picasso was influenced by Toulouse-Lautrec, and Babe Ruth patterned his swing after that of Shoeless Joe Jackson. Models are there for the whole range of us, from the best to the would-bes. In basketball we often think of the biggest name players, those with neon credentials, as the ones with whom we try to identify. And sure, as a kid I tried to throw a behind-the-back pass like Bob Cousy, or, if not to hang in the air like Elgin Baylor, at least to be able to copy that nervous neck twitch he had. But the most significant models are generally those closest to home, those with whom we have the most immediate contact. For me, and some of my friends, that model was Hershey Carl.

When DePaul played the University of Cincinnati with its great star Oscar Robertson in the Midwest regional semifinals of the NCAA tournament in March of 1960, I talked up the game with a close friend at Miami named Jim Schwartz. I told him about Hershey and said that this was a game he must see. And so we found a television set in the dormitory recreation room and sat down to watch.

It was not a wonderful experience. Not for Jim, not for me, not for Hershey Carl.

DePaul fell behind 53–23 at the half and lost 99–59. Carl took 16 shots from the field and made only 5. He even, shockingly, missed 53 of 5 free-throw attempts. He wound up with 12 points, perhaps the worst game of his college career. As the game progressed and DePaul became more and more frustrated at being so outclassed, Carl began to force shots that he normally wouldn't take. And he missed, and missed again. I wanted to cover my eyes. And I felt sorry for Hershey. Robertson, meanwhile, scored 29 points on 12 of 25 from the field and 5 of 7 from the free-throw line. He also had 9 rebounds, and a bunch of assists.

Well before the game was over, Jim Schwartz had formed an opinion. He thought I should have my head examined.

Now, sitting in Hershey's suburban living room, I asked him about that game. From a distance of thirty-five years, Hershey seemed more in admiration of Robertson than chagrined by his and his team's performance. "It just seemed like Oscar wasn't even trying, that he wasn't even running fast or making quick moves, and we had our best defensive player on him," said Carl. "You just couldn't do anything with him. He was just so far superior it was like a man playing against boys, and he proved it. He averaged more than 30 points a game in his sophomore, junior, and senior years, and he never took a bad shot. He never took shots that were far. The farthest I could recall him shooting was maybe a step inside the top of the key. I never thought he was a great shooter, but he was excellent at everything—handling the ball, passing, defense, rebounding. He was just wonderful."

The levels of the game: Hershey was so much better than I. Oscar was substantially better than he was.

Even so, Hershey still got to play in the NBA! He was still suiting up against such stars as Oscar Robertson and Jerry West and Cousy and Baylor and Wilt! He was playing on the same team with Walt Bellamy and Bob Leonard. What an experience, what a tribute!

"It was horrible," he told me. "It was the worst year of my basketball life. I had never sat on the bench like that before."

At home games in Chicago's International Amphitheater, he heard chants from the stands: "Put in Hershey! Put in Hershey!" It embarrassed him. "If I could have crawled under the bench without anyone noticing me, I would have," he said. "I wouldn't play much or wouldn't play at all and it was tough. Here I was on a team in my hometown, where I had always been noticed, and people in the stands were yelling for me to get in the game. And here we were an expansion team, and a last place team, too."

In the previous three years, however, attending one of his DePaul games at Alumni Hall in Chicago had been a ritual for many of us who had played with him. It was not simply a delight to share, however peripherally, in his success, but he was such an entertaining player to watch as well.

While Hershey's deft, no-look passes were always exciting, he would do other things on the court that I had never seen before—or since. I remember the time Carl and a much taller player engaged in a jump ball. As the referee tossed the ball in the air, Carl head-faked as though going to jump. The other player reacted and did jump, as the ball was rising. When the ball reached its peak, the other player was coming down, but Carl was at the height of his modest jump and won the tap.

I loved those moments like the fake on Chamberlain and that jump-ball move. They were spontaneous and creative, the ultimate in urban survival tactics. Some thirty-five years later, Hershey Carl said he remembers neither.

"Well, the high point of my pro career—I guess I could say there was only one high point—was when we played an exhibition game against the Syracuse Nationals at DePaul," he said. "The NBA would try to get at least one game at the college that one of the rookies played at. They figured they would draw. This was about our fifth exhibition game, and I hadn't played much. But in the locker room about ten minutes before we were going on the floor in Alumni Hall, the coach, Jim Pollard, said to me, 'Carl, you're starting.'

"I was kind of shocked. And we went out and beat them— they had Johnny Kerr and Dolph Schayes and Hal Greer— and I had a terrific game. I ended up scoring twenty-two points and looked real good. And then I started the next game. Pollard had to do something because I had played so well against Syracuse. This was I think against Philadelphia. But I played only fair. And didn't play that long, either. And I never played very much after that."

After Hershey left the NBA (he was cut by the Packers before the 1962–63 season), he played a few years in local tournaments and park league games with former high school and college players, but continual leg cramps forced him to give that up. He took up golf, but health problems forced him to quit that, too. In the past several years he has experienced heart problems and wears a defibrilator and a pacemaker, and he also underwent a successful operation for prostate cancer. He has gone through a roller coaster of business ventures, including a long stint as a trader in the Mercantile Exchange, and most recently he was employed by Cook County as a counselor in its criminals program. Hershey has also seen his three children go to college, and his sons, Adam at Bradley and Wisconsin, and Josh at Lake Forest, make the varsity basketball teams.

"I know a lot of guys still are playing basketball—a lot of college and pro guys who are fifty and over," he said. "In my case, I got my enjoyment afterwards, in the last ten years, watching my two sons play.

"You hear, and I guess it's true, that maybe you relive some of your life through them. It was tough to watch, though. You get aggravated: why didn't they do this or why didn't they do that. Like they should have shot, or they didn't run to the right spot. And I'd be sitting in the stands fidgeting, and the other parents are around, and you have to be careful what you say. I think I was a little more intense—a little tougher—on my older son, Adam, than I was a few years later with Josh. I think I learned a little bit through my older son that relaxed me a little more. And when I tried to give advice, I tried to do it in a light vein. Like Josh doing a lot of weight lifting when I thought he needed more work on his outside shot. 'Josh,' I said, 'muscles don't make baskets.'

"Now, instead of being a player, I enjoy watching basketball. Sometimes I'm watching and I can see what the players are going to do before they do it. The good players. I don't ever remember giving the ball up on a fast break to the wrong guy, which I see a lot, and it aggravates me. They will have a three-on-two, and the guy in the middle will throw it to the wrong guy, give it to him a step or a couple of steps too soon, or too late. And the other thing I don't like now is when they have a two-on-one, they won't give the ball up. They want to make the dunk. Or they want to make the layup and get fouled. And you'll see them miss it or get fouled and only make one of the free throws. And this costs their team.

"But the other night the Bulls broke out on a fast break

with Jordan in the middle and Scottie Pippen on his left. I
don't remember who was on the right, but Pippen was behind
Jordan by a little bit. It didn't look like Jordan could see him,
and about in between the top of the key and the free-throw
line, I knew he was going to throw it behind his back to Pippen to dunk it. He was looking the other way the whole time
like he was going to throw it the other way, and sure enough
he fed Pippen for the dunk."

I asked Hershey how he knew Jordan was going to do it.

He smiled almost shyly. "Because that's what I would have
done," he said.

The following day I was back in New York, in my office in at
The New York Times, when my colleague Richard Sandomir
came by my desk.

"I just had this unusual conversation with Governor
Cuomo," Sandomir said.

"Oh," I said. It had been about a month or two since I had
talked with Cuomo in his law office.

"I was asking him about his views on the idea to move Yankee
Stadium to the West Side of Manhattan and what he had
done about it as Governor," said Sandomir, "and then he said
to me, 'Richard, are you through with your questions?' I said
'Yes.' He said, 'Then I have a question for you—How good a
basketball player is Ira Berkow?'

"I said, 'I don't know, Mario, he tells me he plays every
weekend or so. He looks not to be in bad shape, and he
doesn't look his age.'

"And then he said to me, 'Well, how does he take a
punch?'

"I said, 'Governor! I thought you were all elbows!'

"He said, 'Oh no, no elbows!'

"And we laughed."

"That was it?" I asked.

"That was it," said Sandomir.

I thought, well, the Governor is concerned. And then it hit me: this could just be some kind of setup. The governor is very canny.

Or maybe he couldn't get up the inspiration to play a game with me. Couldn't blame him. Out of friendship, though, I decided to send him a note and the *Esquire* magazine story I had written on Magic Johnson, which included a sidebar on that shot I had made in Paris. Of course, that shot in front of Magic hardly qualifies me as a real player. But I thought I'd drop it in the mail to Cuomo, just to stoke his competitive embers even further. I didn't mention his conversation with Sandomir.

I mulled over Cuomo's odd remark about whether I can take a punch, and the notion of weights again began to roll around in my head. I saw Walt Frazier at a Knicks game and asked him about whether he thought it would be helpful for me to start lifting weights. Frazier is now one of the Knicks' radio announcers. "When I was playing, I didn't have the energy to lift weights during the season," Clyde said, looking routinely dapper in a wide-collared, black pin-striped suit. "In summer, I do weights for stretching, but not to bulk up."

The concept of lifting weights continued to remind me of hard work, like laboring in a coal mine.

"I don't have the energy, either," I replied. "And besides, my season is year-round."

So I put weight lifting out of my mind. After all, Governor Cuomo had already observed that I looked like I might be hard to push around.

Like many New Yorkers, Governor Cuomo was a fan of Walt Frazier's, as well as of the great Knick teams of the late 1960s and early 1970s coached by Red Holzman. But another of the Governor's favorite players on that team was the starting small forward, the future U.S. senator, Bill Bradley. I, too, had gotten to know Bradley, and liked him a great deal. We first met in 1968, a few months after we had each come to work in New York City. I had arrived from a job as a sportswriter for the *Minneapolis Tribune;* Bradley, a Princeton graduate, had come from a Rhodes Scholarship at Oxford University.

With the Knicks Bradley had a tough time fitting in at first, particularly because he had been away from basketball for two years while studying in England. Other pro players resented the huge amount of money he had signed for, $500,000 for four years, at the time a record for a rookie. After one of his early games against the Cincinnati Royals, I asked Happy Hairston, who had played him effectively, what he thought of Bradley. "Half a million dollars my ass," he said.

But Bradley was persevering and wise and tough, and he soon became an integral part of those outstanding Knicks teams.

My conversations with Bradley were always enlightening, if not also sometimes strange. We once had a talk about playwriting. He told me his theory that playwrights were not really artists. "There's too much other input from actors and directors and producers for them to be artists," he said. I wasn't sure if he was kidding or not, which is the way it sometimes was with him. "Well," I said, "would you consider Shakespeare an artist?"

Bradley grinned broadly. I assume he did.

One time Bradley met me for a breakfast interview, and saw I had that morning's newspaper. He hadn't seen it. There was something about a prison reform bill that had been passed the day before that he wanted to read about. Had I seen the article? I confessed I hadn't. I had never had an athlete ask me such a question, and never had again.

His wide-ranging interests were matched by his intensity. Another time we had finished lunch and were waiting for the check. The waitress was everywhere but around our table. As the saying goes, even God couldn't catch her eye. Bradley grew more and more impatient. "I'm going to count to twenty," he said, "and if she doesn't show up, I'm leaving." Since I had insisted on paying, anyway, this hardly mattered. But he actually began counting! At about fifteen I said, "Just a minute." I got up and went over and tapped the waitress on the shoulder. And soon the coveted check was ours.

After retiring from basketball and entering politics, Bradley won praise for his hard work and popularity with the voters, but many commentators criticized his speaking style as flat and his sense of humor as wooden. That's not how his humor was remembered on the Knicks. "Bill's not a joke teller, some people just aren't," said Gerri DeBusschere, the wife of Bradley's former Knick teammate and roommate, Dave De-Busschere. "But Dave and I enjoyed his wacko sense of humor.

"I remember when a man began writing and calling Bill at hotels," said Gerri, "and Bill would whisper to the guy on the phone, and they'd have meetings in coffee shops. Dave finally asked Bill who the guy was. Bill said, 'He thinks I'm not Bill Bradley. He thinks I'm really an Albanian spy.' And Bill encouraged him."

Unlike most of the other players, who were dapper dressers, Bradley seemed to have little time for sartorial concerns and would sometimes forget to bring extra socks on the road. (He borrowed DeBusschere's.) When a button broke on his shirt he'd replace it with a paper clip. His raincoat was generally wrapped up in a ball and carried under his arm. On seeing it, Dick Barnett, a Knick guard, would make a sound like a foghorn, an esthetic appraisal of the garment.

After the 1974 playoffs, Bradley, his wife, Ernestine, and the DeBusscheres joined another couple on a vacation to Greece. Gerri DeBusschere recalls that everyone except Bill took at least one suitcase—the DeBusscheres had one suitcase just for their scuba-diving equipment. "Bill came with a little gym bag," she said. "He didn't even have a bathing suit. He swam in his Knick practice shorts."

The three couples rented a cabin cruiser and embarked from the port of Piraeus for a two-week trip around the Greek islands. They lay on deck and watched the islands go by, and from time to time Dave and Bill donned snorkeling masks and flippers, dropped down and explored the Aegean. One afternoon, they spied a church on a hill of a tiny island. The island looked fairly isolated, and the two men decided to get a closer look.

The island was so small that there was no place to dock the boat, so it remained about a quarter of a mile out to sea. Bradley and DeBusschere swam to shore. DeBusschere came up first, and saw a man sitting on a beach chair, reading a book.

DeBusschere removed his mask, and the man jumped up, his book dropping out of his hands. The man's mouth was agape, and he pointed frantically at DeBusschere.

DeBusschere thought that there might be something wrong with the man, or that he was frightened that a 6-foot-6-inch man had suddenly arisen from the sea.

Then, DeBusschere recalled, the man began to stammer: "You're, you're, you're Dave . . . Dave . . . Dave DeBusschere!"

DeBusschere was surprised that anyone on this little island could speak English, let alone recognize him.

"Then Bill came out of the water right behind me," DeBusschere recalled. "The guy says, 'Oh my God! Bill Bradley too! I can't believe this!'"

The man sputtered that he had season tickets under the basket at Madison Square Garden, that he had been postponing his vacation until after the playoffs, and that he was on this island because he had been so overworked that his wife insisted he go to this secluded island for a rest.

"And to see you guys here is—"

"Sure," Bradley said with understanding, "and Willis Reed will be here in a minute."

"The whole team is coming up," DeBusschere told him.

The man said, "Wait, wait right here. I've got to get my wife. She'll never believe this. Oh my God!"

The man flew down the beach, screaming his wife's name.

Bradley turned to DeBusschere. "Let's leave," he said with a grin.

DeBusschere nodded. The pair clamped on their masks and disappeared back into the water.

Gerri DeBusschere happened to be watching this from the deck of their boat. She saw the man now racing back along the beach, dragging his wife by the hand.

He went to the water's edge, looking around and pointing. Meanwhile, Bradley and DeBusschere had returned to the boat and were hiding in a cabin below deck as the boat headed farther out to sea.

On the beach, the man was waving wildly, while his wife was looking at him and then looking at the receding boat.

Bradley and DeBusschere never saw the man again. The next season they searched for him under the baskets at the Garden, but he wasn't there.

"The guy's wife probably thought he had flipped," said Gerri DeBusschere, "and he never came up to Bill or Dave and said, 'I saw you in Greece.' He was probably too embarrassed. He probably thought he hadn't really seen them and that he was just suffering from being overworked."

If Bill Bradley ever runs for president, maybe he'll make it an all-hoops ticket by naming that sixty-three-year-old pickup basketball player from Queens, Mario Cuomo, as his running mate. Now *that* would be intriguing.

My endorsement of Governor Cuomo was put on hold, however, when the mail brought this letter:

Ira,
     Thanks for the note, the magazine and the sidebar. Forget about the one-on-one I offered you!
                              Best,
                              Mario

Of course, I still had to be prepared for the possibility of playing the governor—after all, he might change his mind again. I was also possessed by the nagging idea of returning to Laguna to redeem myself, as well as my general wish to expand my game by driving more and better. To reach these levels, I supposed, I'd have to hone my alleged skills as I may never have before, until my game glistened like a stiletto in a sharp light.

In the meantime, there was work to be done, stories and columns to be written. On one assignment, at Madison Square Garden, I happened to see Bill Walton, who is now a network and Los Angeles Clippers television analyst. Seven feet tall and topped with a head of red hair, Walton is hard to miss. I've known Walton for a number of years and have enjoyed him both as a player—he's in the Basketball Hall of Fame—and as a forthright, knowledgeable man.

I ran into him near the Clippers' locker room and asked him whether he had ever played at Laguna Beach, since I knew that he had grown up in nearby San Diego. I could picture Walton playing on that court, this huge guy with extraordinary turnaround jumpers and just about the best passing skills of any big man who ever played the game.

"We used to play there a lot," he said. "They used to have three-on-three tournaments, and a couple of my friends and I would go down there, as well as up and down the west coast of California, playing pickup games."

I mentioned that there were some very good players there.

"I know," he said, "but I had a winning streak there for years."

"How long was your winning streak?" I asked.

"Years," he replied.

"*Years?*"

He gave me a little smile. "I was once a pretty good player," he said.

If you look it up, you'll find that Walton went undefeated from his senior year at Helix High School in La Mesa, California, through his freshman, sophomore, and junior years at UCLA. I guess you'd have to add the Laguna Beach games to that streak as well. It was only in the latter part of his senior year in college that he finally did lose a game. The UCLA team's record of 88 straight victories, with Walton at center, is far and away the most of any major college team in history. He was also a dominating center in the pros for the brief time that he wasn't injured, and led the Portland Trail Blazers to the NBA championship in 1978.

I told him I had played at Laguna Beach, too.

"Oh," he said, smiling politely.

"Yeah," I said. "Beautiful court."

I decided not to mention my painful experience there. I mean, standing with Walton, who is a foot taller than I am, I thought if I relived that Sunday afternoon right there in the hallway I know I'd just feel myself shrinking. Let sleeping dogs lie.

But I couldn't get Laguna Beach, and some kind of manic retribution, out of my head.

At the game I ran into Walt Frazier again. "I met a guy who wanted to know what kind of basketball player you were," said Frazier.

"And?" I said.

"I told him you were tenacious."

"Me? Tenacious?" I laughed.

"You almost killed me in those one-on-one games," he said.

"C'mon, Clyde, I took it easy on you."

"Yeah," he said, a smile curling at the side of his mouth.

Frazier and I have known each other for about twenty-five years, ever since we collaborated on *Rockin' Steady*. We worked on the book in the summer of 1972, at Kutsher's Resort in the Catskill Mountains. And we played one-on-one games. I was thirty-two and he was twenty-seven, at the height of his career, and in between the Knicks' two championship seasons, 1970 and 1973. Even all these years later I can still take some satisfaction in being somewhat competitive with the all-pro Frazier. The first time we played, the scores were 11–7, 11–0, and 11–6, and the other games pretty much followed suit. He won.

Frazier's agent, Irwin Weiner, told me that he had asked Clyde how I had played. Frazier told him, "Ira made me hustle." While we were working on the book, Clyde even complimented me—on tape!—for "hittin' too good goin' right, so I forced you left." And then, because Frazier's vaunted defense seemed to curtail my jump shot, and every other shot—I thought at one point I was playing against six of him at once—I wound up driving left and throwing up a left-handed double-pump hook shot. And it went in! It may have been the only shot like that I had ever made.

I later told a friend, Ted Margolis, about that shot, and Ted one day asked Frazier about it.

"It was a lucky shot," Frazier said. In that brief sentence Clyde (a) retained his pride of professionalism and (b) told the naked truth. The 11–0 score was also indicative of something: When Clyde wanted to turn it on, it was with all faucets.

Several years later, after Clyde had retired, he told me that Lenny Wilkens had always been difficult for him to defense. "I always knew he was going left, but I could never stop him," said Frazier. I later asked Wilkens about it. "He always knew I was going left," he said, "but he never knew when." In fact, I was a poor mirror image of Wilkens. Frazier knew I was probably going right, and he knew when, too.

But I think Clyde was surprised that I could do anything at all. Big-time athletes are always surprised when a writer shows any signs of physical coordination. I once got a hit off Denny McLain in a pickup baseball game. It was only a little dribbler, but it shocked and infuriated him.

This happened when McLain had been suspended from baseball for gambling, in 1970. And while getting back in shape to return to the Tigers in midsummer, he pitched against college and high school players. I joined in. In between striking out, I hit a ball up the middle that took about twenty bounces and went through for a single. Years later I recalled this glowing moment to McLain, who said he remembered me playing but didn't remember the hit. When I told him about the twenty bounces, he shook his head. "Who was playing shortstop," he asked, "Stevie Wonder?"

As I took my press seat at the Garden, I pondered Clyde's

remark that I had almost killed him in those long-ago games. Did I whack Clyde? If so, I comforted myself, he's probably experienced worse—like going head-to-head with Mad Dog Carter of the Bullets. I thought I was playing tough defense against Frazier. But one man's tough defense is another man's foul. I'm sure he was joking, but the fact is I did try to play him hard. How could I not?

It reminded me of a time when I played Rod Carew in tennis. Carew is a gifted athlete, to be sure, and a decent tennis player, though he played infrequently. I play tennis even less than that, but I can chase down balls and give most hack players a run for their money. Carew won the first set, and as he got ready to serve this one time, I crouched low, ready to pounce on his ball. Suddenly he dropped his racket, bent over and put his hands on his knees. I thought he was sick. "Rod," I hollered, "you OK?"

He looked up. He was laughing. "Yeah," he said.

"What's so funny?" I asked.

"I just looked over at you and you were so *intense*."

"Very fucking funny," I replied.

But I do bring that same competitiveness to the pickup games I play. I try to prove I belong—a common trait among all competitors, anywhere. I play as hard as I can. And if I get fouled in a close game and don't call it, my teammates will invariably want to know why. "If they bustin' yo' ass," a teammate once said to me, "open yo' mouth."

But I have to be judicious all the same. If I were to make a questionable call down the stretch, another guy will say, "Game too close for that, man."

And guys may ride other guys. "A brick," calls one defensive player after his man missed a shot. "Another brick and pretty soon we'll have a project out here."

I try to stay reasonably quiet. But sometimes a remark or a

play can fan the inner flames. One time I slapped the ball out of a young guy's hands—he was about eighteen or nineteen—and he called foul. It was an embarrassment call, I felt, one that is called when you're embarrassed about a good play having been made against you.

"I had all ball," I said.

"Maybe your eyes are getting too old to see it," the guy retorted.

"You wanna get personal?" I said.

He said nothing.

When we had the ball, he was guarding me. I took him low and pump-faked; he went for it, and I made contact but slid in and banked the ball off the boards for a basket.

He didn't say anything. And I didn't say anything. I didn't have to. Not all such encounters have turned out so cheerfully for me, but how sweet when they do.

By long-distance telephone, Steve and I talked often over the next few weeks, as we began to patch up our relationship. I also saw him a couple of times when I was in Chicago covering one story or another for the paper. He told me that the chemotherapy was taking a toll on him. The chemotherapy was designed to kill the bad white cells, but in the meantime it was killing all the cells, and destroying his immune system. His blood was losing the capacity to clot. Without any advance warning, he would suddenly start to bleed—he said he was "leaking." He'd get a nosebleed for no apparent reason, and the blood would drip into his soup. "It can make you crazy," he said.

He was just back from a three-day hospital stay for blood transfusions, to shore up his platelets and try to restore his blood's clotting ability. A normal platelet count is between 150,000 and 450,000. Steve was down to about 10,000. For three days he had been hooked up to the intravenous machine. "My arms are black and blue from all the needles," he told me.

It was hard for me to imagine all this. I asked him how I could help. He said there was nothing anybody could do, except the doctors, of course. And he hoped they knew what they were doing. Now, back at home, he was resting and preparing to return to work.

A few days later I talked with my parents on the phone, both picking up an extension. They had returned home from dinner with Steve and Judy.

"Stevie didn't look good," my mother said. "He's lost weight, and he's losing his hair."

"I didn't think he looked bad," said my father.

"You were sitting right next to him," said my mother. "I was sitting across from him. I could see him better."

"Didn't look bad to me," my father repeated. It sounded to me as if he was trying to convince himself of his opinion, or trying to put a spin on it so that it might relieve my mother somewhat.

When the conversation had moved to lighter topics, I mentioned to my parents that I was going to play basketball later that day in a nearby gym.

"Don't overdo," my mother said.

"You're not that young," said my father.

"Be careful, you can't be too careful," added my mother. "You don't go out when you're sweating."

My father, as if on cue, added, "You know, we have a history in our family."

"I'll be careful," I said.

I didn't need them to worry about me, too.

·   ·   ·

In deference to my parents, I thought I'd make an effort to play ball with someone my own age. There was a story I wanted to cover in Cincinnati, and so I decided to get in touch with someone I knew there who would be up for a pickup game while I was in town. I had met the fellow in the course of my work—he's fifty-seven, a year older than I am—and I learned a few years ago that he played recreational basketball at noontime at the YMCA in downtown Cincinnati. Well, I thought, I'll give it a shot.

"Hello, Oscar?" I said.

"Yes," came the long-distance reply.

Oscar Robertson owns three businesses in Cincinnati, and I had reached him the office of Orchem, the Oscar Robertson chemical-supply company. "The Big O," as Robertson was called, was once regarded as the greatest all-around basketball player in history—until Michael Jordan elevated his game into the stratosphere.

Oscar and I chatted some about the NBA today, and about the Bulls' run for their fourth title. I mentioned Dennis Rodman. "If you just look for rebounds, you can be successful at it," he said. "I tell people that Johnny Green and Jerry Lucas, just to name two in my day, could have done as well in rebounding as Dennis Rodman. But they don't believe me." And when he spoke about the players perhaps giving away too much to the owners in product licensing, I could hear once again the fiercely intelligent voice of the former head of the players' union.

"By the way, Oscar," I said, "are you still playing basketball?"

"Not to amount to much," he said.

"But you play?"

"Yeah. I play with guys of a certain age." He laughed softly. "Most of the guys are forty, forty-five, and over."

"Guys like you who still enjoy the game?"

"Right. There's one guy up there, his wife really hates for him to play. He blows out his knee every four years. But he says he can't stop."

"I blew out my knee, too," I said, "and I still play. But my wife doesn't try to stop me—I wonder what that means."

He laughed. "The way I play is, I always try to get a fast guard, a younger guy. And I fast-break guys to death. But I don't play as much as I used to. Some guys don't care to play with me."

"You mean, you're too good?"

"No, too rough."

"Too rough?"

"It's terrible. They're always calling all these fouls. I tell 'em, 'Whoever told you basketball was a noncontact sport? It isn't.' They accuse me of running into them. But you just have to play hard. They're not used to hard picks. But that's the game. They expect to push you but they don't expect you to push them back. They hit me and hack me. I foul 'em back. They think they know everything about the game. And they know nothing. I shake my head."

I laughed out loud. "Oscar, you sound just like someone in any of my games, complaining about the fouling. It's funny coming from one of the all-time greats."

There was a kind of silence at the other end. I think he was getting steamed just thinking about the hackers.

I remember watching Robertson in college and in the pros, and marveling. At 6-foot-5 and 220 pounds, playing both guard and forward, he was strong, he was confident, he was effortless, and he was competitive. The competitiveness was what I now heard in his voice. He always seemed to get the shot he wanted, even with a battalion of players storming him. He was never a flashy player and always fundamentally sound. He was a pleasure to watch.

Robertson had an effective spin move that first caught my attention in college and that I tried to imitate—still try, in fact. You're on the baseline dribbling the ball and your back is to your defender. And then you spin around him, hooking your hand on his hip. Oscar did it so quickly and smoothly that he was rarely called for it. When I do it, I usually end up with a foul called on me, or an argument. That is the difference between pluck and genius.

After having been a three-time all-American, college player of the year, and three-time major college scoring champion—with a 34-point average—at the University of Cincinnati, Robertson went on to play ten years for the Cincinnati Royals in the NBA. He averaged 30 points a game for the Royals, a scoring output second only to the titanic Wilt Chamberlain, and along with that he averaged about 10 rebounds and 11 assists a game. That is, he *averaged* a triple double for a decade—and about that for his entire fourteen-year pro career. Players often believe it a wondrous accomplishment if they can do that for just one game! Robertson broke Bob Cousy's record for most all-time assists, and he held the record until Magic Johnson topped it. Oscar was traded to Milwaukee in 1970 and, teaming with Kareem Abdul-Jabbar, helped the Bucks win the NBA championship.

Robertson retired from the NBA in 1974 but didn't give the game up, as so many star players do. Oscar just switched from arenas like Madison Square Garden and the Los Angeles Forum and Chicago Stadium to the Cincy Y, of all places.

"I have the greatest respect for Michael Jordan," said Wayne Embry, the general manager of the Cleveland Cavaliers and a former teammate of Robertson's with the Cincinnati Royals. "But I honestly don't know who would be better, Jordan or Oscar. It would be close."

I asked Oscar what his game is like today.

"I can still shoot," he said. "I hit the three-point shot right behind the circle. Most pickup players don't understand how to guard a guy, and they sag off you and I kill 'em with the outside shot."

Do you drive? I asked. I like to think that most older guys are like me and that driving is less an option, but that might be my own inadequacy cropping up. "I drive if I'm fifteen feet in or closer," he said. "But at the top of the key, it takes too long"—how true! I thought —"and guys hack you to death."

This time I didn't laugh but tried to commiserate. "I can imagine," I said.

I asked him if he'd take me up to play in his game at the Y when I came to town.

"Like I said, the games are kinda rough," he cautioned.

"I think I can manage," I replied, not knowing if in fact I could.

"OK, any time," Oscar said. "Just call ahead. I'll round up some guys to play with."

One afternoon in late March Steve was sitting at his desk at Yates School when he started bleeding profusely from his mouth. The doctors ordered him back to the hospital. This was on March 23, three days after his fifty-first birthday.

His blood platelets were very low, and he had also contracted a low-grade pneumonia. My parents called to inform me of all this. "Stevie is very sick," my mother said. "That's what the doctors told us. Dr. Levine said, 'You have a very sick son.' Stevie had a fever which was 103, but it's down to 101 now. And he's in a private room, and we had to wear a mask in there because he's susceptible to germs. And he has trouble walking because a blood clot formed in his left leg."

My father said, "It's a helluva thing, in and out of hospitals. Transfusions —"

"And his blood count is down again," my mother interjected.

"His blood count is down again," my father repeated. "The platelets are around seven thousand."

"Seven thousand!" I said. "That's practically nothing."

"Yeah," my father said. "And you know ma doesn't feel a hundred percent, with her leg." She was experiencing a painful ailment in her right thigh that the doctors were at a loss to treat. "Not good." Neither said anything for a moment.

"Ah, so what are you gonna do?" my father said, with an anguished sigh.

"Nothin' you can do," my mother said. "You just gotta pray."

At times like this, I shared the terrible frustration of not being able to help, not being able to immediately make things better.

I called Judy. "I'm overwhelmed," she said. "I was in the room, and I was looking at him, and he was tied to those intravenous tubes, and he had chills, and I just burst into tears and ran out. I'm so sorry I lost it. Sorry for Steven, to see me this way, to see me not strong. I hate being that way. I don't want to give him anything more to worry about, like me."

I tried to assure her that Steve understood, that he'd be all right with it.

I asked how Shayne—who was now seventeen—was handling the situation. "She's having stomach problems," said Judy. "And she's distracted at school. But she's got some good friends, and that's a comfort."

As for Steve's condition, she said, the doctor told her that the bone marrow should kick in any day. "When that happens," she said, "Steve will be a candidate for a transplant. Right now he's not. But we're hoping."

From then on, I was on the phone with my parents and

Steve every day. On March 27 I called Steve in the hospital. "They're giving me more IVs, more blood, more platelets, more antibiotics," he said. "They're just killin' me more. I still have a little pneumonia. My temperature goes from 103 to normal.

"Today I woke up with a bloody nose, and blood coming out of my mouth. There was so much blood coming out of my mouth I got it all over my hospital gown and the bed. And they're giving me so much medication, but my body is rejecting the platelets they're giving me, my body's eating them up. I'm nauseous. I'm worn out. I'm so weak it's incredible. I'm too tired to even raise up my bed."

What do the doctors say? I asked.

"They said things are supposed to be working," he said. "It's discouraging. And you get mad about it."

I suggested that he try to control his anger, that it's been said that inner turmoil can impede the healing process. He said he heard the same.

"But," he said, "a doctor comes in here and I know nothing has worked yet, and I said to him, 'Am I just lying here waiting to die?' And he said, 'I don't think so.' *Don't think so!*" I could imagine his face contorting in frustration and anger. "Now what kind of answer is that?"

Steve wanted to hear something positive, or more positive, and perhaps the doctor should have intuited this and given him a bit more optimism. It couldn't have hurt. I imagined the doctor being candid, since even medical experts cannot peer into the future. But I could also understand my brother's need for psychological fortification from the doctor in order to fight harder. This doctor had the personality of a undertaker, and an especially morose one at that. I had the impression that he was a very good scientist but that when he learned in medical school that he also had to deal with people, he must have been stunned and resentful, and perhaps never got over it.

But I knew that in the end it was his science and not his charm that could make the difference in my brother's life.

"I'm lying here and I'm going through a lot of stuff," Steve continued. "I did get angry at a lot of people. And sometimes it wasn't necessary."

"Does that include me?" I asked.

"Could be," he said, his tone sounding a little lighter. "But I'm trying to come to terms with that all that. I think I'm doing OK. I know that it might help my condition, too."

He told me that the latest transfusion had brought up his platelets a little.

"That's terrific," I said. "Congratulations."

"Now all I can do is wait," he said.

I had been speaking to Steve from Ike Herschkopf's house, where Dolly and I were having dinner. Ike is the psychiatrist whom I met playing basketball at the Vanderbilt Y and who had recently interpreted my rottweiler dream. He was sane enough to leave the Y when it really got crazy and fights were breaking out, though it took me a little while longer after his departure to leave, too. I'm not sure what that says about me.

Steve and I had been talking on and off about his taking time with a therapist for some psychological comfort. And so on this night I asked if he'd like to say hello to Ike. He said yes. I went in another room while Ike and Steve talked. Later Steve told me that essentially Ike said, "With your condition, Steve, you shouldn't expect a cure overnight. Some diseases are sprints. Yours is a marathon."

Crunch Time

*T*he next morning, Friday, March 28, with my brother still on my mind, I headed to LaGuardia Airport to fly to Charlotte, North Carolina, for the Women's NCAA Final Four basketball championships. But I looked forward to this assignment. I had been to the Women's Final Four in Minneapolis the previous year, and I could still picture with pleasure the little guard for the University of Connecticut, Jennifer Rizzoti. She was all pony tail and knee guards, and with about a minute to go in the game she dribbled the ball the length of the court and through the lunging University of Tennessee players, and finished with a behind-the-back dribble and a driving layup. It was sensational and helped UConn win the game and the national championship, capping an undefeated season.

Like many men of a certain generation, I had grown up with little knowledge or interest in women playing basketball—or any sports, for that matter. Women didn't commonly

participate in sports then, though as a boy in Chicago, I used
to watch televised games of a women's softball league that included The Bloomer Girls, and the stars, the sisters Freda
and Olympia Savona. But not until the 1980s did I feel there
was a true revolution in women in sports.

Back in 1972, I had heard about a whiz of a college player
at Queens College named Debbie Mason, who was called
The Pearl because, it was said, she had moves reminiscent of
Earl Monroe, the original Pearl. I thought I'd check her out.

We arranged to play one-on-one in the Queens gymnasium.
She was a slight black woman, a nineteen-year-old sophomore, who stood about 5-foot-5 and weighed 112 pounds.
She had the beginnings of an Afro and wore a knee brace on
her left knee and a T-shirt that read "Superstar," from the
rock opera *Jesus Christ, Superstar.*

We spoke briefly, and she said, "You ready?" She had already worked up a sweat playing another man on another basket, and I was getting the impression that I was about to get
my pocket picked. It turned out she had a lot of moves. She
dribbled between her legs and behind her back, she shot in
close with either hand. Her jump shot came quickly from behind her right ear after an effective stutter step. She was a
nimble defender and was said to be a hell of a passer.

In fact, we were competitive, and, because she was so
wispy, my greater strength made the difference in the games.

She told me she had learned basketball in the school yards.
She saw the boys at it and wanted to join in. She improved
rapidly. "The guys don't take me seriously at first," she said,
amiably. "But soon they say, 'I'd better start playin' some defense.' By then it's too late."

Men, though, had accepted her playing basketball easier
than women had. "They think I'm insane the way I practice
so hard," she said. "But I want to get ahead. I want to excel. I

find that too many women don't usually work hard at very many things. They don't understand what it takes. And they'll never know that great feeling of driving through a little, little space and then floating high up there in the air."

It was something I had never quite experienced myself, that "floating high up there in the air," but I understood what she was talking about.

After playing Debbie the Pearl, it struck me that this was the first time that I could remember being with a woman whom I regarded as just another human being, and not simply, or simplistically, a *woman*. After one particularly good shot by Debbie, I performed the sportingly chummy gesture of slapping her gently on the backside, as guys do with guys. Out of pure habit. I felt myself suddenly blush after I did it. But Debbie never seemed to give it a second thought. She was a player, and that's an act in the play.

Ten years later I found myself again on the court with women. I had gone down to Dallas to write a story on Martina Navratilova, the tennis champ. She had been living in her three-bedroom town house with Nancy Lieberman, the former all-American basketball player and star of a women's professional basketball league that had recently become defunct. Nancy, the redheaded, green-eyed, 5-foot-10-inch, nononsense operative, was teaching Martina how to play basketball in order to enhance her tennis moves, since there is a correspondence between the quickness and reflexes demanded in each sport. There was something else Nancy tried to teach. And that was "meanness." Nancy believed that Martina had become too passive in her tennis.

If anyone could drive Martina to become more aggressive, it was Nancy, known to some supporters and detractors as Agent Orange. Another nickname was Lady Magic.

They invited me to shoot some hoops at the nearby Southern Methodist University gym. Another girl they knew was shooting at one of the baskets, and Nancy asked her to join us in a two-on-two. The girl was an all-state high school guard in Texas, and she and I were paired as a team.

In the game Nancy was constantly on Martina, like a tough-love coach. When Martina guarded me, I saw that she had a good idea of the fundamentals. When she tried to block a shot, she went straight up so as not to foul, with hand and arm extended. She was also surprisingly strong, with remarkably well-developed thighs. And, like so many great athletes, much of her power came from a low center of gravity.

But Nancy was relentless in her prodding. "Slide, Tini!" "Cut, Tini!" "Don't let him go baseline, Tini!"

At one point tears welled in Martina's eyes, and she stopped presumably to adjust the red bandanna around her head, but I thought it was more to gather herself from Nancy's onslaught. I started feeling sorry for Martina.

"Are you OK?" I asked her.

"Yeah," she said, "I'm just an easy cry."

But Martina continued to battle, which, I imagine, was the point of it all. "It was exciting," Martina said later, which came as a surprise to me. "It adds a dimension."

Nancy had given no quarter to her opponents either, playing in a rough school-yard style. But I felt two could play that game.

In her autobiography Martina recalled the afternoon when we had played basketball together:

I knew very little about basketball, and Nancy couldn't wait to teach me the game so she could compete against me. As soon as I got a reasonable jump shot, I became a target for the full Lieberman arsenal: elbows and hips and knees and plenty of verbal aggression, too: "Come

on, Tini, get inside. Work harder. Get up there. Pass it.
Shoot."

I remember when Ira Berkow of *The New York Times*
came down to do a story on us right after I moved to
Dallas. Ira's a pretty good basketball player, and he
guarded Nancy and tried to stop her from backing in
toward the basket. She gave him a quick shot with her
butt, right where it hurt the most, then turned around
and sank an easy layup. Ira later said he'd never been
hit so hard in that area in his life. He gave her a little
more leeway after that—which was her goal in the first
place.

I had read this while eating alone in a Chinese restaurant
in Cleveland and almost jumped out of my seat. Wait a
minute! Something was missing from that account. I immediately went to a pay phone and called my *Times* colleague
George Vecsey, who had been Martina's coauthor on the
book. I told him I had been reading the Martina book and
came across the part where Nancy gave me this vicious ass to
the balls. "But George," I said, "didn't they mention the
wicked shot I gave her back?"

"Well, no," he said.

"Can't you put that in for the second printing?"

He laughed. "I don't think so," he said, "but I'll put it in
when I write your autobiography."

At LaGuardia, on my way to the tournament in Charlotte, I
called my office for phone messages. There was one from
Marlene Kaplan, a long-time family friend from Chicago. I
rarely hear from Marlene, and called her back immediately.
She told me that my brother was in the hospital.

"I know that," I said.

"He's not doing too well," she said.

"Is something new?" I asked. "I spoke to him yesterday."

"Well, I just thought if you have a chance, and you happen to be coming through Chicago, it might be a good thing if you could poke your head in."

I told her I was headed in the other direction, but gave her the phone number of my hotel in Charlotte.

"I'll be there in a couple of hours," I said. "If there is anything urgent, call and I'll fly up to Chicago immediately."

It was now 10:45 A.M., and I boarded the plane for the 11 o'clock flight. I took my seat, strapped myself in, took a newspaper from my book bag, and opened to the front page. I read something about Clinton or Congress or something else. I don't remember. I read it again, and a third time. No comprehension. My thoughts were on my brother. What was Marlene trying to tell me? Was I dense? Was he—was he dying? I felt my eyes get teary. I was choked up. What am I doing? I asked myself. I'm going to a basketball game and who the hell knows what's going on in Chicago. If he'd survive. If I'd ever see him again.

I grabbed my seat belt and unbuckled myself. I stuffed the newspaper back in my briefcase, gathered my laptop computer and jacket from the overhead bin, and started to make my way back down toward the front door. I was jostling into people who gave me impatient stares as I tried to navigate the opposite way in the narrow aisle.

The flight attendant at the door looked at me hurrying in her direction.

"What are you doing?" she said.

"I have to get off the plane," I said. "Family emergency. Can I make an arrangement to have my luggage sent from Charlotte to Chicago? I'm going to Chicago."

She eyed me as if I might be dangerous. It occurred to me

that the other passengers I had knocked against on the way out had also considered that I might be some kind of terrorist.

"It's an FAA rule that a baggage doesn't travel unless it's accompanied by its owner," she said. "We will have to hold up the plane and take off your luggage."

They held up the plane for about thirty minutes while my luggage was located. I learned that another airline had a plane leaving for Chicago that was about to depart. I raced from one end of the LaGuardia terminal to another—with bag, baggage, and laptop—and just caught the flight.

I had never before missed an assignment. The paper would have to understand.

I landed at O'Hare and jumped into a taxi. I knew Steve's room number from having called the hospital so many times—Room 338—and, dragging my stuff, hurried through the white corridors and took the elevator to the third floor. I had no idea what to expect.

A sign on the door read, A SANITARY MASK IS REQUIRED IN THIS ROOM, and a box of yellow masks hung on the wall. I slipped one on and entered the room. Steve was in the bed to the left and asleep. There were four chairs to the right, and they were empty. No one else was in the room. I assumed that my parents had been there earlier, had either gone home or gone to lunch, and might be back.

My brother had an IV attached to each arm. His arms were black and blue. He didn't look particularly thin, though he did look wan. There were some gift balloons and a novel he was reading beside his bed, E. Annie Proulx's *The Shipping News*, which had won a Pulitzer Prize. Steve had told me that he had read to near the end of it—"It was good, but not great," was his review—when this latest attack hit, and he had not been able to concentrate enough to finish it. His eyeglasses lay on top of the closed book. I dropped my bags and left the room, seeking someone on the floor who might inform me of my brother's condition.

At the nearby nurses' station, I met the nurse who had been attending him. She told me his platelets had dropped again, to around 5,000. His temperature was still around 100, but it was down.

"He's not terminal," the nurse said, "but he could be at any time."

I shook my head and held back tears. My parents had said that they tried not to cry in front of my brother because it might make him sad. I felt the same way. It wasn't easy. I felt that all this was so unfair. He was a good guy. He had a good family—I didn't mean me, but his wife and daughter and my parents. Why should he and they have to endure this kind of torture?

I went back into my brother's room. He was still asleep. I picked up *The Shipping News*, sat down in a chair facing his bed, and thumbed through the novel. The protagonist was a hack newspaper reporter. I wondered if my brother was reading this with any thoughts of connecting it to a particular relative. Proulx described the reporter as having a "head shaped like a Crenshaw, no neck, reddish hair" and "features as bunched as kissed fingertips." I decided that there was no resemblance.

"What are you doing here?" The voice startled me. It was Steve, awake. "I thought you were in North Carolina."

"Plane took a wrong turn," I told him.

Steve went over his condition with me and complained as much about his leg as anything else. "It hurts so bad I can't stand on it, I can't even lie in bed comfortably because of it. This is what I can't do, among other things: can't go to the bathroom, can't lie on my side, can't sit in a chair, can't walk, can't stand, and it's been eight days now. Ira, this is a long time."

I tried to distract him by talking about the Bulls in the playoffs, and "crazy Rodman." "I respect his game," my brother said. "He's an exhibitionist, and I wouldn't want any part of that sweaty jersey he throws to the fans after every game, but he really works hard, and he does get those rebounds."

The door opened, and my parents came through the door. "Oh, what are you doing here?" my mother said. She wobbled in on her recently acquired cane, because her arthritis had been troubling her so much.

"I'm not supposed to be here?" I said, kidding.

"How come you didn't tell us you were coming?" my father said. He looked like he had lost weight, and he had, about ten pounds.

They were happy to see me, I felt, and I explained generally what had happened about my plane connections. We sat around a talked a bit. Then there was a strange humming sound coming from somewhere, perhaps the floor above, perhaps outside. It was loud and it sounded either like men were drilling or that someone was passing gas.

"Is that you?" I asked my brother.

"How did you guess?" he replied.

I looked at my parents. Neither one seemed to be involved in this byplay. Their eyes above the yellow masks looked with concern at my brother. When a nurse came in to give my brother a shot of antibiotics, he glanced away, but my mother stared at it, as though she were suffering the pain of the shot herself. It was a look that disturbed my brother, he told me later, because he felt he was responsible for that anguish. But for now there was simply nothing any of us could do about it.

•   •   •

In the hospital room life went on. Shayne, who was seventeen years old, arrived in a white sweater and bib overalls that had a hip-hop flair to the pants. She wore a strikingly blue nail polish. "What's that?" my brother asked.

"It's moody blue," she said. "Just trying it out."

"Looks beautiful," my brother said, with a rueful smile. He wasn't being judgmental, just playful. She had proceeded through this bad time with a relatively stiff upper lip—at least in front of her father. But Judy worried about Shayne's health—her stomach problems, her distraction at school, where she was finishing her senior year. Yet she clearly brought joy to my brother. The love for her was evident in his eyes, in the way he spoke to her. He had told me that he and Judy shared almost everything with her. "We don't keep much from her," he told me. He had always been very solicitous of her, from as far back as when she was born and was found to have a small hole in her heart. Doctors said it would heal over. My brother was beside himself. But Shayne's heart did heal. And she grew into a tall, reserved, lovely young woman, when, that is, she wasn't being the typical teenager (when, for example, her parents shouted to her to lower the volume on her new Smashing Pumpkins tape while she showered). And now, when she drove the family's second car, Steve had outfitted her with a cellular telephone. When she was leaving work in the deli in Skokie, she had to call home to say she was leaving.

One afternoon in the hospital, I told my family that I hoped one day soon to appear on an amateur night, which takes place every Wednesday in the Apollo Theater on 125th Street in Harlem. I had always dreamed of doing the Hambone, something I learned as a boy from a black kid with thick glasses named Alexander. The Hambone is a kind of hand-jive and the performer flicks his hands with loose wrist on the thighs and chest as he sings, "Hambone, Hambone, have you heard, Daddy's gonna buy me a mockin' bird. And if that mockin' bird don't sing, Daddy's gonna buy me a diamond ring, Hambone. . . ." Few people I know can do it. And my parents had seen my act before, and so had my brother, but I often take any opportunity to perform it.

My father didn't seem impressed. "I can stand on my head," he said.

"But that's not an act," I said.

"*You* try to stand on your head!" he said.

I guess it is an act, then, at that.

I told them about the time, when interviewing Ed Sullivan years ago, I had considered doing the Hambone for him in some wild anticipation that he'd have me on his show. But when, on this winter's day, I was leaving his apartment in the Delmonico Hotel on Park Avenue and as I opened the door, I suddenly remembered something. "Mr. Sullivan," I said, "may I have my coat." He said, "No." He looked serious, or at least deadpan, which was his normal expression. I turned to his wife, Sylvia, for help. "That's just Mr. Sullivan's way of making a joke," she said. "He'll give you your coat." And he did. But I was so thrown off my game I forgot to do the Hambone. And then the show was off the air, and I never had another chance with Ed Sullivan. But I thought I did have a shot at the Apollo, though, having been to amateur night there once before I knew how tough the audience can be. I saw them boo a guy who was singing the Lord's Prayer, for heaven's sake. He moped off the stage without finishing the song.

I looked at my brother. "What did you think of my Hambone, Steve?" I asked.

"It was great," he said.

"Do you think they'd boo me off the stage at the Apollo?"

"Yes," he said.

I thought I perceived a little smile.

"Say," Steve said, "don't you ever work anymore?"

I had been to Chicago several times now during his illness but had been in frequent touch with the sports editor, Neil Amdur, and the deputy sports editor, Rich Rosenbush.

"The paper's been terrific," I said. "I told them I needed some time for personal matters. They were very understanding. I asked, 'Can you get along without me?' And they said, 'Yeah, don't worry about it.' Now I think I'm worrying."

Steve broke into a big grin. It was the best part of the day.

I shuttled between New York and Chicago for the next couple of weeks. One Saturday morning, after having spent several days with my family in the hospital, I went to play basketball with Barry Holt, my old Sullivan High School teammate.

He had called and suggested that I play ball with him at his gym. "C'mon," he said, "it'll relax you from what's going on with Steve." Barry had mentioned playing hoops several times before, as I had come in and out of Chicago during this period. But on this trip I brought my basketball shoes and my knee brace.

Barry took me to a nearby upscale health club and gym of which he is a member. He had told he played in full-court pickup games with "the kids." "Sometimes the games are good, sometimes not," he said. "Passing is not a part of some of their games." Turned out the kids were businessmen, primarily, in their late twenties and thirties. Of course, to Barry and me they were kids. But I had also been playing with teenagers in New York. I suppose the older one gets, the older kids get, too.

Just as I was trying to elevate my game by driving more, Barry had a quest of his own. It was *literally* to elevate his game. He wanted to dunk the ball in a game, and with authority. At 6-foot-3½, he had dunked a few times when he was in college, more than thirty-five years earlier. But that had been in practice, and it was unsatisfying, since at the time he considered a dunk just being able to get your wrist above the basket. "Not one of those great tomahawk jams," he said. "Like Jordan going baseline and slamming one down over Patrick Ewing's head. Now, that's a dunk!"

His blue eyes glowed with possibility. Even at age fifty-eight, and still playing in fifty-and-over leagues, he felt that with effort he might just finally dunk. It would be a personal triumph, a kind of crowning of his career. He believed that if he got stronger in the arms and legs and hands he could do it. I knew Barry was dogged.

"It's like you trying to drive better," he said to me. "We're both reaching for something we've never done to satisfaction before. At this age a lot of guys just fall back on what they could do best. But we're trying to go where we really have never been. It may never happen, and we may embarrass ourselves, and we may expose ourselves, but I mean, what's life about if it doesn't include risks?"

Barry, who has been lean much of his life except when he allowed himself the occasional middle-age paunch, had recently bought a NordicTrack and labored at it every morning when he woke up. He had been at it for several months and reported to me that he had developed a wide array of muscles. "You should see me," he told me on the phone. "I've become a gorilla."

"Can you dunk yet?" I asked.

"Not yet," he said. "But by the end of the season, I hope to be there."

In the locker room as we suited up I noticed that Barry had indeed gotten larger, though "gorilla" might have been overly generous.

He showed me a move that he had recently observed Charles Barkley make. "He starts from outside the end line and pushes his way onto the court and under the basket for position," Barry said, demonstrating for me in the narrow aisle between locker rows. Other guys were coming back from a shower or trying to lace on their sneakers—gym shoes, in Chicago language. It was funny, because Barry was typically intense in the move, as though he had been transported into an NBA playoff game. "Imagine," he said, "all these years playing and still learning something like that."

We went onto the court, which, like the rest of the club, was well appointed. With the three other guys who were on the "next" sign-up chart on the wall, we came together and decided who was going to guard whom. As we broke, Barry turned to one of our teammates, a dark-haired young man, and said, "Let's play smart." The guy looked at Barry as if he had just been addressed in a foreign tongue. "Uh, well, OK," he responded.

I was guarding a good player—clearly a better player than I—who looked to be in his twenties and was about 6-foot-5. He immediately took me into the low post, as he should have. I had no choice but to bump him. And as he pushed me to get better position, I pushed him back. He was strong. When he got the ball, I swiped at it. He got mad. So did one of his teammates. "Hey," said the teammate, "you can't circle your hands around him."

I said nothing, not wishing to argue. But I was not happy. In these moments of supposed recreation, the unconscious is certainly still at work. And I know that I wasn't in the best frame of mind, given the situation with my brother. And I wasn't about to back down from the guy I was guarding.

"Let someone else take him," his teammate called. Barry was about his size, and Barry was guarding a shorter player.

For the sake of the mood of the game, Barry and I switched men.

Barry had opened the game for us with a nice jump shot. It was good once again to see that left-handed shot of his, falling slightly forward, but with good form. It reminded me that Barry had been an excellent high school forward and had made honorable mention all-city his senior year, which was quite an honor. Barry had also made the DePaul University varsity, where he was a teammate of Hershey Carl's.

In our game I missed my first three shots—all of which I thought were on target. I hustled and ran hard up and down the court. If you're not hitting, you should try to make yourself useful in some other fashion. Perhaps, in my enthusiasm to make a contribution, I fought too hard for a loose ball, because suddenly a rival player accidentally swung his hand around and hit me square in the eye. For a scary split second I couldn't see anything out of my left eye. I thought, What the hell is wrong with me, battling like that for a ball. You could get hurt! Then my sight began to clear, though the court remained slightly cloudy.

Barry and a few others were solicitous. "I'm OK," I said.

I tried a drive, and the ball was slapped away. The next time down, I had the ball on the baseline and began another drive. My man backed up, and so I took—and hit—a jump shot. Well, as Michael Jordan had said to me, you take what they give you.

But we lost, 11–10. We sat out one game and then played another game and won, as Barry played better and I played about the same as before, hustlingly mediocre. We'd had a decent workout, though. "The brace doesn't look like it hampers you," Barry said. I mentioned that I felt my shots were on line, though few dropped. "Your adrenaline was flowing," he said. The games plus the shooting around had consumed me for about an hour, and I had that pleasant, slightly tired feeling. I was very glad I had played. Once again basketball had helped relieve tension.

I left Barry and went back to the hospital to say good-bye to Steve before returning to New York. I told him I'd call that night.

On the way to the airport in my rented car, I thought there were a few thin threads hanging from the baseball cap I wore. I felt for the threads. Nothing. I looked in the rearview mirror. No threads. It then occurred to me the threads I thought I was seeing were the remnants of my tussle for the basketball in that pickup game with Barry—maybe scratches on the eye or some blood.

I was concerned, but I know that the eye is supposed to heal itself quickly. I expected—I hoped—that it would. This is one of the dangers of playing the kind of basketball games I've always loved to play. There is contact, there is risk of injury, even serious injury. As I've gotten older, I've tried to balance the aggressive with the cautious. Sometimes I'm overbalanced on one side or the other. But I know that as in writing, if you should err, it's better to err on the side of the conservative. What if I go blind or break my hands and can't type? Or bust up my leg so I can't go to events I have to cover? What if, as the mother of my friend Teddy Schwartz once warned him, the ball will kill you!

What if? You have to go through life trying to do the best and hoping for the best but without being foolish—too foolish, anyway.

Some trick. A full life, as Barry Holt agreed, involves some risk. And if one must cross the street, go—but look both ways before stepping from the curb.

I had been back home from Chicago for a few days when I received a phone call from a voice that I didn't immediately recognize.

"Hello, is this Ira?"

"Yes."

"Hi, Ira. This is Kenny."

"Kenny who?" I said. It didn't register.

"Kenny Garcia."

Now I remembered—Kenny Garcia, the high school kid I played with in the school yard. But how did he get my phone number? I hadn't given it to him, and it is unlisted.

"Where are you?" I asked.

"In the sports department," he said.

"What sports department?"

"*The New York Times!*"

"What? What are you doing there?"

"I work here."

"You what?"

"I'm a clerk. Been here for two weeks. Just calling to thank you for putting a word in for me." A clerk answers the telephones, confirms the stories on the computer that the reporters send in, and does a variety of other jobs.

"How did this come about?" I asked.

"Marie Davitt hired me. They switch me around the building. Yesterday I was on the national desk. But they told me I could stay mostly in sports."

"That's great," I said.

"I owe you lunch," he said.

"La Côte Basque?" I said, joking.

"What?" he said.

"That's a French restaurant."

"I'm thinking Wendy's," he said, with a laugh.

"How do you like the job so far?" I asked.

"I love it," he said. "I want to stay here forever."

A few days later I took him to Yankee Stadium, and he bought me lunch there, a kind of compromise.

I wanted to speak with him about some things he should know about working at the *Times*, but I also didn't want to sound like a pompous uncle. Better a fellow hoopster—or a coach, at the most—one who had had experience playing in this court that was new to him.

I talked to him about the opportunity at the *Times* as I saw it. He could check out the various departments, and not just editorial, but areas from legal to public relations to advertising to photography, too, which I knew was an interest of his. He could seek to work and learn in any of them. I told him that with working there summers and part-time and going to college, this could be a good springboard to his future. I told him that I had just seen a statistic that college graduates make 84 percent more money than high school graduates. He listened.

I also discussed what I thought would be expected of him at the *Times*. "It's like a sign I saw on the door of a Catholic school on Thirty-third Street," I told him. "It said, 'The street stops here.' I think that's the way it should be for you. Remember, even when you don't think anybody's paying attention, they are. But I know you'll be fine."

He was thrilled with his first paycheck, as was his father, an ambulette driver. "When I showed the check to my dad," said Kenny, "he said to me, 'Now you're going to be the one to pay the rent!'"

Kenny was industrious on the job, "punctuous," as he had described himself in his note to me, and well liked. He said hello to fellow workers when he came in and good night when he left, which is not so usual in a hard-nosed newspaper setting. But he ran into some problems. One of the administrative staff in sports mentioned to me that he was still very young and dressed inappropriately, in a kind of hip-hop fashion, baggy pants, sneakers—the way high school kids today often dress. I spoke with Kenny about this. "It's an office," I told him, "not a school yard." The next time I was in the *Times* office, he said to me, "How d'ya like my garb?" He pinched at his shirt. And stuck out his leg to show off his slacks and shoes.

"Is that the best you can do?" I asked.

His eyes widened. I laughed, and so did he. He looked professional, and he knew it.

I also passed along to Kenny some practical advice about working with adults. I told him about one of my summer jobs in Chicago, when I was his age. I was working on a garbage truck with three adult men. The first day, we stopped for a break and one guy bought sodas for everybody. The next time there was a break a second guy bought sodas for everybody. And the third time, the third guy bought. The next time, the first guy bought again. And I thought, this is great, free sodas all time. I was a kid, and adults always did the buying, right?

This went on for a few days. And one of the men on the truck—a middle-aged black man named Donald Groves—pulled me aside. He observed that I was aware how one guy bought drinks, and then the next and then the next. "I want to tell you something, and it's only because I like you," Groves said. "But since you're making the same salary as the rest of us, you should take your turn in popping for drinks, too." It was embarrassing, but I was glad Groves told me. I couldn't wait for the next break in order to buy sodas all around.

Kenny nodded, as I told this story.

"Thanks," he said.

The next fall would be Kenny's senior year at Seward Park High School. He said he planned to play on the basketball team and work part-time at the *Times*.

"What about hitting the books?" I asked.

"I'll make time for that, too," he said.

I felt he would.

At the end of April, I was back in Chicago, where I spent several days with Steve in the hospital. Over the past few weeks I had made several phone calls to Steve's HMO to try to get them to approve a switch of doctors and hospitals. I sat at his bedside as he fed me phone numbers and pieces of information that might be helpful in battling the infuriating bureaucracy. It took considerable effort (and some well-chosen words) but eventually we succeeded, primarily through the volunteered and creative help of Marlene Kaplan's daughter, Rhonda, a lawyer. Steve had also begun calling me regularly to bounce opinions off me, and now he asked me to be a power of attorney for him along with his wife and her sister, Janice, a psychotherapist, with whom he was close. He had a document, and I signed it. We had come a long way from when he wasn't speaking to me, and I was grateful for it.

Steve was getting chemotherapy again, for several days in a row now. "Look at this," he said, as he showed me a bunch of hair that was on his pillow. "It's all falling out now." He had grown increasingly bald. He said, "I told the doctor, 'I didn't say I wanted to look like Michael Jordan. I just said I wanted to play like him.'" At least he still had his sense of humor.

The following afternoon I was alone with Steve at his bedside. We talked about mortality. I recalled to him a diagnosis I had had two years earlier. I had gone in to see a dermatologist, Dr. Philip Orbuch, about a persistent itch on my right leg. It was summertime, and I was wearing a short-sleeve shirt. Dr. Orbuch was wearing those thick magnifying glasses on top of his head and brought them down to his eyes. He grabbed my arm and looked at something on my forearm.

"Doc," I said, "it's not my arm that's bothering me. It's my leg."

"I don't like the looks of this," he told me, indicating a birth mark. "It has to come out immediately. Could be melanoma."

Melanoma? That's cancer! Dr. Orbuch went out of the room to get his instruments. Dolly had told me a couple of times to ask Dr. Orbuch about the birthmark, but I had forgotten. I obviously had not thought it so important. What could I have been thinking—or not thinking! As I lay on the examining table, waiting for the doctor to return, the thought hit me: I might not have long to live! What little I knew of melanoma was enough: it works very fast.

Dr. Orbuch performed surgery on my forearm, right then and there, and scooped out the birthmark, or mole, which had changed shape and had grown darker, though I hadn't realized it until then. He would send the tissue to a laboratory. The biopsy revealed that it was indeed melanoma. It had just begun to develop, and I luckily had caught it in time. If I had let it go for another five or six months, it would have gone through my skin and drained into my blood stream, where it would have been impossible to contain. I would have been dead in about a year.

"When I was lying on that examining table, waiting for the doctor," I told Steve, "my life flashed before me, like a drowning person. And I thought, well, I'm fifty-four years old. I've led a pretty good life, I feel. I've been lucky—good family, good friends, good loves. A lot of people don't live to fifty-four. And if I go, I'll miss a lot of people. And maybe a few people will miss me. But if it's too late, what can I do? Who can I rage to? And the question always is, if not now, when?"

My brother shifted in his bed, and looked at me. "I feel the same way," he said. "I feel I've been blessed, in the same way you feel you've had a good life. But, Ira, I don't want to go now. Not just yet. I still feel I have a lot to live for. Judy and me. We have places we want to go and see. And I want to see Shayne graduate from high school. I—" He stopped and turned toward the window, so I could not see his face fully.

"I know," I said. "I know."

At my parents' home the next evening, as I was getting ready for bed, my mother came over to kiss me good night.

"Ira," she said, looking worn, "is Stevie going to die?"

The question, so direct, fairly took the breath out of me, though I tried not to let her know this.

"Everyone's trying real hard, ma," I said. "We can't stop trying."

"And praying," she said.

My personal religious belief is that God, if there is a God, does not concern himself with fates and actions of human beings. But this was not a moment to discuss such matters.

"Sure, praying, too, ma," I said.

Though things seemed bleak, the situation was fairly stabilized, and so I planned to return to work the next day and to that long-delayed story in Cincinnati. I called Oscar Robertson, and he told me to come down if I still wanted to play, that he'd be in the downtown Cincinnati YMCA gym for the noontime game.

I made two stops in Chicago before catching the plane out of O'Hare. I visited Steve's internist, Dr. David Levine, who is a favorite of the family. I wanted to hear from him as candidly as possible what Steve's prognosis was. From there I would drop in on Steve for the last time that trip.

"Your brother has no immune system," Dr. Levine said bluntly. "He's got no good blood cells, and so of course he is still not viable for a bone marrow transplant."

Why not? I asked. I was ignorant on the subject, I confessed. "Because when you transplant an organ, you do not transplant an entire organ, but a part of an organ," explained Dr. Levine. "And if you still have bad cells in a part of the organ, it will contaminate the transplant."

"What's the prognosis?" I asked.

"The oncologists tell me that the chemotherapy will kick in," he said. "That's all I know."

"Do you tell him everything?" I asked.

"He gets mad if he feels we aren't telling him everything," said Dr. Levine. "But if we told him everything, he'd get depressed."

"Is this going to take a miracle?"

"Miracles happen," said Dr. Levine.

I left and went to Steve's hospital room. He knew I was planning to play basketball with Oscar Robertson the next day. I asked him for advice. He thought for a moment. "The rocker step," he said. "It's your only hope."

"Steve, are you trying to say that it's my only move?"

He smiled—with his glasses glinting from the lights in the room—and said nothing, my kid brother perhaps just trying to spare my feelings.

But he remembered. When I was about fourteen and he was nine, I tried to teach my brother that move: the offensive player keeps his pivot foot in place and then steps forward; if the defensive player doesn't move, the man with the ball drives or pulls back to shoot the jumper. If the defensive player steps back, then the offensive player steps back, too. When the defensive player moves forward, the offensive player then swiftly drives off the leg that his opponent is extending forward, "locking" the defensive player so that he can only fall back on his heels as you sail by him to the hoop. I have seen many players do it. It has worked for me in daydreams and on the rare occasion in a game.

My parents, Judy, and Shayne were in the room as well, all sitting facing Steve, who sat in his hospital gown on a chair beside his bed. He was still hooked up to the IV machine.

I put on my jacket and walked over to him, still, of course, wearing my yellow hospital mask. He wasn't supposed to be touched on exposed skin by any of us for fear of possibly spreading germs to him, which might be fatal. So I stood in front of him and put my hand on his covered shoulder.

"I love you, Steve," I said.

"I love you, Ira," he said.

I felt my throat constrict.

"C'mere," he said. He grabbed my jacket and pulled me to him, and kissed me on the cheek. We looked hard at each other, and then I turned to my family who sat with chairs lined up as in a movie theater, waved good-bye, and walked out of the room. If I had tried to speak, I would have cried. And I just didn't have the heart to do it in front of everybody.

I just said it, I thought, on the way to the airport. I said, "I love you." I had never told my brother that before. He had never told me, either. It wasn't until a day or so earlier that I had thought about telling him I loved him. And I did. But it just had never entered my consciousness. Now it had, and I didn't know if I could tell him. How strange. Those three monosyllabic words. Why was it so hard? Was I too much a macho man? Was he? I didn't think so.

A lot had gone between us, and that now was cast aside, for the most part. There would always be some residual feelings that couldn't be helped, I believe. But, as Dolly once told me, at times like this all that other nonsense is unimportant. I had heard other people tell how they wished they had told loved ones certain things—like I love you—and hadn't. And then it was too late, and they regretted it. I felt a sense of fulfillment, of deep satisfaction, in having expressed my feeling to my brother. And Steve had returned the affection. I had also done it in front of my parents, and I knew it was important for them, too.

I decided to arrive early for the noontime game with Oscar Robertson in order to limber up. After all, if I were going to sing with Luciano Pavarotti, I'd want to get in a few extra warbles before going on stage.

It was a gray, cool late April morning, and I walked the mile or so from my hotel to the three-story dark-red brick Central YMCA building. I walked in hope of trying to digest a blueberry muffin that I shouldn't have eaten for breakfast. I like to eat light before playing ball and finish the meal about three hours before playing. In the hotel coffee shop I had raisin bran cereal with banana, orange juice, and black coffee, which should have been enough. However, the blueberry muffin on the plate of the man sitting across from me looked irresistible. Should have resisted. But maybe the cause of my feeling slightly bloated was out of nervousness, and not the muffin. I mean, it's not every day that I would play in the same game as Oscar Robertson.

As I walked, Ron Rubenstein came into mind. I had played against Rubenstein in the Chicago parks and had competed against him when he was at Senn High School. He went on to start at guard for the University of Louisville. A teammate of his at Louisville, Bud Olsen, once told me the following:

Before a Missouri Valley Conference game against Cincinnati, the Louisville coach, Peck Hickman, gave his players a pep talk, concluding with, "And remember, Robertson puts his jockstrap on the same way you guys do." After the game, the Louisville Cardinals dragged into their locker room. They had been beaten by 25 points, and Robertson had scored at will, passed at will, rebounded at will, stolen balls at will. As

Louisville undressed quietly Rubenstein turned to Olsen, and said, "I don't care what coach says, Robertson *has* to put his jockstrap on differently."

"And," Rubenstein told me not long ago, "I still believe it."

The woman at the front desk at the Y said I could not go into the locker room until my host showed up. Security had become tight. "A lot of riffraff have been coming in off the streets," she said, looking at me through glasses to judge whether I was of that ilk. I sat down on a nearby couch, but a few minutes later she called me. "I'm not supposed to do this," she said, "but if you're a guest of Oscar's I guess it's OK for you go in." I thanked her, and my stomach, which was trying to get that blueberry muffin in order, growled something at her, too. If she heard it, she didn't acknowledge it.

I went to my locker and began to dress for the game. I was adjusting my knee brace when I looked up and saw Oscar come through the door. As we greeted each other, I noticed that he seemed broader than I had remembered him in his playing days and, of course, older, with flecks of gray in his hair. His hand was large and his shake firm. He wore a plaid summer sports jacket, tan slipover shirt, tan pants, brown loafers, and a smile that was, well, cryptic—as if to say, Are you sure you really want to do this? Why did it remind me of a cat's grin, and why did I feel like the mouse? "I'll be dressed in a few minutes," he said, adding brightly, "My guys are waiting for you."

"Waiting for me?" I blurted.

"Yeah," he replied, evenly.

"Oh," I said, as he walked to the back of the locker room. Maybe this was going to be more of a challenge that I had anticipated. But I finished dressing and went to the gym. I didn't stick around to see how Oscar puts on his jockstrap.

• • •

Like a lot of older gyms, this one had a regulation-size basketball court but with only a little room to shoot on the four baskets—two on each side—that hung parallel to the court. The windows let in the sunlight, and, with the yellow-painted walls, there was a sense of airiness and light to the facility.

I noticed signs on the walls: FIGHTING WILL RESULT IN IMMEDIATE SUSPENSION and NO CUSSING. Yes, I thought to myself, a typical Pickup-Games Heaven.

Even before entering the gym, the squeak of sneakers and the faintly gamey smell of sweat were clear indications that a game was in progress. It was a full-court game, and I took in the caliber of play. It was pretty good, though not of the highest level, even by Y standards. There were some older players who looked like they might be close to fifty or in their fifties, and some younger ones, including, Robertson later pointed out to me, one very good thirty-one-year-old. This was Tim McGee, a wiry, 5-foot-10-inch veteran wide receiver for the Cincinnati Bengals and a onetime high school basketball standout in Cleveland.

Shortly after I got in the gym, Oscar appeared. He dressed plainly, in gray T-shirt, gray shorts, and white sneakers. And when we warmed up, he took that jump shot that was so familiar and seemed nearly impossible to block. He cradled the ball in his right hand like a waiter carrying a tray of champagne glasses on his palm. He seemed to hang in the air, not as high as Michael Jordan—not nearly as high then or, to be sure, now—but just as inaccessible. It was vintage Oscar, the shot I had seen him take and score against such as Jerry West and Bob Cousy and Wilt Chamberlain. The ball snapped through the net with an uncommon but customary authority. The one difference, however, was the discernible paunch under his shirt. He told me he tipped the scales now at about

250 pounds, some 30 pounds over his playing weight. He didn't seem troubled by it.

"I come from a family of big people," he explained.

He said he tries to eat sensibly—"lots of vegetables, though I do like ice cream"—and jogs a mile three times a week. Then there's the occasional basketball game. And we had next.

"Oscar," I said, "the floor feels a little slippery, or is it my sneakers?"

"This is the Y," he said, "they never mop it."

Then he spit on the wooden floor—my eyes widened at this—and rubbed the sole of each foot into it. "For traction," he said. Naturally, I did the same. It worked, too.

Oscar had written both our names on a sheet of paper that hung on the wall. Good, I thought. We would be playing together rather than against each other. I thought I'd rather be at the receiving end of an Oscar pass than trying to defend against it, and him. Also, the winning team stays. You get a better workout if you win, naturally, and the chances of winning with Oscar Robertson on my side in a pickup game, I figured, would be substantially better than if he weren't.

We played and lost.

Oscar never seemed to get fully in the game, and we fell, 10–6. The other three players on our team were, like me, your conventional gym rat. As was the other team, with the exception of McGee. The way games are played at that Y, the first team to score 10 baskets wins. Or—and this is something I'd never seen in a Y before—there is a time clock propped against a chair on the sidelines. And it is set for a twelve-minute game. The team that is ahead after twelve minutes wins.

The winning team stays on the court, and the losing team sits and waits for another game. That was us. Our game hadn't even lasted twelve minutes. I had felt a little nervous, as I always do when in a game in a new place, with new people. There is always that thing about proving myself or at least demonstrating that I do belong. Like starting a new job.

The first time I had gotten the ball on offense, I passed to Oscar in the corner. He missed the shot. He took another and missed that one, too. He was playing their tallest man—someone about 6-foot-8, and muscling him out for rebounds. ("I don't jump much anymore," Oscar had told me, "I just lean into people. And these guys up here don't really know how to box out.") As for me, I took a jump shot, and it hit the rim and bounced away. I took another and missed. My shots were just off, and I wasn't feeling confident. I have no doubt that Oscar sensed it. "They'll fall," he said to me as we backpedaled on defense.

The third time down, I passed to Oscar, who motioned that I come around him. I did, and he set a wide screen with his ample body. He cleared out my man and his man and, it seemed, everyone else in the gym. He was setting me up for the shot. I don't remember ever getting a screen like that. I felt all alone, like I was in an empty meadow. I was buoyed. Oscar was, as the saying goes, trying to "get me off." I'd like to think he saw that I had a shot, and that he'd make use of it. I remember Wayne Embry telling me, "He made us all better players."

I shot from about 17 feet away. All net.

But Oscar didn't quite seem to be taking charge. Tim McGee, meanwhile, made three straight twisting, athletic shots. "Get him!" Oscar called out to the man guarding McGee. "He's scoring all the points." I, happily, was not guarding Tim McGee. McGee told me later that Oscar has mellowed in the last few years. "When I first came up to the Y ten years ago, he still had an NBA mentality," he recalled.

"He'd holler at you if you missed a layup. He was in charge. Oh yeah. He's a little cooler now."

The Big O, one of the highest scorers in history, was shut out in our game. Didn't make a single hoop in three tries. But Oscar still had some Oscar left in him. And it became clearer when we were waiting for next.

He was critical of some of the play. "That guy hasn't passed the ball yet," he said of one player.

"Look at that," he said, indicating another player, "he doesn't even try to get back on defense. Unbelievable."

When an argument broke out on the court, he hollered, "Play! Play! The clock is running!" When, shortly after, one of the players slipped over and turned off the clock during another argument, Oscar pounced. "Hey! What are you doing? Don't stop the clock. The clock runs!" And Oscar turned the clock back on. The player said nothing—it was, after all, Oscar Robertson. And Oscar was known to assume command.

But Oscar was also enjoying the camaraderie. Robertson called out to one guy, "Kill 'em, Freddie." Freddie, a lawyer, tried to ignore it. Oscar needled a few others. "Oh, oh," he said, like an announcer, as one team scored several straight baskets to take the lead, "the tide is turning."

When an argument broke out about a player scoring in the final seconds, Oscar turned timekeeper. "Next!" he called. "Next!"

That was our team.

Oscar was more into it now. A teammate was fast-breaking, and Oscar threw a perfect lob pass from half court that sailed just over the outstretched finger of the downcourt defender. I had the ball, and he set a pick for a teammate to cut to the basket and looked at me and pointed to the cutting teammate. I hit him with the pass for a basket. But on another occasion I threw a no-look pass that was wide of the mark. Oscar said nothing. He did shout to me, "Cut through," on one play, but I didn't do it quickly enough and didn't get the ball. Again, I had the ball near half-court and looked to pass. Somehow, Tim McGee seemed to go from one end of the court to the other at the speed of light and stole the ball out of my hands. Outstanding athletes—especially those in top shape—are shocking to the layman in their quickness and strength, especially to the slowing layman.

I was feeling foolish and worthless after that steal, when, on the very next play, McGee stole the ball from Oscar! Off the dribble! Oscar looked not so much sheepish as disgusted at himself as he watched McGee put in a layup. The next time down, Oscar was pounding his dribble in that no-nonsense manner I remembered from his playing days. He got into the lane to the basket and scored on a jumper. He hit two more shots, including one on a rebound—after he missed three straight shots under the basket, getting the rebound each time. He was determined to make the shot.

Oscar's court vision was remarkable. He seemed to know where everyone on the court was, when to get them the ball, and how—lob pass, bounce pass, chest pass. And always with economy of movement. There wasn't an ounce of flab to his game. No frills. Never was. Oscar dribbling the ball between his legs would be as unimaginable as Pavarotti doing rap.

When Robertson was double-teamed, he always found the open man to pass to. When he was an active player, he once told me, "I always know who is guarding my teammates, and so when I'm double-teamed I naturally know who's open." He said it as though to say, "Well, doesn't everybody?"

Oscar threw me a sweet, crisp pass at the chest, just in my stride, and I hit another jumper. I missed my next two shots, however. With the score 9–9—and the game on the line—I passed the ball to Oscar at the top of the key, and he went up for the jumper without hesitation, with the same perfect mechanics he had employed a million times, and swished it for the game winner.

We won the next game, too, 10–7, and I had my best results, scoring three baskets, including the game-ender, a fade-away one-hander on the baseline in which I started to drive and then held up. It felt sweet, though it was the closest I had come to a drive shot that afternoon. In all the excitement my mind had drifted from going to the hoop. And my quest for the consistent drive—or at least one great drive in a game— had, disturbingly, stalled.

According to the rules in that gym, the winning team has to relinquish the court after two wins; we'd been there for over an hour, and it was enough for both of us anyway. Oscar's shirt was splotched with sweat; I could see he was tired. I think I was sapped as much from the tension and anticipation as from the games themselves. I had forgotten all about that blueberry muffin. So I guess it had finally settled.

"How about some lunch?" Oscar asked.

Oscar had said nothing about anything I did on the court, except for his "They'll fall." Which was enough. It elevated my spirits, and, along with his screens and passes, I believe it also elevated my game. I imagine he gave me points for hustling, for I made certain I always got back quickly on defense, though, near the end, the brawny, 250-pound Oscar was having some problem doing so.

"It's really a simple game," he said to me as we went into the locker room. "It's rebounding and defense and maintaining control of the ball."

It's a simple game for Oscar, and, perhaps, in their fields the same could be said for Picasso and Mozart. It's somewhat more difficult for the rest of us.

But I saw that Oscar still enjoyed the game, still delighted in the competition—it wasn't the NBA, but it was still a decent run, even for him. He still enjoyed mixing with the other players in a familiar setting, the basketball court, just as he had when he first began playing as a boy in the "Dust Bowl" playground of Indianapolis, his hometown. And he maintained a competitive sense of himself, even to the pros of today. When I asked Oscar about Michael Jordan, who has averaged 30 points a game in his career, he said he was a great player.

I asked him how many points Jordan would have scored in Oscar's era.

"We had fewer teams, and the talent wasn't as diluted as it is today," said Robertson. "So I think Jordan would have scored about twenty a game."

"Twenty a game?" I said. "But you scored thirty a game in that era."

"Well," said Oscar, with a shrug, "I handled the ball more than he does."

After we parted, I remembered something Oscar had told me near the end of his NBA career. I had mentioned that his career scoring average was dropping. In his last season he averaged 16 points a game, down from 30 after his first eleven seasons in the league.

"I don't feel too bad that it's dropping," he said. "It's to be expected. I'm getting older." He paused. "But you know, it happens to everybody."

"What happens to everybody?" I asked.

"Autumn," he said.

When I returned home from Cincinnati, I visited my internist, Dr. Tuchman, and related my experience with Oscar. "In most pickup games," I said, "guys often seem to be going their separate ways. But with Oscar, there was suddenly a rhyme and a reason for doing things. There was a structure. There was a plan. He seemed to know in advance what was going to happen, even if he couldn't react as fully as he once had. There was form and function. It raised the playing level of each of us on his team. It was a pleasure."

"Hmm," said Dr. Tuchman, leaning forward in his chair behind his desk. "It was like being in the operating room with a great surgeon."

"Yes," I said. "An older surgeon, and a larger surgeon, but a great surgeon. Still."

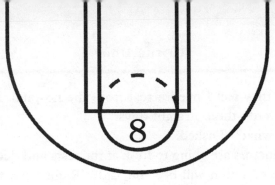

Legacies

*T*he day Oscar Robertson and I played basketball in Cincinnati was a "landmark day" for Steve (as he had termed it), for he was scheduled to learn the result of the bone-marrow test. If it was good, he would be a candidate for a bone-marrow transplant. It would mean a new lease on life.

I was anxious to learn what the doctors had said, and when I called Steve that afternoon, it seemed to take a long time for the call to go through.

Finally, Steve answered the phone.

"It's me," I said.

"How'd you do?" he asked.

"OK," I said. "But how did you do?"

"Nothing has changed," he said, slightly dispirited. "My bone marrow is still filled with the bad white cells. Still not a candidate for a transplant. But they're going to send me home in a few days."

"They are?" I said.

221

"Yeah, they feel I need a rest from the hospital. I've been here for twenty-three straight days."

"Then what?" I asked.

"The doctors are going to look at the tests and decide what the course of action will be," he said. "Right now, they have no answers."

Dolly, who has a deep interest in nutrition, had talked to Steve about a book she liked called *Spontaneous Healing*. Steve had sent Shayne out to buy a copy. The book contains views about maintaining a good diet with vegetables and fruits and the importance of avoiding so-called bad foods. My brother believed there was substance in this.

"I'm changing a lot of things in my life," he told me. "And food is one of them. No more overload on fried chicken and pizza."

He then changed the subject and asked for specifics about how I did with Oscar. I told him we played on the same team, that he set me up for shots, and that I set him up, too.

"I'm sure he needed that from you," said Steve.

"He didn't complain."

"But you played well?" He sounded tired.

"Well enough that I didn't have to be too embarrassed," I said.

"That's great."

"For me," I said, "yeah."

The next night I was back in New York and spoke by phone with Judy. She said that the doctors asked whether I would take a bone marrow test. "That's in case Steven would need a transplant," she said. "You would be the most likely candidate for a transplant. Is that OK with you?"

"Of course," I said. "What a question."

"Well," she said, "some time ago, when you and Steven

weren't really on speaking terms, I mentioned to him that if he needed a transplant, he'd have to ask you. I asked him, 'Do you think Ira would do it?' And Steven said, 'Sure. He's my brother.' "

The next morning I went to Dr. Tuchman's office for a bone-marrow test. I had followed the terrible ordeal of Rod Carew and his family in seeking a donor for a bone-marrow transplant for Rod's eighteen-year-old daughter, Michelle, who suffered from a case of leukemia similar to my brother's. Rod's two other daughters—his only other children—matched up perfectly with each other, but neither matched Michelle. And as month after month passed, accompanied by a tremendous wave of publicity about the search for a match, none surfaced. It was tragically frustrating. And in mid-April, Michelle Carew died.

In the best of all worlds, I thought, a transplant might be the step that saves Steve's life. It was a ray of hope.

On Sunday, May 5, I returned to Chicago to write about the Bulls-Miami playoff series but also to spend time with Steve. My editors at the paper knew my situation and were generous in assigning me stories in and around Chicago. It also helped that the Bulls were so newsworthy.

The first thing I did when I left the airport was go to Steve's hospital room. I found that he had another visitor—his dearest and perhaps his oldest friend, Victor Ostrow. They had gone to high school together, double-dated regularly, and stayed pals after Ostrow moved to Phoenix several years ago. Victor is heavy-set, balding, with an intelligence and gentleness that are readily perceptible. He is also voluble. "Talks a lot, doesn't he?" my brother said, at one point. And he smiled wanly at Victor. I had known Victor for a long time and knew the wisecracking but loving relationship they've maintained over the years.

The two told stories about their common experiences and laughed. My brother told the story of when the two went looking for the supposed treasure in the Lost Dutchman's mine in the Superstition Mountains outside of Phoenix, Arizona, when they were both much younger. They rented four horses, two of which carried their packs. Steve and Victor wore cowboy hats and chaps and cowboy boots. "We looked like something out of a Saturday matinee western," Steve said. The roads leading up the mountain they traveled were narrow and winding. There was a deep ridge, and the horses balked. "I thought we were going to tumble over," said Steve. "We had to get off the horses and coax them up the mountain."

Then they got lost. "And it was getting dark," said Steve. "And we didn't bring enough water. I said, 'It's that way we should go.' And Victor said, 'I think it's the other way.' And we went his way. Thank God he was right." They both laughed. "And when we got to Phoenix, we were hungry and went to the first restaurant we saw. It was a very fancy place. People were sitting at tables in gowns and suits and ties. The maître d' put us at a front table. It was incredible. Here we were all dusty and worn out. But I guess they wanted to show us off, that real cowboys eat in their restaurant."

Victor had surely propped up my brother's spirits. He needed it.

An unexpected development over the last several years is that my parents have become basketball fans. Michael Jordan and the Chicago Bulls have had that effect on them.

"Jordan is like an artist, isn't he?" my father said.

"The games make me so nervous," my mother said, about the playoffs. "Sometimes I can't stand to see it on television and have to go into the other room and shut the door."

"Who ever thought we'd get so involved in it?" my father said. I didn't, since they had taken so little interest in my basketball when I was young.

"Not just us who like it, but our friends, too," my mother said. She mentioned one of her lady friends. "She thinks she knows basketball, but she doesn't know from borscht."

Among other unexpected developments of recent years is the emergence of the author Dennis Rodman. I decided to write a column while in Chicago about what was expected to be, and was, Rodman's madcap, cross-dressing appearance at a book signing for his autobiography, *Bad as I Wanna Be*. A tremendous crowd had gathered, snaking around corners for about five city blocks in downtown Chicago, when Rodman screeched up to the book store on Michigan Avenue on a motorcycle.

He was wearing heavy eye makeup like a drag queen, with a fuchsia boa thrown languidly around his neck. Somehow, it was hard to imagine, say, George Mikan arriving for a booksigning in quite this manner. Or, for that matter, Bill Russell or Michael Jordan. In fact, I can think only of Rodman for such a scene. And then only in the last year or so, when he has become more and more outrageous—and has capitalized on it. I once asked Jordan about Rodman's behavior. "It's all for marketability," he said.

I had a copy of Rodman's book, and I read over parts of it. The next day I had a talk with him in the Bulls' locker room. It's somewhat odd to stand and carry on a nearly normal conversation with a 6-foot-8-inch man with harshly dyed yellow hair sprinkled with obvious black roots, four silver rings in his nostrils, and a kaleidoscope of tattoo squiggles on his chest and arms. I asked him the difference between his book and the one written by his coach, Phil Jackson, *Sacred Hoops*, which was, Rodman acknowledged, a more cerebral undertaking. "Phil's a Zen master," Rodman said. "But he uses bigger words than I do. You can understand the words in my book better."

In the Bulls' organization, Rodman is hardly known as a voracious reader. This, however, is no indication of his intelligence. He is a very smart basketball player—and two of the smartest players I know, Jordan and Isiah Thomas, have told me that they have marveled at Rodman's uncanny ability to be at the right place at the right time.

I asked Rodman about his marketing techniques. "I'm very creative, very crafted," he said. "And until recently I never realized how creative I was." About the cross-dressing, he said, "I'm challenging everyone's fears—and bringing them to the forefront. I'm just trying to show that an athlete is no different from anyone else. And I know people say, 'This loony, wild guy' . . . and in lots of ways I am. But in lots of ways I'm not."

This was hard to argue with.

I asked him who his hairdresser is. "It's Charles," he said. "He works in a shop in Northbrook named Heidi." I wrote this down, and having pretty much exhausted the subject of fashion, we moved on to rebounding.

The next day, I visited Steve. There were balloons bobbing beside the window in his hospital room and on the table beside him were letters from his eigth-grade students telling him how much they missed him. They had made a video that we watched together, in which the kids mugged for the camera but grew serious when they said they hoped he'd be back soon. It was poignant.

I also told Steve about my conversation with Dennis Rodman. At one point in our relationship, I felt he might have resented hearing about what I was doing, and whom I was meeting. But not now. And especially not when it came to Rodman.

When I had related my conversation with Rodman to him, he laughed, though he was very tired. "The man's a lunatic," my brother said, beaming. "A lunatic, but a talented lunatic."

Two of our cousins had come to visit and had been frequent visitors—Ian Levin, now a circuit court judge in Chicago, and his brother, also named Steve, a counselor in municipal traffic court. My brother told me how much he enjoyed their visit.

Later, Ian said to me, "Steve was telling me of all the people who have called and written him. He said he's amazed, that he never realized how many people cared about him. I guess that's just like him. Very unassuming. But people love him. He's straightforward and caring, and once you get to know him, there are a lot of layers to him."

Steve, meanwhile, was getting ready to leave the hospital. The doctors felt that his home environment would lift his spirits. That, I knew, was beyond dispute.

While in Chicago, I had noticed in the newspaper that Sullivan High School was playing a baseball game against Lakeview High School. Forty years earlier I had pitched for Sullivan against Lakeview. In fact, before I ever considered throwing a chunk of my life into basketball, I had first given my heart to baseball, playing it in the sandlots while growing up and then in Little League and the Pony League. I played with modest success as a first baseman and as a pitcher. I could throw better than I could hit. And in late March of my freshman year at Sullivan, in 1954, I saw a posting on the bulletin board in the gym that baseball tryouts were to be held. I oiled my glove but had no idea what to expect.

In the spring baseball broke out at Sullivan High School, "broke" being the operative word because indoor practice was a necessity in the winterlike spring of Chicago, and the baseballs that ricocheted off the walls and plaster of the school gym not infrequently collapsed and fell to the floor.

There was no frosh-soph team, as there were at some larger schools, no B team, just the varsity. So if you made the team, you were in there with all the upperclassmen.

The coach of the high school team was called "Nemo" by the players because of his sunny disposition. He was called Nemo when he wasn't in earshot, since Nemo was the name of the grim sea captain in *20,000 Leagues Under the Sea*. When he was nearby, we called him "Coach."

His real name was Alex Nemkoff, and I can remember him entering the small Sullivan gym for the baseball team tryouts. Coach Nemkoff wore a plain black baseball cap with no insignia, the bill pulled low to shade his eyes like a riverboat gambler, and, under the bill, one would find a dark scowl, the stub of a dead cigar, a sweatshirt, and a whistle around his neck.

He also carried a baseball bat that in his hands, looked like a dangerous weapon. The gym was filled with players in sweatshirts and jeans and sneakers and baseball caps, to keep the glare of the ceiling lights from their eyes, I imagine. Several balls were being thrown at once, with balls smashing off the metal coverings of the broad windows and careering off the walls as the players dived out of the way. The place resembled a pinball machine.

Nemo began hitting ground balls, the ball bouncing on the wooden basketball floor with an unnatural thud, thud, thud. "Around the horn," Nemo grumbled. "Show some life!" And to a kid who flubbed a fungo: "Hey, buddy, did you ever play organized ball before?"

I made the team and got a uniform with a shirt that didn't quite match the pants—the underclassmen took what we could get from a pile of old uniforms in a back closet. I told the coach that I was available to pitch or to play first base and the outfield.

I remember ball games on cold days in the spring. The wind came whipping in off the lake, and the lake always seemed to be across the street, even when you were miles from it. There were snow flurries. A fire had been lit in a garbage drum behind the backdrop so we could warm our hands. After an inning in an early-season game, Rob Sanders came jogging to the bench from his position alongside another outfielder, Herb Fagen. "Gee, Herb," said Rob, "it's cold in right. Is it cold in center, too?"

Nemo wore his low-lying baseball cap and a long overcoat buttoned at the collar. Sometimes he'd shout encouragement: "C'mon, you jokers, get a hit." He'd give a signal to the base runner to steal, and often the runner had forgotten the signals, if he had ever learned them in the first place—in my first couple of years at Sullivan it was that kind of team—and Coach Nemkoff pulled a handkerchief from his pocket and began to wave it at the runner. "Hey," he'd shout, "Steal!" Such macabre humor led us to believe that Nemo wasn't quite the ogre he seemed to want us to believe.

Barry Stein, the pigeon-toed second baseman, often ignored Nemkoff's tactics. He had another agenda. He invariably had money-making schemes that he would discuss at the pitcher's mound. He once tried to convince me to go in on one while rubbing up the ball for me at the pitcher's mound. "Listen to me," he said, "and we'll be farting in silk underwear."

One of our two catchers was Cal Feirstein, a stocky, streetwise guy who looked about forty years old for as long as anyone had ever known him. Nemo called him "Wooden Arm," because his throws to second base often ended up in center field, and Feirstein accepted the name as a badge of honor. It was hard to insult Cal.

But for all of Nemkoff's bleakness, from my view, he had his adherents, especially my cousin Ian, a rangy, 6-foot-3, red-haired third baseman who was a semester ahead of me. Ian believed that Nemo was a good strategist, that our practices were organized, and that if you had talent, Nemo recognized it. He certainly saw talent in Ian. While some others in the school, including the basketball coach, Art Scher, thought that Ian was less than a serious-minded student-athlete ("They thought I was a screw-off," he said), Nemkoff saw an intelligent, solid citizen with leadership qualities and even named Ian player-coach the few times Nemkoff was unable to be at a practice.

Years later, when Ian became one of the most highly re-spected judges in Chicago, the *Chicago Tribune* endorsed his reelection to the Cook County Circuit Court bench and cited his "integrity," "scholarship," and "hard work." So Coach Nemkoff proved to have a certain farsightedness, too.

I characterized myself primarily as a pitcher, though on a team like ours, with limited resources, one had to be prepared to play any position at any time. But I dreamed of pitching for Sullivan one day. As a freshman, though, and a fairly skinny one, I sat on the bench and watched the juniors and seniors play. But one day, about midway through the season, I got my chance, in the last inning of a game against Waller High School. We were getting soundly beaten. "Hey, you! Warm up!" I looked around to see which you he was speaking to. "Yeah, you!" said Nemo. It was me. "You're pitching the next inning."

When I entered the game, I stood on the mound and peered toward home plate. It seemed about seven miles away. Not only was my heart thumping, but I discovered I had made a grave error in warming up on the sideline. I had mistakenly thrown from about 50 feet away, rather than the requisite 60 feet 6 inches. I had also warmed up throwing downhill.

When I pitched, it was the Fourth of July. The Waller hitters boomed and rocketed my pitches all over the field. It was all like a dream, and, in retrospect, memory commingles with fact, and I can see that one ball was miraculously caught by an outfielder in a tree; a line drive was snared by an infielder who threw up his glove just in time to save his life; and someone else made another impossible catch, and thus the inning ended. Three up, three down. Nothing to it.

Nemo didn't acknowledge the performance, and, as one game followed another, I didn't pitch again. A few weeks after the Waller game, however, the coach collared me in school on the morning of the last game of the season.

"You're starting against Von Steuben this afternoon," he snarled.

"Sure, coach," I said. And he was gone.

Starting? Von Steuben? They're meaner than Waller!

After two innings, the Sullivan fielders were dying of exhaustion from chasing base hits, and Nemo, scowling but showing uncustomary humanity toward them, yanked his freshman hurler.

I played three more seasons for Sullivan and Coach Nemkoff. And I had some games that I am fairly proud of. One was in my junior year, when I played first base and hit a solid double down the left-field line off one of the best pitchers in the state, Jim Woods of Lane Tech, who led his team that year to the Illinois state high school baseball championship (and he later played briefly in the major leagues as a third baseman for the Cubs and the Phillies). Lane beat us 9–0 in that game in which I hit a double—oh yes, I also popped up and whiffed my other two times at bat.

It also happened that in a game in which I was pitching in early May of 1956, shortly after the Lane game, I was on first base when the pitcher tried to pick me off. I dived back head first, and avoided the tag by jerking my shoulder away from the ball that was being swiped at me. I heard some sounds in my shoulder, like the ripping of clothes. I went back to the mound the next inning and felt a lot of pain, but I finished the game and won, raising my record to 2–1. In the days to come, the shoulder didn't stop hurting. I tried to warm up to pitch a week later but could hardly lift my arm.

I didn't realize it then, but this was the end of my pitching career, such as it was. I was diagnosed as having torn tendons—today, it would be called a rotator cuff. I started at first base the next season and never threw the ball overhand again. I was concerned that my bad shoulder would affect my basketball shooting, but it didn't, for good or for ill, because the shot is more of a push than a throw and I didn't stretch the shoulder when looping the ball to the basket.

I learned years later that while I was beginning and ending my pitching career on the North Side of Chicago, over in a South Side suburb, another kid, also a six-foot-tall, right-handed high-school junior, was having better luck. In April 1956 two weeks after I had pitched a game against Lakeview, he had pitched a curiously similar one for Bloom High School against Argo. Each of us gave up three runs on five hits and pitched complete games. The difference was, I lost 3–0, and he won 6–3. Six summers later he would be pitching for the New York Yankees and I would be once again working between college semesters on the garbage truck (where I imagine I would have been regardless of any arm injury). That other pitcher's name was Jim Bouton.

I have gotten to know Bouton over the years, and I was intrigued to learn that at age fifty-seven he was still pitching in semipro leagues. After winning 21 games for the Yankees in 1963 and 18 in 1964 (winning a couple of World Series games and pitching in an All-Star Game as well), Bouton lost his fast-ball, and his career apparently had come to an end when he was released by the Houston Astros in 1970. But a few years later he became determined once again to make it to the big leagues, this time as a knuckleball pitcher. He played for several minor league teams and then, by the grace of Ted Turner, who appreciated an unconventional spirit—"This Bouton's no dummy," Turner was heard to say—Bouton found himself on the mound for the Atlanta Braves in 1978, eight years after his last big-league appearance. He was thirty-nine years old and won a game for them at the end of the season while losing three. And then, dream realized, he went home. But he has never stopped pitching.

One day not long ago I went to visit Bouton, who lives with his wife, Paula Kurman, in a house on a hill in western Massachusetts. Bouton is still trim and engaging. I asked him how he had done in his outing the night before while pitching for Mama's Restaurant in the Twilight League in Clifton Park, New York. "Not well," he said. "I lost. It wasn't working. My knuckleball made one of its trips out of town. And didn't tell anyone. Not a note, nothing. Sometimes I wonder what the hell it's doing."

I had the impression that this is the way I sound when my shot is not on target. I don't know if there are any more baseball pickup games in America, as there might have been a quarter of a century or more ago, but if there were, I could envision Bouton doing exactly what I do with basketball games. Instead, he plays in these semipro leagues, against players including former college and minor-league players and who are some twenty-five years younger than he.

"When I'm on my game," Bouton said, "they have trouble hitting me. But when I'm not, I get ripped. I can't just throw my scrapbook onto the mound and expect to win."

Are there times, now, I asked him, when he returns home and tells Paula, his wife, "This is it, I'm hanging up my spikes"?

"It's never that definite," he replied. "I usually say, 'I think it might be over.'"

"And what does she say?"

"Well, she's heard it before. More than once. And she says, 'There, there. It'll be OK.'"

He laughed.

"But I don't say it much anymore," he said.

"Oh, what changed? More confidence?"

"No," he said. "I think she just got tired hearing it. And I guess I got tired saying it. Now I just think it."

"Yes," I said. "I understand."

"I'm scheduled to throw again next week," Bouton told me. "I'm hoping for the knuckler to come back. I'm thinking it just took a vacation. It's happened more than once."

In *Ball Four* Bouton wrote that beautiful, poignant ending that described for all time a ballplayer's love of a sport. "You see, you spend a good piece of your life gripping a baseball, and in the end it turns out that it was the other way around all the time."

Since I have relatively small hands, I can't palm a basketball. But I can grip one with two hands. And I believe that Bouton's baseball metaphor worked for basketball and me, too.

The news from Chicago was not good. Steve had been home for five days, but then he showed signs of internal bleeding, and his new oncologist, Dr. Jacob Bitran, gave my brother some of the facts of his situation and told him how he planned to proceed.

"It will be very aggressive," said Dr. Bitran.

"Good," said Steve. "I want it as aggressive as possible. So whatever you say."

Dr. Bitran readmitted my brother to the hospital.

I returned home, and the next day we spoke by telephone. "The hospital rabbi came to see me," Steve said. "It was part of his rounds. He asked if it was OK to talk with me. He said he had seen that in the admittance registration I had written 'Jewish' for my religious affiliation.

"I said sure, sit down. I told him that I wasn't deeply religious. And we talked about that, about my ideas of God and religion."

"What did you say?" I asked. I had never spoken about this with Steve.

"I said that I believed there might be a creator or something or other that exists in the universe," said Steve, "but I wasn't sure. I don't know if I ever will be. The rabbi said I was cerebral. It's funny, I just thought I was being straightforward. Does anybody really know any more than that?"

"I don't," I said.

"But I enjoyed the visit with him," Steve continued. "I thought he was a warm guy. We spoke for about an hour, and I got a little emotional, too. I cried twice."

"You did?" I asked. "When?"

"Well," he said, "once when the rabbi held my hand."

Then there was a silence.

"And the other time?" I asked.

"The other time," said Steve, "was when I told the rabbi about you."

Four days later Steve was put on a respirator. His pneumonia was critical and had spread from the right lung to the left. He had been sedated and put into an induced coma because if he were conscious the tubes of the respirator would be too uncomfortable for him to accept. He had also been put into a state of enforced paralysis so that he didn't move around and knock out the tubes that curl down his throat. My father had called me with the news.

"Dad," I said, "I'm coming to Chicago." When he replied, the sound in his voice suggested to me that he didn't want to be saying this: "I think so."

I left immediately. At the hospital I went up to the seventh floor where the ICU was and saw Judy, Janice, Shayne, and several of Shayne's schoolmates and one of their parents in the family waiting room. Their faces were drawn. Two of Shayne's friends held her hands. It was late, and a school night. I thought it was a warm thing for Shayne's friends to be there with her, and at this hour. My parents were home, unable to be at the hospital since my mother was in bed suffering from agonizing arthritis in her leg and my father was at her side.

"Where's Steve?" I asked. Judy took me down the hall to his ICU room. It was heartbreaking. His unseeing eyes were about three-quarters closed. His hair was very thin, and he looked very pale, paler than I had ever seen him. But he looked like he was resting. I was told he was in no pain. The life-support tube was taped to his mouth. I counted thirteen different machines to which he was hooked up, some of them showing wavy graphs and accompanied by periodic, eerie beeps.

I was told that he was breathing 100 percent from the life support. At this point, he could not live without it.

A doctor named Wolfram talked with me and told me that they were doing everything they could to keep my brother alive. "If only we can get rid of the pneumonia," he said. They were pumping antibiotics and other medicines into him to try to knock out the pneumonia.

I spoke to Steve, though I had no idea whether he could hear me or not. I'm not sure what I said, but it was just something like, "We're all fighting for you, Steve, we all love you. I know it's hard, but don't give up fighting."

His eyeglasses were on the table near him. Good, I thought, when he gets better, he'll have his glasses right there. He would want that.

Two nights later Steve's vital signs were fading, and Judy called me at my parents' home. She asked if I could meet with her and Janice that night in a coffee shop, the three of us with power of attorncy over Steve's life.

It was close to 10 o'clock when we slid into a booth in the restaurant. "It's time," said Janice. She meant, it was time that we let Steve go. Judy nodded. She had lived with all of my brother's suffering—physical and emotional—through all of these months in a way none of the rest of us had. For the last several days she had been sleeping in Janice's lap, too much in pain to crawl into bed. I agreed that tomorrow we would suggest to Dr. Bitran that they begin to remove the life-support from my brother. "From all indications," I said, "Dr. Bitran tomorrow will tell us it is irreversible."

It was wrenching to think it, to say it. It was like the light of hope at the end of the tunnel had been sealed off.

"You know, one of the things I'm saddest about," Judy said, "is that Steven will not be able to enjoy seeing sunsets anymore. He and I used to love that."

The next morning, Saturday, we assembled in the family room of ICU ward for Dr. Bitran to tell us what we assumed would be the inevitable bad news. Vic Ostrow had flown in and was with us. So was Marlene Kaplan, the family friend whose call had pulled me off the plane to Charlotte six weeks earlier.

"Steven," said Dr. Bitran, seated before us, "has shown slight improvement." We were stunned. Was there hope? "His kidney is working a little, his heart appears a little stronger, the infection in his left lung has cleared up from the medication."

Janice asked what this meant. Should we allow Steven to hang on longer? "Yes," replied the doctor.

Someone else inquired about whether there had been brain damage at this point.

Dr. Bitran said we could not know about that until Steve emerged from his coma.

"We don't want him to be a vegetable," someone said.

"Of course, I understand that," the doctor said. "But if we were to take him off life-support now, it would be like executing him."

The comment was stark, and Janice, for one, was taken aback by it. I didn't have a problem with it. This was Dr. Bitran's professional opinion, and he wanted to state it as forcefully as he could.

"Have you ever seen anyone come out of a situation like this?" asked Victor.

"Yes," said Dr. Bitran.

"And lead a normal life?"

"And lead a normal life."

Dr. Bitran said he would increase the dosage of chemotherapy to try further to wipe out the bad blood cells and allow the marrow to build some kind of immune system to combat the pneumonia.

"I feel that Steve is talking to us," I said to the group, after the doctor had left the room. "His body is obviously fighting.

And I know that he had put himself fully in Dr. Bitran's hands, to be as aggressive as possible. Steve only has one life. I think we must continue to carry out Steve's wishes and do what Dr. Bitran thinks is the way to go at this point."

And so it was agreed. We would wait and see.

The end came on Tuesday, May 21. The day before, Dr. Bitran had told us, "Nothing has worked. The few things that had improved are failing again. We are no longer involved in life-saving; it's just life-prolonging."

Dr. Bitran had hoped to be a miracle man. My brother had hoped he would be his miracle man. Instead, he departed sorrowfully, defeated, as we all had been, by an insidious act of nature. Modern medicine, for all its marvels and brilliant practitioners, was unable to vanquish the cancer.

"Stevie has always been such a good boy," my mother said, holding her head. "God doesn't know what he's doing."

This chilling remark stayed with me as I walked over to Shayne, curled up in a chair in a corner of the room. Her eyes were filled with tears. "Shayne," I said, taking hold of her hand, "I know how hard this is for you. This is so hard for all of us. Your dad was a real fighter through all this. And he was such a good father. I think you will remember how lucky all of us were to have had him as long as we did." She nodded, unable to speak. I hoped I hadn't said too much.

In a little while, the machines that had kept Steve breathing would be unplugged. And so it was now unnecessary to wash our hands before going into Steve's room. We saw him alive for the last time. I could still see the whites of his unseeing eyes. His breathing was regular. I held his hand, which felt warm. I told him he had been brave and dignified. I told him he had been a loving brother. I told him again that I loved him.

I kissed him on the forehead good-bye. My parents stood nearby and wept. My mother, her eyes red, held his hand. I could hear my father saying under his breath, "My baby, my baby."

I felt a deep sense of loss and sadness, and also frustration. I thought of how much more my brother and I could have shared—and would have shared, if he had survived this. Barriers had been broken between us. I would have delighted in his offbeat sense of humor and in sharing his joys and his problems, as well. But I was glad that we had come together in the last few months the way we had. And, of course, I had him to thank for that. Judy had told me that Steve, sensing something terrible, had called me because she felt he "wanted to get his house in order." I thought that given another situation like that, I, too, would make a greater effort at conciliation or understanding. In the end the younger brother had taken the role of the older brother and taught me a significant lesson. I hoped I would not soon forget it.

I returned with my parents to their home. Several weeks earlier Steve and Judy had talked openly about the possibility of his death, and Judy had made him a promise that if the end was near, she would be with him when he died, holding his hand.

She called my parents home at about a quarter to one that afternoon. I answered the phone.

"Steven died," she said, "at 12:32."

It was left for me to tell my mother and father the expected and quietly shattering news.

The night before the funeral, I was thinking about what I wanted to say in my eulogy for Steve, and I couldn't sleep. I earned my living as a professional writer, but this kind of writing was different from my general run of columns and articles.

I had always tried to write from deep within in order to capture people. I had always tried to remember Robert Frost's observation: "No tears in the writer, no tears in the reader." So if the writer doesn't truly feel the emotion, the reader won't feel it, either. I didn't have to recall that now. I was living it.

I arose at about 3 A.M. and went into the kitchen and began to take notes on the small yellow notepad used by my parents for telephone messages.

"Writing what you're going to say tomorrow?" It was my father. In pajamas and slippers, his gray hair mussed from sleep, or lack of sleep, he was squinting at me in the light through his glasses. He had seen the kitchen light shining and had gotten up to check it out. He stooped slightly, looking shorter than his normal height of 5-feet-9, about as tall as my brother had been.

"Yes," I said. "Trying to put some thoughts together."

"Will you be able to get through it?"

"I'll have to," I said.

The day of the funeral was miserable in Chicago—rainy and windy. The funeral was scheduled for one o'clock in the afternoon, but people began arriving at 11:30. The immediate family, as is traditional, occupied the front-row seats, and, with Dolly beside me, we greeted people who filed past, extending sympathy.

Soon the chapel was filling up. Steve's friends, his schoolmates, people from far back in his life, arrived. Some of the kids from his school, in shirts and ties, in sweaters, in dress shoes, entered, looking somewhat lost and respectful. Steve's entire eighth-grade class came in, having arrived in a yellow schoolbus. "More of the kids wanted to come," one of the students told me, "but the principal said they couldn't have the whole school empty."

My cousins Ian and Steve Levin and Errol Halperin were

there, of course, along with many of my friends, including
Hershey Carl and Barry Holt and Stuart Menaker and Dick
Brandwein and Rob Sanders. I was moved to see them and
hugged them, giving in to the comforting feeling of affection
that coursed through me.

The chapel was standing room only. Old and young, men
and women, boys and girls, blacks and whites, a slew of reli-
gions. It was wonderful.

The rabbi made some opening remarks and then introduced Janice, who spoke warmly about how Judy and Steve
had met more than a quarter of a century earlier, at a mutual
friend's home, and how over the years they had laughed and
cried and dreamed.

I spoke next. I recalled my brother's seeking of the Lost
Dutchman's legendary treasure in the Superstition Mountains
in Arizona. I began: "My brother never found that treasure,
but he found other treasures: treasures in his work, treasures
in his friends, treasures in his family."

I spoke about the kids in his class and how they had made
a video for him in which one of them had said, "Mr. Berkow,
hurry back, we miss you yelling at us." He yelled at times,
they understood, because he cared. One of the boys in his
class who was at the funeral, Luis Pedraza, told me, "But we
always knew Mr. Berkow was with us."

I talked about how proud Steve was of his daughter,
Shayne, who had made National Honor Society at Niles North
High School and was captain of the girls' tennis team there.
He once told me that during his illness Shayne had been
"magnificent." He said, "She has gone from a seventeen-year-
old kid to a seventeen-year-old woman." And I spoke about
Judy, his wife of twenty-five years. "Steve told her a few weeks
ago, 'You're perfect,' " I told the mourners. "And he meant
every word, and she has been."

As for me, his older brother, I said, "I remember him as a little boy who wore glasses from the time he was two years old. He was someone I felt I had to protect. There was the winter day when he was about six or seven and I was eleven or twelve, and he and his friends were building a snow fort in someone's yard on the West Side. An older boy—older than I, and bigger, too—came by and began to kick in the fort. My brother and his friend began to holler and cry. I was nearby and came to my brother's aid. I pushed the older kid away, and we began to fight. We fought for one full block on Springfield Avenue, from Roosevelt Road to 13th Street, with me backpedaling all the way. And when it was over, and I looked around for my brother, I didn't see him. He had stayed with his friend to rebuild the fort. But as an adult, the tables were sometimes reversed, and he would be supportive of me. He was an astute reader and always encouraging.

"What he was," I concluded, "was a good and blessed and brave man. He never found the Lost Dutchman's Mine, but he found something better. He found happiness, he found love, and he found peace."

About two weeks later I flew back to Chicago to attend Shayne's high school graduation. While I was there, I wrote a sports story for the *Times* as well. It was about Steve Kerr, the Bulls' role player and standout three-point shooter, with whom I had earlier that season talked about driving to the hoop. We now spoke again, a few days before the Bulls would open at home against Seattle in the first game of the NBA finals, but part of our conversation had to do with family, his and mine. I told him about my brother, and about Shayne. I thought he could relate to her, since Steve Kerr's father had also died tragically, and suddenly.

At three o'clock in the morning on January 19, 1984, Steve

Kerr was awakened by the ringing of the telephone in his dormitory room, at the University of Arizona, where he was a freshman and substitute player on the basketball team.

The caller was a family friend. "Your father's been shot," he said.

"Is he OK?" asked Kerr, suddenly wide awake.

There was a pause. "Your father," said the caller, "was a good man."

With that, the young Steve Kerr broke down sobbing.

Malcolm H. Kerr was fifty-one and the president of the American University of Beirut when two unidentified gunmen fired two bullets into his head while he was walking to his office. Shortly thereafter, a male caller telephoned a newspaper office there and said that the slaying was the work of Islamic militants. The gunmen had made Dr. Kerr a symbol of the American presence in Lebanon. He left a wife and four children, Steve being the youngest.

My brother and Steve Kerr's father were the same age when they died. Shayne and Steve Kerr were the same age, eighteen, when their fathers died.

What can one say to Shayne? I asked him. "Only that time passes," said Kerr. "And you have to go on and live your life the best you can. It's what any parent would want. But it is always with you. I think of my dad just about every day. He was a big basketball fan. I know he would have tried to come to all my games." He smiled. "He would have been a regular on the Beirut-to-Chicago shuttle."

A few days later, after a shoot-around in the late morning, I saw Kerr at the Bulls' practice site. I had told him previously that Shayne was graduating that night, and with honors. And that I would be a kind of substitute father to her, since her father had been buried less than two weeks earlier. Steve Kerr remembered.

"It's going to be kind of bittersweet tonight, isn't it?" he said. I said yes, it is.

And it was. I sat with the family as we watched Shayne, pretty and grown up in her white graduation gown and blue mortarboard with the yellow tassel, as opposed to the standard blue one, signifying her membership in the National Honor Society.

"Steve would have been so proud," my mother said, bringing a handkerchief to her eyes.

And he would have been proud a week later when the graduation ceremony at Yates School was dedicated to him.

Judy and Shayne were invited there as honored guests, and, onstage, against the backdrop of burnished-gold drapes, each received a bouquet of roses. Upon hearing of Steve's death, a boy in his class in Room 118 had taken down the American flag in the classroom and folded it up. At the graduation he presented the flag to Judy.

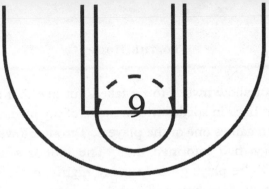

To the Hoop

I hadn't played basketball in several weeks, though I had occasionally done some jogging. I had put aside the pursuit of a passion in my life while my brother was in the last, deadly phase of his struggle to hold on to life. Now I returned to the courts in New York, and primarily the school-yard games at the New York University Medical Center.

On this warm June day there was no one on the court. An adjacent building cast a shadow over half of the full court, and I chose the basket on the sunny half, as a kind of affirmation of life, a bow to my brother, who, as Judy had said sadly, would never again experience the pleasure of watching the sun set.

Within a half hour three more players had shown up, and soon we were in a two-on-two game. They were a nice bunch and pretty good players. It felt good to feel the basketball again, to shoot it, to try to make a move off a defender. I hit a jump shot, missed another. I got faked out, and I felt a shiver of embarrassment but also of competitiveness. That not only would I not allow myself to be faked out like that again, but I'd get him back in spades with a move of my own.

Between games one of the players, Tyrone Flowers, a clerk in radiology, had informed me, "The indoor schedule has changed. We're playing on Monday nights instead of Tuesdays," he said. "Look to seein' ya."

One of the joys of pickup basketball is to be chosen in the games, even when some of the players, like Tyrone, are thirty years younger and also of a different race. Basketball was the bridge that spanned our different experiences.

More players soon showed up, and the intensity of the games increased.

An argument arose over the score.

"It's 5–4," one guy said.

"It's 5–5," said another.

"He goes to school and he still don't know how to count," the first guy said. "Countin' backwards."

"C'mon," said a third. "Play y'all."

Somehow, after what had been going on for the last few weeks in Chicago, even a dispute like this was a pleasure.

The routine of my life, meanwhile, returned off the court as well—family and friends, work and recreation, though the specter of Steve's death was often in my mind. He was so young, really, with so much more to live for and so much to give. It wasn't fair. But I felt that for myself I would try to do more with my life, whatever that might be. And, as silly as it might have seemed, one thing was to continue to become a better basketball player, which included driving more to the hoop. Who knows, I told Dolly with a laugh, it might even make me a better person.

I flew back to Chicago in late June to look in on my parents. Fortunately, they had a network of friends who helped ease some of their pain. But none of it, understandably, was easy. My mother had found a photograph of Steve and me, with my arm around his shoulder, which had been taken a few years earlier. She told me she loved that picture. "You both look so good," she said. What she meant, I thought, was that the picture showed us in an affectionate pose. She had had the picture framed and placed it on the coffee table in the living room.

Before returning to Chicago, I had called Stuart Menaker, my friend and old high school teammate. We had discussed playing one-on-one again, as we had so many times when we were kids, and we agreed to play when I came in on this trip.

Stuart had recently retired as the head basketball coach at Schurz High School on the North Side of Chicago. He had won 350 games in twenty-three years as the varsity coach there, but his career ended in a bizarre incident in 1993, when one of his players, a 6-foot-3-inch senior forward named Desean Watson, made menacing gestures to him in the parking lot after a game—even though Stuart was going to drive that player and a few others to the elevated train for their journey home. A scuffle ensued, and here the stories diverged. Watson filed battery charges against Stuart, charging that Stuart had hit him with a golf club for no reason. Stuart asserted that he was defending himself from rocks thrown by Watson as he was placing equipment in the trunk of his car and had just grabbed a golf club that was there.

The fact that the players were all black and Stuart white made this a national story: white coach beats up black player. I had heard about the incident from friends in Chicago, and then read about it in the New York papers and *USA Today*. It did not sound like the Stuart Menaker I knew.

I do know that changing times and attitudes had affected him—discipline was slipping; players and students talked back and cursed him and other teachers; he had problems keeping his players from being tardy to practice or not showing up or dropping out of school. Although I hadn't spoken to him in several years, I called to see how he was. "Terrible," he said. "The *Chicago Tribune* printed my address, and the television cameras and the reporters are all over my lawn and up and down the street. Jackie and I have to crawl around on our knees to avoid being seen in the windows."

Stuart said he was innocent. Sure, he had been on Desean's case because he could have tried so much harder, been so much better. "But I just couldn't get anything out of him," said Stuart. "And he has talent. That's the really sad part. I had taken him out of the game and he was mad about it." Ironically, Stuart and his wife Jackie had befriended several of the players, regularly having them to their home for dinner, including Watson. "The neighbors used to look out the window at thise group of black kids coming over our house," Stuart had told me, "and they were nervous."

After a six-and-a-half-hour bench trial, the judge found Stuart not guilty. Watson's testimony was contradicted by that of several eyewitnesses, while Stuart drew significant support from his principal, other teachers, and students. But he was scarred by the experience. He quit coaching. He sought and received a transfer from Schurz to another high school, where he became a student counselor.

While he was at Schurz, Stuart had still played in practice sessions with his team when a tenth man was needed. And, he said, he more than held his own. He was still in decent shape, still playing ball on occasion, though spending more time in a gym with weights and light jogging. I now phoned Stuart to let him know I was in town and to find out whether he would be available to play the next day.

He said he was.

"But," he said, "I haven't played in a while."

"Yeah," I said, "and the next thing you're going to say is, 'Do you want to play for money?' "

"No, no," he protested, with that great laugh of his crackling across the telephone wires.

Later that day I visited my brother's grave site. It had been about a month since he was buried, and the plot where he lay was covered with dirt. The grass had not yet had time to grow. There was a simple marker—a larger one would be put down in a few months—which read, S. BERKOW. It was all still so unbelievable. I began to choke up.

A pot of flowers sat beside the grave, placed there by Judy and Shayne a day earlier. I had made a copy of a photograph from a sports magazine and now took it from my pocket and placed it in a crevice of the grave. It was a picture of Paavo Nurmi running a race.

Stuart picked me up at my parents' apartment, and when I got in beside him in the front seat of his gray Pontiac Grand Prix, it felt as if the years had melted away. I was grateful, though, that I was not sitting in the Menaker family's green 1953 Pontiac, in which the steering wheel would sometimes come off in Stuart's hand as he made a turn. This car seemed to have the steering wheel screwed on tightly to the column, which was a nice touch.

Stuart and I had always played intense, competitive games and were rather physical with each other. We had had a natural rivalry, being about the same height and weight, playing the same position, and being just two months apart in age. We had also been the closest of friends in high school, teammates in baseball and basketball, double-dating through nearly four years, going on vacations together, living nearby, and visiting

each other's home as regularly as we did the refrigerator–
which was quite often.

When I was playing ahead of him in basketball, in frosh-
soph, Stuart later told me, I had become his motivation to improve: he was going to be better than I.

And when he began playing more minutes than I did in
varsity basketball when we were juniors, even though I started
the games, he became a miserable thorn to me.

But through all that our friendship remained as fierce as
our rivalry. And we started together at guard as seniors.

Now, he was wearing a white T-shirt, blue shorts, and low-
cut white basketball shoes. Stuart had grown substantially
broader than when we played in high school, and he was lifting weights. He now wore glasses, his hair was streaked with
gray, and there was a small patch of baldness at his crown. If
not for his new muscles, he might have looked professorial. I
wore a T-shirt and my maroon nylon sweat pants. I told him
about my knee with the severed ACL. "I always wear long
pants when I play to cover up my brace," I said. "I guess it has
something to do with vanity; with gray sideburns and an obvious look of middle age, I don't want to look even older."

"It's a good idea to cover it up because if some guys see a
weakness, they'll give you a whack there," said the coach, who
is accustomed to looking for an edge.

"I hadn't thought of that," I said.

"Which knee did you say it was?" He turned to me with a
kind of diabolical smile.

I laughed. I knew he was kidding. Maybe.

The day before I had driven around the North Side and
the northern suburbs checking out hoops. Some baskets were
too high, or the court was slanted, or there were no nets. I saw
one that I liked, but Stuart said he had another court in mind
that would be just right. It was in a little park on the North

Side called Paschen Park, on Lunt and Damen Avenues, a few blocks from where my parents lived.

There were two baskets, and one was occupied by two players. When we arrived, they asked us to play two-on-two. But Stuart and I had other plans.

"This is a grudge match," he told them with a smile, referring to himself and me. "Maybe later."

It was a good court with a firm basket, and Stuart had wisely chosen a place that had some shade. The leaves of a large, lush maple tree covered half the court from the sun that on this late morning was already hot. The temperature was close to 90 degrees. We warmed up slowly, starting with lefty and righty layups around the basket, then moving out for jump shots. I squinted into the sun, which was at our backs, and I was thankful that my left eye, which had been banged up with those "hanging threads" while playing with Barry Holt, had healed almost completely.

Stuart and I settled on the same rules by which we used to play: 11 baskets wins, by ones, and if you make the shot, you take the ball again—it's called winner's out or "make it, take it."

I hit my first shot, missed a few after that, and then I hit a few in a row. I went ahead in the first game, but he was on his game, hitting from middle distance. He had a favorite move when we were kids and still had it. He dribbles and then stops and throws a head fake while never giving up the dribble. He anticipates that his man will jump for the hesitation fake, and he'll go around him. I had seen that move too many times and remembered it too clearly to be faked by it. He would have to try something else. Which he did. He came back to win.

Our games, it seemed, hadn't really changed that much in all these years, except for our having gotten slower and, one hopes, a little more canny and a little less physical. He won the second game, too, but he seemed to be laboring a bit. The games were, as always, hard fought, but neither of those games was as close as I had hoped to make them, much less a victory.

And Stuart still drove well, with superb body control—a kind of body control that I never possessed—hanging for a moment and drawing a foul, and sometimes banking the ball off the backboard for a basket. And he could still make long one-handers and jumpers.

And now I was trying to drive more than I ever had with only moderate success. I got inside, but he was there. And I had to spin for a shot or fade away. And not everything went in.

We played relatively quietly, being so concentrated. It was like a chess match. Very little talking, few "Oh shits," but an ample number of simple grunts. We were both deeply involved in the game. And since we both respected the other's knowledge of the game, we called no fouls—you call your own fouls in such games—because there were no hard, or intentional, fouls. It was more or less no harm, no foul.

I won the next two games.

"Can you go another?" I asked.

"Sure," he said. "The rubber game." This was to decide our minichampionship.

In the fifth game the score was 1–1, and he had the ball on the side. He made a fake, I slapped him on the arm, but he still got the shot off, all right.

"I'm going to have to take that one," he said.

It was the first foul called that morning. Things obviously were heating up.

He proceeded to hit six straight shots from beyond the high school three-point circle that had been painted on the concrete court. I pushed him back a little, but I couldn't get too close because I could no longer defend his drive to the basket any other way.

Stuart finally missed. I got the ball back, and I did make a little flurry of a comeback—including a left-handed driving hook across the lane—but the game was soon out of reach. Stuart beat me 11–6.

We both were drenched with sweat from the intensity of the morning's heat and from our effort. And as we leaned against the park's wire fence, we toweled ourselves off.

"I thought you were finished after the fourth game," I said. "You weren't killing yourself on loose balls."

"I was trying to conserve my energy," he said. "I knew it was going five games."

Later, I had some suspicion that he had eased up in the third and fourth games, the games I had won, but then I remembered him calling that foul in the fifth game—an act of determination—and reconsidered. My suspicion was further alleviated when he told me that when I was on offense, he tried to angle me into the half of the court that was sunny to try to tire me out a little more. Ever the coach, I thought.

And ever the aging athlete. "My hips and back hurt," he said afterward. "I'm going home and taking Tylenol."

But we had had a beautiful time. It was a remembrance of things past, but remarkably we were still able to re-create a semblance of it. And without animosity. Two old friends participating in an activity that had drawn them tightly together forever but had also retained the tartness of old rivalry.

When he pulled up to my parents' apartment house to drop me off, we shook hands good-bye. I wanted to hug him—but he was still kind of sweaty. I told him I was going to mention these games to some of our friends.

"Who should I say won?" I asked.

Stuart smiled. "Let your conscience be your guide," he said.

Thinking about those games, I decided that even now, as

adults, he seemed to need the conquest more than I did. Perhaps he felt he should win. After all, he had devoted his life as a coach to the playing of the game, while I was a sportswriter, supposedly a sedentary observer. And maybe he was still going to prove that he was better than I—as he had done when we were boys. I thought I saw that intensity in his eyes. I felt it as he barreled to the basket. That's why he won, I was convinced—that and the fact that still, after all these years, he had more talent than I did.

But I was feeling relaxed about hoops. Oscar had helped open new possibilities and confidence for me, and so did my games with Barry Holt. And of course Stuart had helped tap a reservoir of youth. And kinship. Even brotherhood.

I felt ready to make a return to a place that had never left the back of my mind, a place that to me represented a certain frustration and vexation.

Yes, I would go head to head with Laguna Beach.

A few weeks later, as I dressed to go to a Broadway play with Dolly, I informed her that I had purchased a cheapie weekend airline ticket to Los Angeles, got a cheapie weekend rate at a hotel near Laguna Beach and, because of car rental certificates through my frequent flier program, I could rent a car free for the weekend. I was going back. I wanted to prove that I could play better there than I did the last time, six months earlier.

"You're not really going to do this," she said, at dinner in a neighborhood Italian restaurant. She remembered the funk I had been in after that one disaster of a game I had played on that gorgeous Laguna Beach court.

"I am," I said. "It's something I feel I have to do."

"But why?"

"I don't know. Stupidity, I guess."

"Hmm," she said, mulling that one over.

"I remember once interviewing Kurt Vonnegut after he had just had a book of his panned in the New York press. He said it made him feel like a bad neighbor. He was feeling as though he had committed some unfriendly act and hoped his next book would cause people look at him with kindlier eyes."

"Do you think you committed some kind of basketball transgression?"

I had to laugh—a low, bitter kind of laugh. "I guess, yeah, in a way I'm going back to the scene of the crime." I knew I wouldn't be playing with the same group of guys—I had no idea who I'd be playing with—but just for myself. What did I want to do? Redeem myself? Reclaim a certain sense of self? Make atonement? Seek vindication? Get revenge? Maybe all of the above. Or maybe there was nothing more to it than just seeking to change my mental vision of that dream basketball court and turn it into something cheerful and not, as it had become, a bleak experience.

"What happens if you play poorly again?" Dolly asked.

"Then I play poorly, and I go on with my life."

"You do?" she said.

"Well, maybe."

She looked at me with what I took to be a combination of sorrow and pity in her beautiful brown eyes. Then, contemplatively, I swirled a forkful of linguini and stuck it in my mouth.

I toted my knee brace on board the airplane with me, in a carrying bag with my basketball. I didn't want to chance having the brace banged around by luggage handlers, especially after Dolly had brought it in to be rehabbed. The Velcro had begun to lose its stickiness, and a patch of foam had mysteriously disappeared from a little wheel contraption that fits into the right side of the knee. So Dolly had taken the brace to an of-fice on 57th Street where such devices are made whole again—it is like an emergency room for knee braces and other orthotics.

On the plane my mind focused on the various things I wanted to remember when I got to the court. I wanted to play more aggressively, from the very first throw-in of the game. I thought about the guy on my team the last time saying, "Go strong!"

I wanted to remember to have that good snap of the wrist when I shot and to arc the ball instead of releasing it flat.

I wanted to remember to get up close on my man on de-fense, because one basket in a short game could make the dif-ference between winning and losing, between staying on the court for more games and waiting a long, long time for next.

I wanted to remember that when I drive, I should stay low on my drive. I think that as I get older, I get stiffer, and the flexibility that I once possessed is not quite there anymore. But I know I could get still lower on my the drive, as Michael Jordan does, but I'd have to concentrate.

For light reading on the plane, I took along Larry Bird's how-to book, *Bird on Basketball*, which I had only recently ac-quired; my ancient copy of Red Auerbach's *Basketball for the Player, the Fan and the Coach*, which has made the cut every place I've moved, and a copy of my unconventional collabora-tion with Walt Frazier, *Rockin' Steady*. I say "unconventional" because the book includes not only Clyde's basketball stats but also his wardrobe stats, such as his forty-nine suits (one was made of goatskin), fifty kicks, and eighteen lids; and, since he was believed to have hands so fast that he could catch flies, we had diagrams of him catching flies while they were in a sitting position as well as in midair.

As in writing—or catching flies—technique in basketball is

paramount. Bird's advice on outside shooting is to aim at the basket with your shooting elbow. I had never heard that one before, though some coaches advise trying to "stick your hand" in the basket on the shot while others say to aim with your forefinger. I just aimed at the front rim, tried to put an arc on the ball, and let fly. I like Bird's notion because the technique helps to keep your elbow close to your chest, which is better than having it hang out. I practiced it before leaving, but it felt slightly awkward. I thought I would keep it in mind anyway.

Bird, after all, was one of the best players I had ever seen. "You couldn't stop him," Magic Johnson once told me. "You did this, he'd do that. Inside, he has too many moves, and outside he could get the shot away so fast, and it was dead accurate."

I also recalled what Bob Woolf, Bird's agent, had told me about Bird the perfectionist. "One time I walked into Boston Garden with him, and as we walked across the old parquet court, he threw himself to the floor," Woolf said. "Then he did it again. I was amazed. I asked what he was doing. He said he was just checking for dead spots, so he'd know where they were when he was guarding a dribbler, or dribbling himself." I felt there were only certain things I myself would do in the name of playing a better basketball game, and throwing myself on the cement court at Laguna was not one of them. For a moment I worried that I might not be hungry enough, but then I decided that a broken arm in pursuit of a dead spot would not be beneficial to my game.

One of Bird's great skills was knowing how to handle himself in a variety of situations. I once asked him, for example, what it was like going back to his hometown, French Lick, Indiana, after his rookie season in the NBA with the Boston Celtics in 1980. Bird had played high school basketball in

French Lick and had played college ball at Indiana State in nearby Terre Haute. This was actually his first time living for any period of time away from Indiana. And he had set the NBA on its ear, turning the Celtics from a mediocrity into one of the league's strongest teams. Bird was one of the league's top scorers and rebounders and was named Rookie of the Year. He was on the cover of numerous national magazines, including *Sports Illustrated*.

"When I came back to French Lick," he told me, "I went to the pool room where all my buddies hung out. I walked through the door, and they looked up and saw me. They didn't say anything. As I walked closer, I realized that they were waiting for me to say something first, to see if I had changed. I stopped, looked 'em over, and said, 'How ya doin', assholes?' That broke the ice. They knew I was the same."

My in-flight tutorial continued with Auerbach. Here he is on driving to the hoop: "Keep your weight forward, knees bent, and abdomen inward." The weight forward part, and even the abdomen inward part, come fairly naturally. But it's the knees being bent that becomes harder as one ages. But I would try to remember it, as well as another piece of instruction from Auerbach on the drive that I believed crucial: "The first bounce after a fake should be a long one."

I have been guilty of short to normal first bounces after a fake.

And I checked Frazier on driving to remind myself of what I had helped him write. Clyde said, "The first move must be explosive." He recommended that one should dribble about "knee-high or a little higher." He said, "You can practice this by letting a little air out of your ball so that it doesn't bounce as high. You could let out two pounds of a standard nine-pound ball." Why hadn't I reread Clyde's book earlier? If I had spent a week practicing my dribble, I'd be in better shape than I was now. But now, well, I knew it was too late to form a new habit.

I thumbed through *Rockin' Steady* for some other pointers. On shooting the hook shot, Frazier said, "I never could shoot a hook shot." And we had left it at that. But I remember his advice on defense: "Everyone has a certain rhythm that he dribbles to." We are creatures of habit, whether we admit or understand it or not. And what is a part of our nature off the court—when we are being faithful to our tendencies—will hold true on the court.

Over the years I've covered and written and read about people in sports who made comebacks, who avenged previous defeats or embarrassments and regained a sense of self. But in the entire history of sports, I'm not sure there was anyone who sought vengeance quite the way Boo Morcom sought vengeance.

Richmond (Boo) Morcom finished sixth in the pole vault at the 1948 Olympics in London after having been the favorite and having broken the world record in the Olympic trials. He had suffered a knee injury shortly before the Olympics, and on the day of the event, it rained heavily, creating a wet track. "I was shattered when I came in sixth," Boo told me years later. "Vaulting was my life." Since he was too embarrassed to return home to New Hampshire, he arranged his own post-Olympic tour, visiting each foreign athlete who had beaten him, challenging him man-to-man, and toppling each one.

In the process Boo became the first man to vault over 14 feet above the Arctic circle when, wearing two pairs of long johns, he beat the silver-medal-winning Finn. And Boo overcame a problem in Norway when his man was in jail awaiting trial on a drunk-and-disorderly charge. Boo dug into his own pocket, bailed out the competitor, whipped him, and then left for Sweden to knock off the next guy.

"I got the idea of going into the backyards of the guys who beat me and beating them. It was evil pride combined with a grand passion," Boo said. "Two Americans were first and third, but they knew they were lucky that day, and besides I had beaten them many times before. So nothing to prove."

After beating the Norwegian, the Swede, and the Finn, Boo was invited to the house of the Finn, Erkki Kataja. "By this time," Boo recalled, "everybody in Europe was calling me the world's champ. I went to this kid's house and met his grandmother. She went to the cupboard and brought out his Olympic silver medal. She asked to see my Olympic medal. She didn't realize I didn't have one. That really put me in my place. I laughed. It showed what kind of bastard I was. But it was beautiful. I could beat him, but I couldn't beat that."

I took some inspiration from Boo Morcom's determination, but still I had anxiety. It's amazing how much pressure one can put on oneself. I was going to a place to participate in a little recreational sport. That essentially was it, right? No one knew who I was. No one cared. This was hardly the finals of the NBA or the NCAA or even a park league. I was just going to be out there on a pleasant Sunday for some carefree fun. If anyone had the slightest idea that this guy—graying at the sideburns, of more-or-less average size, wearing sweatpants in the California heat, who might appear to these other, younger players as being perhaps a shade this side of shuffleboard competition—had flown 3,000 miles to avenge one lousy half-court game six months earlier, why, they might have called the paramedics to get my head examined.

On the other hand, the other guys would want to win, to keep the court, to prove something to themselves and others—you do that every time you're in a game. I liked to think that this was just a microcosm of life itself. And I imagined that those in the game in Laguna were of the same general ilk as I—even if they only traveled from a few blocks or a few miles away, and not from East 30th Street in Manhattan.

I rented a car, motored down the coast, and took a hotel room in Newport Beach, about a ten-minute drive from the basketball court at Laguna Beach. It was a Saturday morning in July, and I wanted to get in a day's practice at the courts there in order to get a feel for the environment—the liveliness of the rims, the deadness of the backboards, a sense of the court's surface. I wanted to feel as comfortable as I could for the big games—I hoped there would be more than one—on Sunday.

It was a typically beautiful Southern California day, sunny and mild, with little breeze to speak of, which still struck me as odd as it did the last time I was here, since the court was so close to the ocean. But as a guy whose game primarily is to shoot from the outside, I had no complaints. The sailboats were plying the ocean, bathers lolled on the beach, and the basketball players toiled, scraped, and grunted on the court. The two half-courts at the Main Beach Park looked as beautiful as I had remembered, the even surface painted blue with white foul lanes and three-point circles.

The atmosphere was more casual than I had remembered, and the games were not quite at the level I recalled. Sunday, it was clear, was the high octane day, when the best players showed up, and the crowds came in their beach chairs and rimmed the court. For me then, Saturday, would just be the warmup.

And I was happy for it. There were two games being played that day on both of the baskets. The half-court games at Laguna are customarily four-on-four. You call your own fouls, games are to 11 baskets, and it's winner's out, with winners staying on the court until they lose—or, as in the case of Bill Walton's quartet, until they suffer exhaustion.

I missed some shots, I hit some. I was guarding a player who was about 6-foot-6, some six inches taller than I. He was the biggest man on the court, and he scored and scored again. I tried to belly him away from the basket, and I tried to bother him by poking at the ball when he held it. He scored again. One of the players on my team hollered to me, "C'mon, stop him." I said, "He's not going around me—he's going over me! How about some help!" Someone else hollered, "Switch." This is always disheartening, since the feeling is that you can't stick your man. I reluctantly but silently switched. And the 6–6 guy scored again, off a new defender. I turned to the guy who was now guarding him and who had hollered to me "Switch" and shot him a look. The look said, "OK, dick-nose."

We won some games, and I was starting to look pretty good, I thought. My confidence was rising, and I hit my jumpers. On one play I faked the shot and drove the baseline. I wanted to practice the drive because it would be the center-piece of my comeback.

I got the step on my defender, and when I went up for the shot, he went up, too, and hammered me into the pole sup-porting the backboard. But the cord that tied the padding on the pole had become loose and the padding had slumped; when I hit the pole I hit all iron. I fell to the ground, and some guys came over to see if I was hurt. I thought I had bruised my shoulder, but I was all right, and I shook it off.

After one of our games, the guy guarding me, someone named Iggy, who looked to be in his early twenties, came over and said, "You torched me for ninety per cent of the points."

I smiled. "Friendly rims," I said.

"When guys see some gray hair, they don't think you can

play," he said. I imagined he was talking about that switch. "But I have an uncle about your age, and he still plays and plays pretty good, too."

"How old do you think I am?" I asked.

"Fifty-four, fifty-five," he said.

"Fifty-six," I replied. This was a little disturbing for me. I have imagined that people look at me and think I'm younger than I am. I also know that many young people can't tell if someone is thirty-five or fifty-five. But Iggy could. My guess is that like most people, I don't see myself the way others see me. And when I've seen obviously older guys on the court, I expect less from them. Their bodies aren't as flexible. They aren't as quick to get to balls as others. They grab a helluva lot more. But I wasn't one of those—or was I? And yet if you can hold your own, what difference does gray hair at the sideburns make, anyway? The trick, of course, is to hold your own.

I thought of a fifty-year-old woman I know who wants to look like a twenty-year-old, wants to hang on to her youth. She wears miniskirts, but the texture of her thighs gives her away, though she is unaware of it. But if she'd drop her hem to her knees she'd still turn heads, but for the right reasons. When she went into the hospital for a life-threatening operation, she called a close friend at three in the morning and said, "If I die, don't you dare tell the newspapers my age for the obituaries!"

She later admitted to me that she was "in denial." Some go gracefully, some go raging. Which for me?

But neither grace nor rage were topics for me to think about now. I was in the throes of seeking my atonement. Philosophy was out. Physicality was all. I had worked up a good sweat, departed on a positive note and treated myself to a terrific ice-blended mocha coffee with a dollop of whipped cream on top. I then drove back to my hotel.

I wanted to rest, eat a careful dinner, get a good night's sleep, and be primed and ready for the next morning. For The Game. There was a Mexican restaurant across from the hotel, and while I like Mexican food, I thought that anything spicy might disturb my sleep. I decided that chicken burritos would be okay. I also like Margaritas. Well, one wouldn't hurt, would it? On the rocks and no salt, please. I cooled it on the salsa and chips. Then I went to an early movie, and saw *Striptease* with Demi Moore. If my sleep was going to be disturbed, it was going to be because of Demi Moore, and not the Margarita.

I slept well. I had wanted to get up early and be one of the first to get to the courts. I'd been told that guys show up by 8 A.M., so I phoned the front desk for a wake-up call for 6:45. When I woke up the digital clock in my room said 6:40. I lay there until 6:45. But there was no wake-up call. I was lucky to get up when I did, I thought. And I was miffed. Well, I figured, you can't rely on wake-up calls. I should have brought an alarm clock.

I did stretching exercises, concentrating on my back— which has a tendency on occasion to stiffen up—and my legs. Especially my right leg, the one with the bad knee. Then I soaked myself in a warm bath. My friend Charlie Miron had told me that a sauna or hot bath or shower loosens the muscles. I didn't want to jump into a game cold as I had done six months earlier.

Next, I shaved lightly. I don't like the looks of a salt-and-pepper sprinkle of whiskers when I'm playing with younger players. It makes a guy not only look like an old fart but also a scruffy old fart. Maybe even a homeless one. One must take pride.

After I'd been up for about an hour, the phone rang. It was my wake-up call! I couldn't believe this! An hour late? What kind of service was this, anyway? Then I looked at the digital clock. Did it read 6:45? I put on my reading glasses. It *was* 6:45. Damn. I'd made a mistake. I had awakened at 5:45! I guess I had been anxious.

I went to the lobby, where they served coffee, poured myself a cup and took it back to my room, where I ate half a blueberry muffin that I had bought the evening before. Anything more would make me logy. Anything less would make me weak.

Then I strapped on my brace, pulled on my sweatpants, laced up my sneakers, stuffed my ball in my bag, and went out the door. This was it.

The morning was gray and a little cool. But I knew that once it broke, it would be fine. On the drive down Pacific Coast Highway, I noticed the palm trees. They hardly moved. Good. I didn't want a wind playing tricks with my jump shot. As I came upon Main Beach Park, I saw the courts and noticed that there were already some players on it. It was 8:30. I noticed something else, something that concerned me. On both courts lay small puddles of water.

Wet spots on the court. This made me nervous, for two reasons. One, you might take a dribble and the ball splashes but doesn't come back up. The other is, you could get hurt. I had a close friend who played tennis on an outdoor court somewhat slick from a rain the night before, and he slipped and broke his hip. I wasn't going to go to the hoop on a court like that. I had come 3,000 miles to play on a perfect court, and it was blemished. But I had no choice. I had to play. I wasn't going home. Not now.

I parked the car and walked to the courts. Shooting around with the other players, I was told that it hadn't rained the night before, but that the puddles were the result of an accumulation of dew. "It'll evaporate in a while," one guy said. "No problem."

He was right. The sun came out, the water nearly disappeared. By now we had enough players for a game and chose up sides. My team consisted of a red-haired guy and a black guy, both about six feet tall, and a white guy named Eric who was about seven feet tall. He looked to be in his early twenties and had decent moves to the basket and a good touch on his hooks and on jump shots from 15 to 20 feet out. He was a good seven or eight inches taller than our opponent's tallest man. We won the first game. More guys came. Different players. We won the second game, and the third and the fourth.

There were the usual arguments.

"Steps!"

"No way steps!"

"You walked like a train!" The thought instantly flashed through my mind that a train runs. Did you ever wait on a platform and check your watch and say, "The train is walking late"? But I didn't have time to mull this one over. Someone threw the ball in, and play resumed.

Then something was said that made me wince. The ball went out of bounds, and the two guys closest to it just looked at each other. Neither moved to retrieve the ball that had bounced onto the grassy area.

"Your team's ball," said one. "You the one to get it. You like an old man."

"Hey," said the other, "*you* the one like a thirty-five-year-old."

Thirty-five and an old man? I said nothing. The ball was eventually retrieved.

Now the area around the court was beginning to look like the picnic grounds that I had remembered from the last time I was here. Players and their girlfriends or spouses and children, as well as kibitzers and other spectators started to ring the court. They brought colorful sun umbrellas, blankets to lie on, coolers, beach chairs, radios. Some sat on the stationery wooden benches along the walk beside the sandy beach.

I was playing OK. I hit several shots in a row, and a player from the other team said, "Lights out!" when I popped another. I also shot an airball that I couldn't believe I shot. And I let my man drive the baseline on me and score. I looked up and saw Eric turning his head away with what I perceived to be an expression of disdain.

We were playing a team with a good-size guy with a green basketball shirt who was guarding Eric. When one of our players drove, he swatted the ball onto the grass. Another time a teammate of mine took a fadeaway from the side. "Better shoot that fadeaway," said green shirt. "Keep that shit outta here."

I had tried to drive and wound up having to try a hook shot, which missed the mark. I was still smarting a little from the drive the day before in which I wound up being smeared onto the pole like a stick of butter, but I wanted to make a legitimate drive, with a finish. If not a flourish. I wasn't about to punctuate a drive with a dunk. But maybe I could get in there and pump fake and lay it sweetly off the boards like Hershey used to, or Clyde or Magic. It was what I had envisioned doing for the last six months—the perfect ending to this cross-country journey.

And then at the top of the key I faked a pass to the right, and my man moved to his left. He was off balance, and before me I saw nothing but open space! I started to drive. It was incredible. It was as though there was no one else on the court. I didn't know where green shirt was, and didn't think about it. The Catcher in the Rye whose job was to protect the basket had vanished.

I was on the left side of the basket and driving left-handed.

And looming ahead of me, inviting me, was that beautiful rim and net. I swept in as cool and lovely as could be and took off for the easy layup. I was on the left side and so naturally laid it up left-handed. It was a shot I had practiced hundreds—thousands—of times. A piece of cake. A step-in.

And I missed it!

The ball caromed off the backboard, bounced on the front rim, hung for just a moment, and then fell away. I jumped for the rebound. By now the other players had regrouped, and I was not alone. I didn't get the rebound. In fact, I had fallen to the ground and felt stupid down there. When I rose, I felt some hot stares at my back from my teammates, though I might have been imagining it.

I sulked to myself. I had taken off for the layup on my right leg, the one with the brace. But I couldn't blame my damaged knee for my not sinking the shot. Fact was, I hadn't extended my arm high enough. That was the problem. I knew it immediately. I could just envision a slightly bent elbow as I shot the ball. My arm should have been straight as a string. It was the way Itzhak Perlman had described Reggie Jackson's swing at the plate and his own movement with the bow. Extension, extension, extension!

When, a short time later, I grabbed a rebound and banked in a shot, and Eric said, "Good take," I still hadn't got over that missed layup.

This was our sixth straight game, and we lost, 11–9. I wasn't thrilled. I felt I could have helped my team more.

"You were on fire," said Eric. "Nice game."

I felt he meant it, and I felt better about it. We chatted briefly. He told me he had just graduated from the University of New Hampshire and had played there. Out of curiosity and journalistic instinct, I later called the school to find out what his career was like.

I was told that he was from Newport Beach and that he was a five-year "project." He hadn't started until late in his senior year, on a team that wound up only with 5 wins against 16 losses. I was told he might play in Europe. I thought Eric was still learning the game, and perhaps his best days were ahead of him. But I liked playing with him on those courts, and winning. While it doesn't ensure victory, it is of substantial help to have a coordinated seven-footer on your team. And you definitely get a better sweat playing as a winner than watching as a loser.

Eric went to a lawn chair he had brought and sat down at courtside. It appeared he might play again. But I was through for the day. It was sunny and hot now, and my white shirt was nearly black with sweat. I had helped my team win some games. I had played decently.

And I had driven to the hoop! But I still missed the shot. I know in my heart that I will make that drive some other time. That is, I will try to make that drive some other time. Life, I knew, is not a lyric series of fulfillments. I hadn't run away from the challenge but had met it head on. Someone once said that true pleasure comes not in the winning but in the striving. Yes, of course. But dammit, I lusted to make that layup.

I gathered up my ball and bag, tugged on a baseball cap, and departed the court. I left with a decidedly lighter step than I had six months earlier.

As I left the court, I saw that the little guy named Jude had arrived. He was the fellow who had picked me on his team the last time I played here, only to be bitterly disappointed at my performance. And the team's quick exit: one game and gone.

"Hey, Dude," he said to someone nearby. He high-fived him with his right hand, and someone else with his left. Jude wore dark glasses, and his hair had been dyed a more neon blond than when I had last seen him. He wore a mustache and goatee and a silver earring on each ear.

He looked my way but didn't seem to recognize me. I wasn't unhappy about that. Old mortifications die hard.

Epilogue

I heard a siren from an ambulance headed to the emergency ward of the hospital. And there was the rumble and honk and exhaust emissions of the cars on the F.D.R. Drive, as well as a foghorn from a boat on the East River. The sun was slowly dipping behind a building at the New York University Medical Center, and I sat against the wire fence waiting for next at the school yard basketball court. Some guys I've played with came by and joked with me about something, maybe the quality of air there, which probably should not be bottled.

I saw Stuart Golbey, a radiologist, with whom I've played at NYU for nearly twenty years, from the time he was a student there. I asked how he was feeling. Golbey had tripped running backward on a recent Saturday and banged his head on the cement court and partially lost consciousness. He was hurried to the nearby emergency room, where X rays were taken. He lay on the gurney, sweating and shivering under a blanket. A nurse came by with the X rays and told him that he'd have to wait for the results of the test because no radiologist was available at that time in the emergency ward. He said, "May I see those please?" He read his own X rays and determined he had suffered a slight concussion and diagnosed that he would be OK. And here he was, back on the court.

And I was back from Laguna, feeling as if I had given as much as I could to my quest to come back from my knee injury, to go to the hoop.

At Main Beach Park I had missed that one shot, that left-handed drive, that might have one day sent me grinning broadly to that great outdoor court in the sky, but I looked at it as a kind of triumph. I did penetrate, even though I didn't finish.

Thirty-five years ago, when I first wrote to Red Smith and sent him two of my columns from the Miami student newspaper, he wrote back:

Dear Ira Berkow,

When I was a cub in Milwaukee, I had a city editor who'd stroll over and read across a guy's shoulder when he was writing a lead. Sometimes he would approve, sometimes he'd say gently, "Try again," and walk away.

My advice is, try again. And then again. If you're for this racket, and not many really are, then you've got an eternity of sweat and tears ahead. I don't mean just you; I mean anybody. . . .

And, as I do in writing, so I'll continue in basketball, I'll try again. Still striving to penetrate and finish, but perhaps being just a little less hard on myself. After all, things can end in a flash. My knee gave me evidence of that, as did the melanoma that was luckily caught in time, as did the tragedy of my brother.

So every day on the court for me is a day that I ought to perceive as blueberries on the cheesecake. Every day that I can enjoy a sunset should be embraced that way.

The aging basketball player, meanwhile, is the aging human being. (Yes, I believe he deserves the benefit of the doubt on that.) And I wonder sometimes how much more there is left, how many more minutes in the game. After all, nothing is forever, unless it is forever itself. And after I play now, I know consciously or otherwise that this might be my last game. There may be a final injury. Or if I play poorly, I think perhaps it *should* be my last game.

I spoke about this with a neighbor, Larry Freundlich, a writer and book editor and avid golfer in his midfifties. He could identify.

"Not long ago, I was having a very good round, and then I hit a bad shot from the seventh tee," he said. "You can't hang your head, or it will begin to work on your psyche. And you can't moan about it because that immediately labels you a bad sport, and a jerk, probably, too. I just smiled at my partners and said, 'I knew I had that in me.'

"We all laughed. But I did that one time, after I had been having a very good round. The fact is, if I hit a bad first shot off the tee, I get sullen, isolated, mean, and silent. I just don't want to talk to anyone. If you tell me a joke, I get this vicious grin across my face. I don't want to hear it. I am a perfect gentleman, and I am perfectly amusing when I am playing well. Otherwise, I will shut up and I have a terrible time. I want to give up the game. Most golfers are that way."

Bill Mulliken, a contemporary of mine at Miami University, remains an ardent swimmer, getting up with his wife, Lorna, at 5 A.M. to swim before going to work—he's a lawyer, she's a conservator at the Art Institute of Chicago. Bill won a gold medal in the 200-meter breaststroke in the 1960 Rome

Olympics, where he had beaten Japan's Yoshihiko Osaki, the
favorite, by six tenths of a second. Bill told me the story of
when he traveled to Japan in 1986 and raced in a masters
meet in which Osaki was entered. Twenty-six years later,
Mulliken finished behind Osaki, but neither won: a third
swimmer came in first. "I lost but I didn't really lose," Bill
said. "I swam faster at age forty-six than I did the first time I
placed in the nationals when I was sixteen. That's not losing.
Someone just swam faster."

Bill has slowed down a bit in the last ten years, but he's still
at it. He still loves it. "I keep trying to streamline my move-
ments in the water," he told me. "The trick now is to stay out
of your own way."

Terry Diamond, meanwhile, scales steep mountains for
pleasure. Terry and I have been friends since we were in high
school and played basketball together in the parks. He was
one of the first friends I made at Green Briar Park when my
dad took me there to play with him when I was thirteen years
old and had just moved to the North Side. Terry is now a financial consultant in Chicago and a mountain climber, having
come to that sport along with his wife, Marilyn, as they approached fifty. They have climbed some of the world's most
formidable mountains, including Kilimanjaro, the highest
mountain in Africa.

"We all set limits on ourselves," Terry said to me one day.
"You know, my father, Solly, used to say, 'Why don't you
shoot for the moon? You might fool yourself and get it.' I think
that when you see what your body is capable of doing—and
again only if you prepare for it—it's amazing. There is an aspect of climbing that says, 'If I can do this, I can do anything.'

"There are a lot of people who are fearful of doing things
that they don't have to be. And fearful of failure. It is living
life to the fullest."

Diamond related an expression that mountain climbers use to describe the exhilaration of their sport: "The higher you get, the higher you get." But that wasn't the case especially in December of 1995, when Terry and Marilyn climbed Pico de Orisaba, an 18,400-foot mountain in Mexico. It got particularly scary at one point. The air got very thin, the mountain got treacherously steep, and Terry was uncomfortably wearing a cloud for a hat. At such times mountain climbers begin to say a mantra of their choosing to keep focused and to inspire and drive themselves higher and farther. "My mantra," said Diamond, "has usually been, 'You've gotta want it. You've gotta want it.' This time, it was, 'Never again. Never again.'" He laughed. But six months later he and Marilyn were scaling the Grand Tetons in Wyoming.

And, as time goes on, basketball becomes like that for me, too. Like Diamond and Freundlich in their sports, I returned to hoops.

But then I can hear Barry Holt:

"Look, one day Michael Jordan scored 55 points, and the next day he scored only 18, and he missed a big shot at the end of the game," he said. "It's all relative. We all have our good days and our bad days, at every level. But that's a helluva lot better than having no days at all. If you had a bad day, it means you care enough and think enough of yourself to be pissed off at your performance. If you are not, it means you have no self-image, it means you have no standards. Your standards are always going to be higher than what you can attain. So you keep reaching. You're alive.

"When you see a bunch of old people get together at a reunion or any time, you can usually tell what people are doing by how old their stories are. When some talk about what great times they had twenty-five or thirty years ago, that is sad. Because they are talking about when they had fun. I know that all of the guys that I play ball with and that's not just our team, they are talking about, 'I can't wait until the next game' and when you lose, 'I'm going to get back. I'm going to get better before next time.'

"The less time elapses between the time you are doing something that you enjoy and the time you die, the less time you have been old. I think age has never been a matter of years, age is a matter of not giving in."

Even Michael Jordan could look down the road toward the end of his career and view it with a kind of equanimity: "It's a matter of getting older," he told me, "and knowing you have very little time left in playing at this level and might as well enjoy it and not overlook anything. It's one of the last opportunities, and don't pass it aside."

Jordan's respect for basketball and for its lessons is great. "Because of your competitive nature," he said, "you think you can come back and do what you wanted to do. But the game teaches you not to take it for granted."

My *Times* colleague Richard Sandomir had another conversation with Governor Cuomo. And at this point Sandomir was not beyond acting as a kind of *agent provocateur*. "Governor," he said, "you know that Ira Berkow played basketball with Oscar Robertson recently."

"He did?"

"In a pickup game in the Cincinnati Y. That's what he told me."

"How did he do?"

"Well, he didn't look too unhappy. So I suppose he did OK."

"If he said he did well, then he's lying! Against Oscar Robertson? Sure!"

Sandomir wouldn't let it alone. "Well, Governor," he said, "when are you going to play Ira one-on-one?"

The governor rose in indignation. "Any time! I'm ready!"

Sometime later, another friend told me he had met Cuomo at a political fund-raiser in Manhattan. After Cuomo spoke on behalf of someone running for state office, my friend recalled to me what happened next. He introduced himself to the governor and said, "Sir, we have a mutual acquaintance."

"Oh?" said Cuomo. "Who's that?"

"Ira Berkow," he replied.

Immediately, my friend said, Cuomo's demeanor changed. "The cocktail party veneer slipped away from his face. He had become deadly serious."

Cuomo asked, "Have you ever seen him play basketball? You know, I promised to play him one-on-one."

"No," said my friend. "I haven't."

"I need to find out if he has any weaknesses in his game," said the governor.

Then, according to my friend, the governor's political skills kicked back in, for he put his arm around his shoulder, conspiratorially, and said, "Listen, maybe we can work together on this. If you find out anything that might help me play him, you'll let me know, OK?" And then the governor shook my friend's hand.

So, I thought, everything I've heard about Governor Cuomo is true. He is one fiercely competitive but very wily guy. And brilliant, to boot. I'm sure I did not psyche him out. And all this business about acting concerned is, I believe, a smoke screen so that when we do play—and I am guessing that he is lusting for the game—he will try to force me to give him points, to allow him to choose the referee, and to pick the gym.

Well, I have news for him: not so fast, Governor. I'm not

falling for it. I wasn't born yesterday, to coin a phrase. And anyone who has to ask if his basketball opponent can take a punch is the one who should have to give the points, play with the other guy's referee—and on the other guy's hoop!

And that, as of press time, is where the governor and I stand on this parliamentary issue.

Early in the 1995–96 season, Reggie Miller had not yet found his shooting rhythm. A story in the *Chicago Sun-Times* began: "Having reached the age of 30, Pacers star Reggie Miller has found himself being labeled 'old' and 'on the decline' by some critics."

"I laugh at that," he said. "I believe that my better days are still ahead of me. I'm almost like a fine wine. I get better with time."

Will he say that when he's fifty-six years old? Perhaps he won't have to. Or maybe he'll be haunting the pickup-game courts. Reggie told me that he and his siblings indeed used to wipe out the competition at numerous basketball courts in their home area of southern California, but Laguna Beach happened not to be one of them, since he had never played there.

Isiah Thomas, who had grown up in my old neighborhood, was only thirty-five in 1996, but he had retired as an NBA player. "To keep in shape," he told me, "I run track sprints, and I rollerblade. I play golf a little—I'm just learning it. And I still shoot around with a basketball once every two or three weeks. I try to get into a pickup game, but with former pro or college players. Basketball still gives me the most thrills. A certain type of glow when you're on the court that I've never gotten anywhere else. It's a nice feeling."

Surely, Reggie Miller's last game is well in the distance. But one game will be the last. When the body is not responding to the summons, to the inner whip and lash, it can be a long, frustrating day. It becomes *memento mori*—a sign of death or one's mortality.

But it is natural to try to keep age at bay. So one exercises, and, as Satchel Paige used to say, one tries to think cool thoughts. Diet is also important. And while my intentions often outdistance my performance in that area, I was struck last April by a story I read in *USA Today*, with the headline: "Theory of Eat Less, Live Longer Evolves":

> Experiments since the 1930s show that cutting calories by one third transforms short-lived insects and rodents into lower-kingdom Methuselahs. But, until now, research has not shown whether it might do the same in primates and humans. . . . If future studies prove caloric restriction works in humans—say 3,000 a day to 2,100—the maximum life span theoretically could be extended to well over 150 years. . . .
>
> But what about the quality of life? [The study leader] says rodent Methuselahs are just as quick at learning new mazes as when they were young.

Could I still be shooting jump shots at 150 if I walk around with a calorie counter? Would I want to?

Red Smith once wrote that he admired the way his friend Grantland Rice died—at the typewriter. Smith didn't die that way, but nearly did, writing a column nearly on his deathbed. I haven't quite decided how I want to die, other than painlessly, perhaps in my sleep, with several angels tooting on cornets.

I think of Steve, and of the mental and physical anguish that he and the family suffered—the anxiety, the transfusions, the respirator—and then his dying at such a young age, at fifty-one. "He had so much more to live for," my father has said, more than once.

Many of Steve's seventh- and eighth-grade students sent letters to Judy after his death, testifying to the role he had played in their lives.

"He was not only a teacher," wrote a student named Muriel Reyes. "He was my best friend. Every time I needed help he would never let me down."

"He was a great influence on my life," wrote Eloisa Perez.

And Reynaldo Garcia, a father of one of my brother's students, wrote, "I met Mr. Berkow through my children and in him I met a strong and firm man. The kind of man that in some ways reminded myself of me. He said what had to be said and stood his ground. I like that in a person. Many of the kids thought he was too strict, and my son Reynaldo was one of them. But I knew as they do now that he was just doing things his way—the right way. He shared an evening with myself and my family at my daughter's Sweet 15. And made her very happy."

A girl named Raquel said, "Losing Mr. Berkow is like losing a part of my heart."

None of us in the family had any idea how great an impact my brother had made on his students, how he had so profoundly affected their lives. I'm not sure he realized it. "He had told me individual instances," Shayne told me, "but the reaction from the students was so deep I think it might have surprised him."

I considered anew the meaning of important people and the so-called heroes. And the people we honor who are in the spotlight—who often go about their lives in selfish or isolated or even childish pursuits—and about people like Steve, who make a hands-on difference and for whom no monuments are built, no streets are named, no parades thrown.

When Steve graduated from college with a degree in English, he decided to teach school as a stopgap and to keep from going into the military. This was not an uncommon dodge. Serving in the army was not a pleasant notion for many of us, including me, who did it. And if you were a schoolteacher until you turned at least twenty-six years old—when you were no longer eligible to be drafted—you could avoid the service. So Steve got into the schools, and for one reason or another, he stayed. For the first several years, he looked around for other things to do, but nothing else either satisfied him or worked out. And then slowly, he grew more and more committed to his work with kids, until, well, it took hold of his mind and heart.

And watching my brother's struggle to live, and doing everything I could to help, but with a terrible feeling of helplessness, of inadequacy, made clear to me the fragility and the transience of my own life.

But even in chaos, even in disaster, even in sorrow, life doesn't stop. Living still must be left to the living, and accepted, if sometimes with great difficulty. I imagined Dr. Tuchman in Auschwitz looking toward the snow-capped mountains through the barbed-wire fence and hoping and dreaming that one day he would be skiing again, and how that anticipation provided an impetus to survival. For a long time, he told me, he sought to block that experience from his thoughts, but as time went on, he realized that it was important for him to recall it. "It's true that as we get older," he said, "we begin to reflect on our past. There's not much future ahead, so in order to kind of maintain the longevity, we borrow on our past. Suddenly the present isn't taken for granted, and things come into focus."

And I understood that continuing to throw myself into life, as fully and as passionately as I could, for as long as I could, was what I wanted the rest of my time here to be about. And if I could still play basketball and experience pleasure on good

days and think that the pain of the bad day was only an accident, I would be happy. And when there wasn't basketball or
another sport, there would be writing. I know I am happiest
when I am outside myself, thinking about another game of
hoops or another story or another person.

It is not morbid to think of dying, or how one will die,
since dying is a part of living. And I know it would not be impossible for me to die on the basketball court. And perhaps
not so bad, either. I remember having that thought when the
spectacular Pistol Pete Maravich, the floppy-haired, floppy-
socked former player who seemed never to age, collapsed and
died in a pickup game in 1988 at the age of forty.

He had a congenital heart problem that had somehow
gone undetected.

When he was a rookie with the Atlanta Hawks in 1970, I
wrote a column about him in which his coach, Richie Guerin,
told me that one of Pete's problems was that he gets himself
"stuck up in the air." It was a great trait for a moon, but not
necessarily for a basketball player. Ah, but how he improved.
In one game against the Knicks, he scored 68 points. He
made shots from so far out, and from such strange angles, that
it amazed everyone there, including the handful of Knicks
who tried to guard him. Walt Frazier, one of those who tried
to contain him, recalled, "The Pistol was taking shots that we
wanted him to take."

And then on that January day in 1988, on an outdoor court
in Pasadena, California, Maravich, seven years retired from
the NBA, not having played in a year at that point, and having
struggled through personal problems, including alcoholism
and a divorce, once again had the chance to soar and hang in
the air.

"I feel great," Maravich said, breaking a sweat. A few minutes later his heart gave out. Pistol Pete died on the basketball

court, where, it is not a stretch to say, for so many years his heart had been.

One day recently, in the late afternoon, I went to the NYU court, and it was empty. These are often some of my favorite times. I dribbled the ball the length of the court, up and back, up and back, up and back, switching hands, lefty to righty, righty to lefty. I worked on my moves, I worked on my shots. A righty hook, a lefty hook, a spinning fall-away. A jumper from the top of the key. Another from the right baseline corner, the left baseline corner. I watched the ball float toward the hoop and swish musically though the net, or I chased the carom off the rim. I dreamed. I soared. I sweated. I drove.

The sun had not yet set.

Acknowledgments

Casey Stengel, the improbable manager of the New York Yankees of old, once said that he couldn't have done it without his players. And in writing this book, I couldn't have done it either without the help of many people.

I thank my editor, Paul Golob, whose sense of nuance and structure and whose friendship and firm editing pencil were indispensable.

I thank Paul Berczeller, who was a catalyst for the concept and direction of this book.

I thank Bennett Ashley, the best combination of basketball fan and agent I can imagine. And I thank Bennett, Dr. Peter Berczeller, Bill Brink, Richard Close, Nicky Dawidoff, David Fisher, David Fox, Larry Freundlich, Dr. Isaac Herschkopf, and Lawrie Mifflin for reading whole or parts of the book and making important suggestions.

So many people contributed to the text and body of this book over some fifty years that it would take more pages than can be accommodated here, and while many appear in the book itself, I wish to call particular attention to some.

I start with my parents, Shirley and Harold Berkow, for it is indeed with them that this autobiographical book lovingly started.

I wish to extend heartfelt appreciation to Judy and Shayne Berkow, and to Judge Ian H. Levin.

I am also grateful to Seth Abraham, Paul Berko, Stu Black, Frank Blatnick, Edgar M. Branch, Jimmy Burke, Sam Carl, Michael B. Cohen, Vivian Crowe, Curt Cyr, John Diamond, Tim Duggan, Henry Feldman, Matt Fogg, Ginny Fox, Maxine Friedman, Bob Goldsholl, Myrna Greenberg, Steve Greenberg, Ernestine Guglielmo, Jerome Holtzman, Selma Holzman, Richard Huttner, Mike Isakoff, Will Kenigsberg, Michael Mamett, Ted Mann, Curt May, Ed Menaker, Howard Noel, Harry Randall, Dr. Craig Rosen, Ted Schwartz, Herb Sirott, Jerry Snower, Dr. Lee Stern, Bob Stone, Ilene Strauss, Gary Stutland, Fern Turkowitz, Joe Vecchione, John A. Weigel, Milton White, Jack Wilkinson, and Gilson Wright.

I want to add my appreciation to the morgue directors of the *Chicago Sun-Times* and the *Chicago Tribune* for allowing me to rummage through their microfilm for pertinent old high school and college baseball and basketball stories, box scores, and line scores.

Finally, and above all, I want to thank my wife, Dolly, whose encouragement and understanding lit my way.

Index

Ira Berkow has been a sports columnist and feature writer for the *New York Times* for more than twenty years. In 2001 he shared the Pulitzer Prize for National Reporting with his article on "The Minority Quarterback," later published in *The Minority Quarterback and Other Lives in Sports*. Mr. Berkow's work has appeared in numerous sports and literary anthologies, and he is the author of almost two dozen books—including the best-sellers *Red: A Biography of Red Smith* and *Maxwell Street: Survival in a Bazaar*—and a new play, *The Shakespeare of the Press Box*, about Red Smith. Born in Chicago, Mr. Berkow studied at Miami (Ohio) University and Northwestern University's Medill Graduate School of Journalism. Before coming to the *New York Times* he worked for the *Minneapolis Tribune* and Newspaper Enterprise Association. He lives with his wife, Dolly, in New York City.